# Stirrings of Culture

## Essays from the Dallas Institute

# Stirrings of Culture

Robert J. Sardello
Gail Thomas
editors

The Dallas Institute Publications
The Dallas Institute of Humanities and Culture
Dallas

Cover:
    Painting by Joe Guy
    Photograph by Lee Clockman, courtesy of Dallas Museum of Fine Arts
Design by Mickey Bright, Patricia Mora and Maribeth Lipscomb
Production by Susan Dupree and B. Ruth Rinehart

ISBN 0-911005-07-2

Library of Congress Cataloging-in-Publication Data
Stirrings of Culture.
    "The articles in this volume have all been previously
published in the Institute newsletter'--p.
    1. Culture.  2. City and town life--United States.
3. United States--Social conditions--1980—
4. Dallas (Tex.)--Social conditions.  I. Sardello,
Robert J., 1942–    . II. Thomas, Gail.
III. Institute newsletter.
HM101.S786      1968       306       86–24028
ISBN 0-911005-07-2

The Dallas Institute Publications,
formerly known as The Pegasus Foundation,
publishes works concerned with the
imaginative, mythic, and symbolic sources of culture.
Publication efforts are centered at:
The Dallas Institute of Humanities and Culture
2719 Routh Street, Dallas Texas  75201

# Contents

# Economy
— 100 —

# The City
— 132—

# Dallas
— 164 —

# Street Life
— 185 —

# The Body
## — 209 —

# Contributors Notes
## — 245 —

# Introduction

Sometimes you can know a book by its cover . . .

A book jacket, most often, serves as an illustration designed to attract a potential reader by first exciting the visual imagination. Usually, one cannot know a book by its cover. The work of art that is the cover of this book is not usual. It needs to be addressed. Entitled "Echo," it is the work of Dallas artist Joe Guy. Unquestionably beautiful, breathlessly so, it seems to me to be a perfect presentation, not an illustration, of *Stirrings of Culture*.

Art critics have said the following about the work of Joe Guy: some technical details—he stretches paper over wood frames and coats it with graphite and wax; the mixture of graphite and wax can cause the black undercoating to become almost a reflective surface, while at the same time it is an absorbing absence; some influences—critics locate Guy's painting within the modernist tradition, liken it to that of Ad Reinhardt or Mark Rothko, with an infusion of Oriental aesthetics; what his paintings present—it is a return of the spiritual to art. His paintings are objects of contemplation rather than objects of perception. To see them, one must enter into their own spirit or soul.

In addition to "Echo," some of the titles of Guy's paintings include: "Waiting . . . Listening," "Concealing," "Shelf," and "Homage." Each series of wall reliefs takes on a particular shape such as a folding screen, a diptych, an altarpiece, or a fan. These shapes are not representations but minimal structures through which the subtleties of spirit and soul resound.

What of the particular painting, "Echo?" The critic can help us to see, but finally it is up to us to see. The fan shape of the painting places us in the presences of the wind of the spirit, its breath. To indicate the character of this breath as it actively creates the actual world, the Chinese call it "the breath of nature." The breath of nature, in its inhalation, is the change from nothing into being, and in its exhalation, the change from existence to non-existence. At the top of the fan, at the centerpoint, rests, with great energy, a fan-shaped void. From this void radiates the fan which we see, backed by the energy of the void. The substantial fan, at the top, inclines upward; and if the point of view of the space above is taken, it inclines downward. The fan which we see actively engages with an invisible other half impressing itself downward, embraced by and creating that which we see.

The strength and power of what lies invisibly above must be tremendous, for two small details, in the vicinity of the void have the purpose of providing a right relationship with what presses from above, utilizing the energy in a manner that makes rather than destroys. At the left of the void is a small notch, and at the right of the void, a small key. The notch receives what comes from above; the key returns what is given back to its source. Between the notch and the key stirs the tension of the whole work. To the far right, at the edge of the top section of the fan, lies another notch, which does not receive energy, but gives it back, allows the key to penetrate the void. A third notch lies at the very bottom center of the painting, and has more to do with the dark radiating lines, particularly the center line, which is the deepest. All the energy of the tension above gathers at this place, and the fan which we see is equivalent to the small key above.

The vertical direction of the painting, if left at that, would indeed give the impression of a purely spiritual work. And the texture of the painting would be ignored. The shape of the void repeats in the shape of the fan; as well, we could say the void receives the shape of the fan. But, it is the texture of the tension between that counts most. The fan is sectioned, vertical sections, projections of the notch below, producing the beauty of the material world, full of subtle sensuousness, where light is simultaneously reflected and absorbed, where the deepest density of matter shines with the sparks of vitality. While the work may be spiritual, or a presentation of meditation and contemplation, it nevertheless belongs completely to this world, not so much an object in the world, an entity to be perceived, as the perpetually nascent state of physical things.

A significant detail, one difficult to see in the photograph of the painting, concerns the manner in which the nine sections of the work hold together. 1300 paper hinges link the sections. Many other techniques, far easier, can be imagined, so this method must be considered essential to the presentation. It produces the sense of great strength, the body of the painting, and the signature of labor . . . both in the sense of work and in the sense of birth.

"Echo" does indeed echo the character of this book, *Stirrings of Culture*. Over the past five years—in conferences, seminars, lectures, The Dallas Institute of Humanities and Culture has worked in the vortices between prevailing institutions and guiding ideas of society such as education, medicine, city planning, economics—and the primary originating imagination from which society draws its vitality. Culture stirs between the imagination and the enactment.

Critics sometimes view the process of culture as occurring in three phases—the visionary, the aesthetic, and the technological. Certainly, the stages are not progressive; as in the painting, "Echo," all three go on simultaneously. The Dallas Institute gathers together people with the capacity of incorporating all three phases in a unified vision to address the major concerns of society. In many instances conversation is promoted among those who, on their own, may be restricted in imagination to one of these planes, but who, nevertheless, have courage and desire to go beyond known boundaries. Such conversations intend to stir culture—not to produce it or affect it in any immediate fashion. Combining vision, imagination, and know-how, the work has been to prevent any one mode of thought fragmenting from the rest. The Dallas Institute has sided, for example, neither with occult or alternative medicine on the one hand, nor with current technological medicine on the other; and in education it has prompted thought as diverse as art and classics; it has heard proposals in economics from the benefits of establishing local currency to the necessity of global economy; it has considered design in the city all the way from movable chairs in public places to skyscraper architecture.

Diversity is not equivalent to eclectic; imagination determines the difference, and this difference reveals itself in language. Eclectic language is specialist, self-serving, the promotion of a singular view patronizingly presented along with other views. Imaginative language is symbolic, metaphoric, encompassing, and suggestive. This language is determined by and centers on the thing itself and requires submission to something larger than oneself. In order to shelter the centrality of real things and their language, The Dallas Institute refrains from addressing causes, engaging in political stances, and resolving disputes; it abdicates both power and control. Such a modest endeavor may thus seem to be of no practical value. The value lies in value itself. An institute concerned with culture—not as culture refers either to individual or group development, but to the well-being of society as a whole—can do very little to direct it. It can draw attention to culture, serve it, remember it, and engage in those modes of knowing which illuminate the necessities of the human condition and have the power of restoring human reality to human life. The Dallas Institute exists for the purpose of stirring culture.

The articles in this volume have all been previously published in *The Institute Newsletter*. They represent five years work of the Institute and condense a lifetime of labor of the authors. Each article has been carefully excerpted from a more lengthy writing in order to provide a core thought for consideration. The intention has been to produce, in each case, a memorable image to be contemplated, to be returned to and re-read with ease. Most certainly, the reader will be motived to search out more extensive writing of some or all of the authors. This volume, though, presents a community of thought.

*Robert J. Sardello*
*Dallas, Texas*
*1986*

# Introduction

On June 10, 1980, a diverse but like-minded group met in the old White Swan Coffee Roaster warehouse of the North End in downtown Dallas to read manifestoes to each other. Some were literary pieces, some were scientific, others held a psychological persuasion, and others still were outlines for academic programs. All were imaginative and freshly conceived, and all adhered to a common theme—the need for the renewal of culture.

It was a gathering of unique persons: Donald Cowan had been president of The University of Dallas for sixteen years, and had built that fledgling school into a major institution of higher learning; Louise Cowan had formed the Literary Tradition program there, requiring all students regardless of major to study the important texts of the western world and had created The Institute of Philosophic Studies, an interdisciplinary graduate program involving five disciplines; Robert Sardello had established a unique program in psychology combining phenomenology and archetypal psychology; James Hillman, former director of Studies of the Jung Institute in Zurich had come as Distinguished Visiting Fellow; Joanne Stroud had purchased the rights to translate and publish in English the works of Gaston Bachelard; Gail Thomas, as head of The Center for Civic Leadership, had been linking the work of the graduate programs with the city offering seminars in Dallas City Hall.

These became the Founding Fellows of The Dallas Institute. They were joined by Robert Scott Dupree; Lyle Novinski; Eileen Gregory; Leo Paul and Helen de Alvarez; Marianne Beard; Patricia Berry-Hillman—all of The University of Dallas.

Filling out the circle of Fellows were Thomas Moore from Southern Methodist University; Robert Armstrong from the University of Texas at Dallas; A. C. Greene, Billy Porterfield, Patsy Swank, John Bruce Moore, Wick Allison, and Frank Ryburn from the community, and Jacques Barzun, Mortimer Adler, William H. Whyte, O'Neil Ford, James Lehrer, C. West Churchman, Bernd Jager, Arthur Erickson, Kathleen Raine, and Christian Norberg-Schulz from other points of the world.

The Institute opened its doors in January of 1981, offering lectures, classes and seminars for those in the city who wanted serious study and thought without regard for academic degrees. The first series of six courses attracted more than two hundred people and the Wednesday night lecture series addressed over-capacity crowds. It was clear that Dallas wanted a center for imaginative study in the city.

Additional Fellows were invited to join: William Burford, Brice Howard, James Pratt, John Tatum, Mary Vernon, Patrick and Judith Kelly, and Robert Romanyshyn from the Dallas area and Adolph Guggenbühl-Craig, Vincent Scully, Ivan Illich, and Wendell Berry from all quarters of the globe. The "What Makes a City" annual conference of Fellows was initiated, an occasion bringing together the Fellows of the Institute for four days of retreat, papers and conversation, ending with a public seminar in downtown Dallas for city officials, civic leaders, and interested citizens. These annual conferences have created the arena for many of the papers included in this collection of short essays:
"What Makes a City: Architecture and Poetry," 1982;
"What Makes a City: The Economics of Taste," 1983;
"What Makes a City: Water and Dreams," 1984;
"What Makes a City: Growth and Undergrowth," 1985; and
"What Makes a City: Money, Myth, and Mana," 1986

From the beginning, the Founding Fellows of the Institute decided to risk critical inquiry about the nature of contemporary culture, cities, and individual attitudes and mores, and to be unafraid of controversy. If the enterprise was to have a short life, that life would at least be fruitful! Amazingly, the city and the nation have supported the Institute's programs beyond its own expectations.

The task of the Institute has been, from its inception, to reflect on all aspects of our culture—education, architecture, downtown street life, city planning, money, business, economics, the media, art, music, theatre, film—using the particular perspectives of literature, poetry, physics, psychology, art history, philosophy and political philosophy as a way of seeing. The Fellows meet frequently at the Institute to read papers or discuss an idea presented for discussion. The Dallas Institute Forum, a series of six monthly lectures drawing citizens of the city who are concerned about the vicissitudes of modern life, offers an occasion for the Fellows to engage members of the community in conversation, a rare opportunity in Dallas for open inquiry free from pre-programmed yea-saying.

The focus of this attention is the city, the gathering place for the making of culture, with primary emphasis in three areas—education, the city itself, and the pursuit of ideas for their own sake. The concentration on education is seminal to the Institute because of the interwoven relationship between education and culture. After five years of public seminars, free lecture series, consultation with the Dallas Independent School District, week-end seminars for teachers, and three summers of a month-long institute for teachers, a Teachers Academy has been established to provide a place for learning and revivification for teachers. Focus on the city grows naturally from an awareness of the need for the renewal of culture, viewing the city in its most vital form as the place where the spirit of the individual, the group and the tribe become visible, where new forms emerge and cohere with the old, where imagination congeals. The city offers immediate confrontation with the "stuff" of ideas—an immersion in things themselves, events, and ceremonies. The "What Makes a City" conferences have, for the past five years, allowed the exponential powers of the city to play around with ideas. Ideas, then, are at the center of the activities of the Institute, ideas for the pleasure of thinking, for the joy of good conversation, for the power of language, for the movement of images, ideas for entertainment, for play, for creating a vision, for knowing the way.

The Dallas Institute has been a bold experiment, operating without the credentials of an academic institution, without financial security, and without a known constituency. Perhaps this uncertainty has been the secret of its vitality. This relatively small house on Routh Street has been, in a way, a microcosm of the city—gathering diverse individuals together, celebrating their unique particularities and simultaneously inviting diverse ideas to join together as well. Farmers and gardeners rarely engage in the futile attempt to count the seeds which are planted. Their eyes are on the yield. They know the reward of their labor at harvest time. We at The Dallas Institute rarely have the opportunity to count the seeds or weigh the yield. We know, however, that the work here is having its effect not only in Dallas but beyond. These short essays reflect that work. Brief and seemingly insignificant, they contain powerful ideas. We call them the stirrings of culture.

*Gail Thomas*
*Dallas, Texas*
*1986*

# Ideas

The very notion that there could be an institute for the cultivation of ideas—not an academic establishment, a think tank, or a consultation group—but a gathering of like-minded people giving time and a place for thoughtfulness about the world, certainly must be counted as unusual. Further, imagine placing this enterprise, not in a sequestered lake-side, mountain-side, forest-scaped retreat, but right in the center of the city, Dallas, of all places, and the notion begins to appear odd indeed. What may be odd, though, is that every city does not initiate such care for thought. Ideas are not private matters, but essential ingredients, the very essence necessary for community development. The presence of such a place serves as a daily tangible reminder that ideas belong to life and have definite, though unpredictable, effects in the world. Reflection, brought about by the presence of ideas, makes culture possible.

Ideas have fallen into decline—replaced by planning, social reform, design. Central to the work of The Dallas Institute is the resuscitation of the action of ideas. The decline is marked by the separation of action from thought, producing hyperactivity and its attendant diseases of stress, heart attack, and burn-out. And while such diseases are treated with more mindless activity—exercise, jogging, diet-watching, the cure may well be found in the act of contemplation, focused, not on an inner spot of nothingness, but on the actual things of the world. Such meditative activity breathes life back into the things of the world. The point of thinking about things is not to derive new plans of action, but to see the ideas themselves as potent action.

This chapter focuses on ideas themselves, ideas of ideas, if you will. Such reflection is necessary both as a prelude to considering other topics and, as well, to provide the element of self-reflection that makes the difference between promoting a subjective stance and true cultural criticism. By being true to ideas themselves, the possibility of criticism based in an interior vision rather than a perspective alien to the matter at hand is enhanced. Architecture should be reflected upon in the language of architecture, not sociology, politics, or city planning; and similarly for any other endeavor. Each field needs rich ideas of itself, with which to reflect itself. Each field contains its own logos, and it is this logos alone which can do justice to the variety and depth of the many facets of culture. Without this vision, we cannot see. And without being aware that we are always in the embrace of an idea, we cannot know what we are seeing. This awareness of an idea as what is seen as well as that through which one sees, constitutes the definition of insight. The Dallas Institute exists for the sake of insight. It is well, then, that we begin with a consideration of ideas.

*Robert Sardello*

# Entertaining Ideas

## *James Hillman*

Our society offers places where you can let your feelings out. You may go to group therapy or to sensitivity training; and, no matter how silly or strange the feelings, they are received. There are also places where you can improve your will: the gym or spa to work out, willing yourself to lift that contraption another twenty times; or to an EST meeting to develop your self-control and willful determination.

But where do you go to play with ideas? There is Church, where an idea may be presented to you in a sermon —more likely, though, it's a judgment, not an idea. There is TV; on "60 Minutes" there may be three ideas, presented as pro's and con's, as if the point of an idea were to force you in-to a choice. Newspaper editorials urge ideas on you. But you aren't shown how to play with them. Where can we go to imagine an idea and move it further? In none of these places —Church, TV, Newspaper—do you let the idea swim way out and reel it back in again. You don't just relish the delight of the idea in itself.

Now what we're doing here at The Institute is entertaining ideas. One of the great difficulties in our American life is that we don't have places for entertaining ideas. And that is precisely what we're supposed to do with an idea: entertain it. This means having respect for ideas themselves: letting them come and go without demanding too much from them at first, like their origins (who said that first), their popularity (what if everybody thought that), their logic (but that doesn't fit with what you just said). Why can't they be a little crazy? We admit our feelings are crazy. We all have crazy feelings that might want to do this or say that. But maybe our ideas have arms and legs, too, and are crazy and want to get out and meet other ideas, air themselves, spend time with each other in public. The ideas themselves, not the people in whom they occur. Just the ideas wanting to appear and be received, welcomed, entertained for a while.

What we usually do with an idea is put it into practice. Someone says: "Oh, that's a good idea!" and he means: "Oh boy, I can save four bucks this way!" or "Smart. I can do some-thing now that I couldn't have done before because I had a bright idea. I can hang the strap like this instead of like that."

That's what makes a "good idea" in our society. A good idea means useful, practical, immediately applicable. Isn't it a shame that we can value ideas only when we have them in a harness. I think it breaks their spirit. We don't let them run loose, to see where they might take us if we just fed them with a little attention and trusted their autonomy.

If you watch one of the more intelligent interviewers on TV, Dick Cavett, say, even he, when an idea breaks in, often says: "Well, it's just an idea I had." They move away from it. There is a little anxiety that the idea might get out of hand. "What will I do with that!" There is no skill in handling it, no way to dribble around the floor with it.

The media do not really favor ideas. They mix them with opinions. We have plenty of opinions and are taught very early to have an opinion on most everything—but opinions are personal. We get pugnacious. They involve belief. Ideas are much easier to live with: they don't ask to be believed in, and an idea doesn't belong to you even when you "have" one. You can become friends with an idea, and after a while it will show you more of itself, or you and it may get tired of each other and separate.

One thing is sure: ideas don't belong to academics. You don't have to have academic knowledge to have ideas.

Knowledge might help work with the idea, enrich it, discriminate it more finely, or recognize its history—that it's not the first time that idea ever moved through someone's mind. So knowledge may save you the embarrassment of inflation and help you pick up some skills about polishing ideas. But knowledge is not necessary. You can distinguish things you have learned from ideas you have. Keeping these distinct—knowledge and ideas—ought to help you to feel that you can ideate without an academic degree. When an idea comes to mind, it asks first of all to be listened to and that you attempt to understand it. If knowledge helps do this, then fine. But first entertain your visitor.

That word "entertain" means to hold in between. What you *do* with an idea is hold it between—between your two hands. On the one hand, acting or applying it in the world, and on the other hand, forgetting it, judging it, ignoring it, etc. So when these crazy things come in on you unannounced the best you can do for them is think them, holding them, turning them over, wondering a while. Not rushing into practice. Not rushing into associations. This reminds me of that: this is just like that. Off we go, away from the strange idea to things we already know. Not judging. Rather than judging them as good and bad, true or false, we might first spend a little time with them.

As I said, a "good idea" is a bad idea! I mean, a good idea tends to imply a better mousetrap, ingenuity. "Genius"—which is your own guiding spirit, a daimon or angel, and who may be the transmitter of the ideas that come into your head—has now become "ingenuity," being clever, solving a problem. We lose the genius in ingenuity. Putting the idea in practice stops the play of ideas, the entertainment from going on. We put them into practice, however, in order to test them. In America we don't seem to know other ways of testing except by practice.

How else could we evaluate an idea? Is the idea fertile, fecund? Does it generate other ideas? Does it make you think? Is it surprising, shocking? Does it stop you up from habits and bring a spark of reflection? Is it delightful to think it? Does it seem deep? Important? Needing to be told? Does it wear out quickly? Especially: What does the idea itself want from you; why in the world did it decide to light in your mind.

This requires that you ponder it, which means weigh it, feel its weight, that it is substantial and has some gravity. Pondering is an action of its own and keeps you holding the idea, from letting it go into other kinds of action before it is fully appreciated. Meanwhile, you get a better feel of the idea.

The word idea supposedly originates in the Greek word *eidos*, which means both something seen like a form and a way of seeing like an eye, a perspective. So, ideas are not only things you can pick up and ponder. They also give you eyes, new ways of seeing things. Ideas are already operating in our perspectives, the way we look at things. We take our usual ideas for granted, and so, ideas have us rather than we have them. One thing we want to be doing in this Institute is getting to know the ideas that already are in our perspectives. We shall be trying to see the very modes by which we are seeing into our own ideas. I expect it to be entertaining.

# City Beasts

*Robert Sardello*

Universities have writers-in-residence, museums, artists-in-residence; symphonies, composers-in-residence. I speak as the fool-in-residence at The Dallas Institute. The city needs its jesters, particularly the successful city; and The Dallas Institute is the abode of the foolhardy. That is why it is an institute and not a civic institution. Its sole purpose lies in instituting ideas of the city. Since our work concerns ideas, we need to distinguish ideas from other kinds of realities. I would like to spend a few moments doing exactly that. The ancient philosophers exerted much effort separating ideas from opinions, belief, faith, and knowledge. They knew this was an important task, a guide to whatever they needed to develop. I am no philosopher, merely a psychologist of imagination, and thus will attempt to imagine what ideas are like.

Ideas are very strange creatures indeed. In order to be able to listen to them, we first need to tell them apart from other urban creatures with whom they are most often confused. Certainly, ideas are not the same as opinions. Opinions are tenacious beasts with large saber-edged teeth; they seldom smile, are generally unapproachable, almost impossible to tame. I have heard stories of people who have been attacked by these beasts; they are really quite terrible because upon sinking their teeth into you they contract the disease of lockjaw. Release from them requires a most painful operation. The operation is in fact so painful that, when bitten by a small opinion, most of us prefer to let it hang on to us for the duration of our life, provided of course that it is not too noticeable. This beast roams the city; reportedly, the whole population has been affected to one degree or another.

Another urban creature often confused with ideas is the fact. Several species of this animal exists in the urban environment, the two most notable being *factus informatius* and *factus knowledgeius*.

*Factus informatius*, a very flat, grey creature, lacks any vivid coloration. Their behavior is quite uninteresting, and only collectors become intrigued with them. They do not appear to be dangerous or aggressive except in large groups. They may be related to rabbits, for their favorite pastime is self-reproduction. The favorite habitat of the fact in the city is the computer, where they seem quite content to rest undisturbed. Facts feed mainly on paper, often using reams at a time.

The more aggressive of the species is *factus knowledgeius*. While flat and grey like its closest relative, the *factus knowledgeius* appears more attractive because it is able to camouflage itself so that it looks exactly as we think an idea would look if we could see one. This species likes to act like it knows something, imitating a form of life which they themselves do not possess. This beast is related to the vampire, for it is a creature that looks substantial but actually casts no reflection. It pierces the neck of the unsuspecting victims, secretly draining away the lifeblood of the city.

The next animal we must consider is the plan. It is not certain whether the plan actually qualifies as an animal. Its name in fact comes from the word *plant* (there, you see; I was just attacked by a *factus knowledgeius*, a fact acting like it knows something). It lies always close to the ground and consequently sometimes goes by the name of ground-plan. It too is thin and flat; it moves by spreading itself like a thin membrane over the city. While slower, it is related to the centipede. When it walks over the city it leaves the imprint of the grid. Once caught by a plan, it is almost impossible to get out of its grip. It produces the

chronic disease of conformity. The plan can be very colorful. Just last week, at the planning session for the urban neighborhood of the near east side, I saw a large picture of one that was red and green and blue and yellow with black stripes.

Finally, let me describe the creature known as the goal. It is a speedy little creature; reminds me somewhat of a road runner. It is always on the move, going somewhere, traveling only in straight lines. And it always travels upward, never downward. Very few people can catch a goal, though it makes for great sport. Whenever you get close, it jumps a little higher. I know of many people in the city who spend their life trying to attain a goal for their trophy case. A few people have large collections of interesting varieties. Goals themselves, however, are not very interesting creatures; the pleasure comes from chasing them.

Now, ideas are the most difficult of all to describe. They are nearly extinct within the city. Almost everyone considers them dangerous, though in all of the sources which I have consulted there is not a single report of anyone ever having been harmed by an idea. We fear them; sometimes they act wild or crazy, and when they attach themselves to you they will not let go. Sometimes they bounce off walls. Everyone likes big ideas, and few are interested in small ideas. I myself prefer the little ones because you can hold them in your hand, and they are absolutely delightful. One of the few places you can find them in the city is over on Routh Street, often on a Wednesday evening, where they love to gather. What is most amazing about these creatures is that they are able to talk, and love to have conversations with each other.

Now, I have not provided a very good description of ideas, and I really would like to do so in order that you will have no trouble recognizing one when you see it. Well, from what I have already said, you know that it does not have sharp teeth, is neither flat nor grey, that it does not reproduce by itself, is not flashy in color, does not spread itself over a large area, does not move in straight lines, and does not soar to great heights. You would think that the best place to get a good look at them would be in the university. When they were thought to be dangerous to the city they were all gathered up and placed in the idea sanctuary because no one wanted to be accused of idea-cide. I went out to several of our local universities to see if I could observe them carefully because I really did want to provide you with a clear description of this creature. When I asked about them at our local campuses everyone remembered them and spoke very fondly, almost reverently of them. They recalled how you could play with them and contemplate them and delight in their curious ways. But, alas, I was told that ideas have not done well in the university because almost no one knows how to care for and

feed them. Some thought it best that they be kept locked in cages called books, and whoever got the most into books and journals would be rewarded by being appointed professor of ideas. Others thought that they ought to be put into computers in order to make instruction in ideas more efficient. This was an example of *factus knowledgeius* killing off ideas. Still others thought the best place to keep students safe from ideas was to imbed them in film and tape—audio-visual aids, I believe they were called.

Well, I am sorry to report, I did not get a look at an idea in the university. I did hear them though. In just a couple of classrooms—where students were not pounding away on computers or looking at filmstrips—as I stood outside the door, I heard the most wonderful conversations. I do not know what the creature inside looked like, but they simply could not have been opinions, facts, plans, or goals. I could only hear scattered words through the heavy doors, but I am quite sure it was the voices of ideas. I heard words like truth, imagination, city, love, care, evil, goodness, soul, holocaust, leadership, war, peace, death, hope, psyche, thought, memory, poetry, mystery, history, dwelling, god, myth, human, life, birth, sky, polis, suffering, wisdom, eternity, understanding, time, celebration, ritual. I don't know why, but just hearing such words made me cry with joy. And there were long moments of silence in that room, as if ideas need lots of time and quiet. But there was also laughing and arguing coming from within the room. And absolutely no one in that room said anything like "what do you do with all this talk," or "how do you implement these ideas," or "what is the practical value of this conversation."

So, I come before you now to plead a case for the reintroduction of the species idea into the city. And I have to do so lacking the clear description I had hoped to gather. Even if we cannot see them, why don't we try to reintroduce them into the city on a trial basis. Let's close off a small space, call it The Forum, keep out all the beasts —opinions, facts, plans, and goals—and see if the kind of language heard outside the classroom visits us. Ideas seem to be very closely connected with conversation, so we will have to talk with one another in these Forums, and when we find that this talk takes on a life of its own, then we will know that ideas have entered.

Now, I don't think that we can talk directly about ideas—they are probably too shy and self-conscious. But we can talk about the city—maybe the crisis of public education or leadership, or the imagination of the city, or criticism in the city. If they don't think that we are talking about them, maybe ideas will join in, and we might get a glimpse of them.

# Power and Insight

## *Louise Cowan*

The Irish poet William Butler Yeats has written that it is "only those things which seem useless or very feeble that have any power." And he would go on to attribute to the very immateriality of things their ability to move the world. He speaks of the way in which a lyric impulse, conceived in solitude, the feeblest and frailest of things, grows, by its encounter with other impulses, into the larger forms such as epic and finally, as he says, "flows out with all it has gathered, among the blind instincts of daily life where it moves, a power among power." Yeats is of course speaking in images and metaphors, as befits a poet; but what he describes applies to all creative thought: the way in which a flash of intuition, which has come to hidden and relatively powerless men in moments of contemplation, finally "makes and unmakes mankind," as he puts it.

We are prone in our current age to evaluate things solely in terms of size and hence tend to underestimate the enormous effect of the necessarily small but intense effort by which insight must be generated. By their very nature institutes and academies are small—unburdened with the massive paraphernalia which accompany the task of education in colleges and universities. The institute makes no pretense at anything other than the pursuit of that one thing for which it was established—the interior action of the mind.

We might at first think that institutions of learning are in competition with each other, and that perhaps only the established schools can hope to accomplish anything of worth, with the small new institutes and academies merely diverting energies and resources that would be better engaged elsewhere. But true learning, when it occurs, adds to the total value of human culture—its total capital, if you will; all of us are richer for it; nothing is taken away from already existing institutions. Rather, we all gain from the act, as we gain from a small portion of the air's being purified (for we all breathe it), or from the planting of trees or the cultivation of a park—or the acquisition of a precious painting, say a Cezanne, by a single art museum among many other museums in the area. We cannot really limit beauty, truth, and goodness to groups or organizations or institutions, as we cannot limit insight.

And as for the ability of these secret, invisible deeds to affect the very cities in which we dwell, Yeats (I call on him again) testified that he once asked a medium to enquire of one of the spiritual powers surrounding her what would come of the apparently trivial labor of a friend. The answer came: "the devastation of peoples and the overwhelming of cities." Small and apparently impractical actions can change the world. And thinking, though it appears weak, useless, and private, is the most powerful action in which the human person can engage.

# Talking as Walking

## *James Hillman*

It seemed it might be useful to say something about why our Institute puts so much weight on psychology, why so many of us are psychologists, even psychoanalysts. How does psychology fit in with the tasks of the Institute and the life of the city.

Psychologists are engaged in the business of consciousness. People come to see us about this or that problem, symptom or trouble in order to become more conscious. We take things apart, that is, analyze problems, feelings, dreams, so that they become more conscious.

Now what is this consciousness? What actually goes on in becoming more conscious? Actually, what goes on is conversation. If you listened to a tape of an analysis hour, an hour of becoming conscious in therapy, you would hear a conversation. That's all it is: conversation. You become more conversant with your dreams, about your relationships, your fears and needs.

Consciousness is really nothing more than maintaining conversation, and unconsciousness is really nothing more than letting things fall out of conversa-

tion, no longer talking about something—or what Freud called repression.

Now it seems to me that this is precisely the job of the Institute: keeping a conversation going and not letting things remain unsaid, unspoken, repressed.

You see, we aren't really a think tank. We don't take on problems in order to come up with specific answers, recommendations. Answers anyway don't really keep conversations going as well as questions do. Answers are stoppers. It seems, at the Institute, we spend more time coming up with new questions than with answers.

And we aren't really a cultural center either, with a program of adult education—except when we initiate something on architecture, or manners, or education, or economics, or the media, so as to initiate conversation.

Now conversation isn't easy. You know how hard it is in a family, what an art it is to keep a conversation going. You know the tortures of the family dinner table, how more and more is left unsaid—so, of course, Freud found repression mainly in the family. It's a place where conversation often has a hard time.

Or, at a dinner party. Striking up a conversation and keeping it flowing —not a monologue, not only opinions and sounding off, not only firing questions but conversation at an exploration, a little risky adventure, discovery, an interesting happening. Parties are terribly important in a city for keeping its conversation going, keeping the consciousness of the city at a certain intensity, moving its mind adventurously toward deeper discoveries.

What doesn't work, we also pretty well know: Personalism: just talking out loud about what we feel. Complaints. Opinions. Information doesn't work: simply reporting what's new, where you've been, what you've heard. And lullabies don't help either: singing charming little stories to prevent anything from entering the heart or the mind. And boosterism isn't conversation either: broadcasting, self-advertising what we are doing, have done, going to do. You can't converse with a sales pitch of positive preaching. All these kinds of talk have to be cured in therapy: they interfere with conversation.

So, not just any talk is conversation, not any talk raises consciousness. A subject can be talked to death, a person talked to sleep. Good conversation has an edge: it opens your eyes to something, quickens your ears. And good conversation reverberates: it

keeps on talking in your mind later in the day; the next day, you find yourself still talking with what was said. That reverberation afterwards is the very raising of consciousness: your mind's been moved. You are at another level with your reflections. So, what helps conversation?

Here we need to look again at what conversation is. The word means turning around with, going back, like reversing, and it comes supposedly from walking back and forth with someone or something, turning and going over the same ground from the reverse direction. A conversation turns things around. There are versions in a conversation: various turns to it. And there is a verso to every conversation, a reverse back side.

It is this verso, this exposition of the reverse version, that is, I think, the work of the Institute—and also what the Forum is about.

What we expect from these lunches is not information, facts, personal opinions, and boosterism, not even education, but rather whatever keeps us walking together with something and turns things around, upside down, converts what we already feel and think into something unexpected, the unconscious becomes conscious.

And to keep turning means that it's no use having fixed stands, definite positions. That stops conversation dead in its tracks. Our aim is not to take a "stand" on this or that issue, but to examine the stands themselves so they can be loosened, and we can go on walking back and forth.

And that is why the style of our conversation here has to be somewhat upsetting, turning around the first expected direction of a thought or a feeling. And that is why we have to speak with irony—even ridicule and cutting sarcasm. Shocking even: because consciousness comes with a little shock of awareness, keeping us on edge, acute, awake, and a little awry. Psychotherapy doesn't use electroshock, but psycho shock—that little twinge or flash that makes a situation suddenly seem altogether new.

One small institute, one small lunch each month among a few friends and acquaintances, can hardly turn the city around, raise the level of its self-awareness, its reflection and insight into its unconscious repressions. Or might these Forum conversations already be at the cutting edge of raising consciousness? For if we here are working at curing our talk and less at talking of cures (for this or that problem) we would be engaged in true conversations, the very activity that does turn all things around.

# On Culture and Chronic Disorder

## *James Hillman*

To make a point already at the beginning of these notes: I'm not going to begin by defining my main terms "culture" and "disorder," but shall start with an image. The image of the back ward in the state asylum, clinic, mental health home—and it doesn't matter whether today or when you were a child and there was a brick building for the criminally insane, the crippled children's home, the county asylum for the incurably insane, or whether your image be Bedlam, Bellevue, Brookhaven—there is a back ward. The retarded, the drugged, the indolent in strange postures; monuments of unaging neglect, refuse, and decay, noiseless confusion, an underworld of benches and beds and ugly walls, glassed-in nurses, the defeated like ghouls under nightlights, odd clothes on shapeless bodies, odours unusual and sick, ridiculous the waste sad time stretching. . . .

You may brighten the image with cheerfulness programs (youth in training), with occupational crafts and ward music, fresh pastel paint, little jokes on signs. You may have no chains, no mass showers, replaced all by tiny, glossy color-keyed pills. Still the back ward remains a fixedly recurring image —wherever it be located: on a Roman slave ship, in a Czarist drunken city, in Orwell's Paris hospital, a VA unit in hometown USA.

Now, let's move that image inside, as we psychologists are fond of doing. Let's move the back ward into our own backwardness. Let us envision our own retarded, crippled, "incurvature" as Robert Burton called our conditions as they age, the incurvature, the incurable, permanent conditions of human backwardness, that cannot be cured, that cannot be endured. Here is our chronic disorder whether it appears in our marriage knots, family reactions, fears of the dark, erotic fantasies, blank long depressions, inhibitions, compulsions . . . there is a backward look, a terror of the back ward in us each which appears in the chronic disorders of our human natures that bespeak the eternal return, the *ricorso*, of primordial conditions.

**I**

The issues that now arise are these three:

a. how to look at this back ward; then
b. how to deal with it, and
c. what has the back ward (and how
    we look at it and deal with it) to do
    with culture—the purpose of our
    meeting today and with this institu-
    tion which we are inaugurating.
So now to *a*: how to look at backwardness.

First, we may assume the chronic
area is defective. Either sociologically
backward, deprived, underprivileged,
underdeveloped, and owes its nature
to external forces. Or, we may assume
a genetic defect, a hereditary taint,
again owing its implacable nature to
forces outside its own condition. Or,
we may take a Darwinian position
that the back ward is the unfit. As
Jung says, nature is aristocratic, profli-
gate, throwing up countless attempts,
but only few seeds survive and even
fewer rise to genius or culture.
Human life is a vast area of failed attempts. In this view the back ward is
as it is, a demonstration of nature, of
natural laws which have little to do
with the individual case.

Second, we may regard the chronic
area as cursed. This gives to the
natural laws a moral meaning. The
back ward is a circle in Dante's Hell,
an area of the human soul as por-
trayed by Dostoevsky or, in another
mode, by Graham Greene, in which
God's purpose is working.

Third, we could imagine the place
of irremediable disorder to be the
shrine of a specific God: Saturn,
Kronos, Chronos. Here Saturn reaches

our lives and we would not find him
otherwise but through the retarded,
crippled, unchanging chronic factor.
Or the God may be Fate, the Furies,
Ananke, that is, again in Jung's language, there is a God in the disease
(which is not to say that God *is* a
disease, or the disease *is* a God and
must be worshipped as disease, for this
is to idolize disease and to limit the
God to his shadow).

Each of these ways of looking at the
chronic back ward implies *b*: modes of
dealing with it.

The first of these is heroism: Let's
get in there and do something. Let's
not accept the chronic disorders to
begin with. In psychiatry, this notion appears in the refusal to accept
any genetic governance of behavior,
no hereditary taints, no karma—
everything is changeable. It is a protean, mercurial view of the soul. All
nature is subject to transformation
by human will so that transformation
tends to be equated with reformation.

We need at the Institute to give
time to this theme because for me
heroism of this sort is the prime
enemy of culture. Only in passing
then let me characterize the theme:
Heroism, and the American mono-
myth of doing away with trouble;
Heroism, and disappointment, or
burnout and despair; Heroism, and
move-out: the Sunbelt, New Frontier,
Westward Ho! Get away from what
drags—away, away with it. What actually is shot by troubleshooters? The

heroic denial of chronicity seems to be a fundamental American tenet. "We must keep this nation on the move," say the slogans. And then the reverse: not going down with your ship, for the flag, at the Alamo, a heroic stasis that leaves no culture either.

Heroism comes in a second style. Contrary to heroic redemption is heroic *suppression*. The chronic is accepted as it is: incurable, so let's not waste time on it. Let's stuff it away, euthanasia, concentration camp, ghetto, slavery—make it work for us, or get rid of it. Will power, control, clean the stables in one way or another. But keep it cost efficient.

A third way of dealing with chronic disorder we may call welfare. Here is our main modern approach, a fantasy of humanistic mediocrity, of democratic kindness and practibility. Welfare says the back ward is the price we must each pay for success, for our tough competitive ego. Some parts are weaker—not defective, but not quite able to keep up. So we must create a place for the chronic disorders, "remedialize" with programs the slower stupid parts, and re-integrate, with half-way houses at the threshold, the back ward closer to the front-line cutting edge of the advancing civilization.

Welfare is both external in society and internal in the way we meet our individual backwardness. With the expectations of improvement, we administrate it, arrange for it, or "put it away." Mainly we have some sort of adjustment fantasy, progressivist,

toward the civilized goals of conformism.

Welfare misses that the chronic is a different form, serves other Gods. The blind, the crippled, and the mad have other measures than unafflicted human norms. For that reason we can learn from them—the blind poet, the crippled artisan, the mad prophet. They imagine in wholly other ways. As Bachelard said, the imagination works through deformation, but welfare works in terms of reforming and conforming. Chronic disorder is precisely that which does not fit into progressivist humanism, precisely proof of the survival of the unfittest and that even the Platonic ideal of "fittingness" does not here apply. Hence the recidivism, the eternal return, of chronic disorder in ourselves and society.

Welfare fails and there is deep bitterness over its failure. "I've tried and still nothing worked . . . I've been decent, tolerant, kind." Welfare must fail because it remains within the heroic attempt to change, though this be a secularized, castrated heroism, subdued, adjusted, mediocratized—the heroic mission to *save* has become to *help* or to *improve*. Mission without mission and without hero. Mission becomes administration, institutionalized feeling. Welfare is finally a guilty-ego event, not an archetypal passion like an ascetic (burn it out) or a redemptive Jehad holy war (convert or die). Mere civility, mere good will and programmatic gimmicks.

We've now reviewed heroic

redemption, heroic repression, and welfare or secularized heroics. Now we come to a fourth way of dealing with chronic disorder, and the one I recommend to your hearing.

If there is an archetypal basis of the chronic, if it has its own nature, is its own form, it then requires its own kind of handling. Let us say it will be like living with an incurable cripple. (Is that why freaks and cripples have been coming into prominence in our films and theaters—are we American heroes being reminded of chronicity?) This kind of handling is a caretaking, nursing, compassion, charity—charity rather than welfare. Recognition of the God within the condition which God is not to be violated by cure or conversion. Drive out the Devil and drive out the Angel too. Sacredness of the back ward, for even Hell belongs in God's vision. Amelioration performed through charity (not tolerance) and compassion which says: "here is something to be lived with because of its very difference, its utterly foreign alienness, which leads me to want to be closer to it for what it offers." The mission changes into a transformation, not of the disorder, but of my norms of order.

"The Elephant Man" affects the doctor and the actress because they have accepted his irremediableness, that his complaint is chronic, death the only cure. Irremediable does not mean unredeemable. Redemption would not change a condition; it blesses as it is.

The first step of blessing the state-as-it-is leads to a second: interest in it,

curiosity about its nature, desire to stay with it longer (becoming chronic oneself), that chronicity we call fidelity, to move it to show itself further, let it speak, enact, grow its wings. In other words, the ground of love is in the very irremediableness, its chronicity.

## II

We are now led to my third question, and the one which most concerns this Institute. First we tried various ways of looking at the back ward, then we tried various ways of dealing with it. Now we ask *c*: What has the looking and dealing, and the chronic disorder itself, to do with culture?

Here I suppose you expect some notes toward a definition of culture. But all I want is to give the word a penumbra, a connotative atmosphere. It evokes "cult"—and it evokes the "occult" (hard to see, deliberately hidden, esoteric, mystery)—and "culture" also evokes fermenting organic forms that grow in intense, warm, richly fed unnatural vessels.

Culture takes us back to another place, another time, once upon a time, a golden age, to being beyond our usual existence, to forms in fermentation, and it refers to fundamentals, traditions handed down. As such, culture is always trying to revive, reach back, attempt again by serving in cult, or to repeat or resurrect as in a laboratory culture, forms that do not simply happen along in daily natural life.

May I here interject a quick distinction between culture and civilization (a risky thing to do, but others may make the distinction in other ways).

Culture evokes an intelligentsia or initiates—and these may be everyone in a society, not only an elite priesthood of "the cultured"—who appreciate, maybe even live in terms of, the occulted (what is not simply naturally given, like ideas, qualities, soul, virtues, forms). That is, *invisible values and the value of invisibles*. Because the occulted is not simply naturally given, because it refers to something artifacted, it is confused with art—but art is the visibility of the occulted, culture literalized, civilized, and does not necessarily indicate the presence of culture.

Here now some "hard facts" taken from *The Humanities in American Life* (Report of the Commission on the Humanities, pp. 113–28), published by the University of California Press. These humanistic improvements show the advance of civilization; are they also evidence of culture?

More than 750 new museums have been founded since 1969. In the single state of Wisconsin, there are more than 170 historical societies; in 1950 there were 59. Great books groups now number 2500 in the nation. In 1978, museums counted 360 million visitors which is six times the number of spectators attending professional baseball, basketball, and football games. More Americans attend performing arts events than spectator sports. In 1967 one million persons in the audiences of modern dance and

ballet; ten years later there were fifteen million. Opera attendance has increased five times between 1950 and 1978, and there are close to 1000 opera companies in the United States today. In 1968 there were twenty-four professional theater companies; 1978, over 300. There are 1400 professional symphony orchestras.

These figures raise a question we must consider here: What is the relation between humanities (arts) and culture? The name of this Institute includes them both; will it serve them both, as a "both"? Might this confuse them, substituting one for the other?

Culture takes place in closed, even closeted places, involving the alchemical *putrefactio*, or decadence as the body of fermentation. Generation and decay happen together; and they are not always easy to distinguish. What goes with civilization are irrigation systems, monuments, victories, historical endurance, wealth, and power as a cohesive force with common purpose. Civilization works; culture flowers. Civilization looks ahead, culture looks back. Civilization is historical record; culture a mythic enterprise.

They may interrelate, but they also seem able to do without each other. Civilization without culture is all around us. Culture without civilization? I think of the Tierra del Fuego Indians found by Westerners in the eighteenth century, with hardly fire, clothes, shelter, tools or vessels, always starving, always sick, yet whose vocabulary was more numerous than Shakespeare's or Joyce's, and whose culture was altogether myths of every sort.

Culture, as I have been speaking of it, looks backwards and reaches back as a nostalgia for invisibilities, to make them present and to found human life upon them. The cultural enterprise attempts to peel, flail, excite individual sensitivity so that it can again—notice the "again"—be in touch with these invisibles and orient life by their compass. The key syllable in culture is the prefix "re."

To build an argument upon a pun, the back wards display the backwards toward which culture reaches. For here is a display of recurring forms that do not change through time and which repeat in every age and society. (All societies, by the way, have some sort of psychopathology.) This universality and chronicity is expressed by both the physical view, backward as "genetic defectives" and the moral view, backward as sin, fall, or eternal damnation. If the Gods have become diseases, then these forms of chronic disorder are the Gods in disguise; they are occulted in these misshapen, inhuman forms, and our seeing through to them there—in all forms of chronic disorder in ourselves and our city—is a grounding act of culture. The education of sensitivity begins right here in trying to see through the manifestations of time into the eternal patterns within time. We may regard the discontents of civilization as if they are fundamentals of culture.

It may be surprising to associate the diseased with the divine and culture with deformity. We do so want the Gods to be pristine, models in marble on Olympus, pure as driven snow. But they are not without their shadows, their afflictions and infirmities. As they are beyond time (*athnetos*, immortal), so these shadows of disorder that they portray in their myths reappear in those human events that are not affected by time, that is, in chronic disorders. Since we are created in their images, we can only do in time what they do in eternity. Their eternal afflictions are our human infirmities.

So, my point is coming clearer: it is in dealing with the back ward that culture grows. I do not mean going off to apprentice oneself in an asylum, to become a therapist—although I understand what students are asking for by wanting to enter a training program. Not merely to help people— that's the welfare reason. Rather it is to move from civilization toward culture. By being present with the chronic castaways of civilization, they become present to the timeless incurable aspect of the soul. I may make this yet clearer to you if you think again of your own backward back ward. Nursing and sitting with it, dwelling upon it, tracing the invisible mystery in it, letting compassion come for your own chronic disorder—this all slows down your progress, moves you from future thinking to essential thinking about our nature and character, upon life's meaning and death's, upon love and its failure, upon what is truly important, and upon the small things in words, manners, act, necessitated by the limitations of your inescapable disorder. We begin to hear differently, watch differently, absorb more sensitively. Confronted with the unbearable in my own nature, I show more trepidation—which is after all the first piece of compassion. In regard to others, my manners alter, my language more attuned and precise, I become more sophisticated and artful—as a cat steps, a bird perceives, a dog follows invisibles in the air. I look to arts for understanding, to ritual for enactments, and to the lives of men and women of the past and how they came through. I need something further than community and civilization for they may be too human, too visible. I need imaginal help from tales and images, idols and altars, and the creatures of nature, to help me carry what is so hard to carry personally and alone. Education of sensitivity begins in the back ward, culture in chronic disorder.

Finally, if you allow me one more paragraph, I come to appreciate the chronic itself. More than slowing down, more than an occasion for tolerance or instruction in survival, I come to see that things chronic are things that have nothing to do with civilized time, either future time when it will be better, or present time and adjustment, disguise, or complaint— but rather the timeless structures of being which accompany us, keep company with us, in forms that do not change and do not go away, seemingly so out of place, out of step with civilization and its courageous march toward its inevitable destruction. For civilizations do eventually decline and perish. Cultures, by existing always in decay, in disorder, may continue beyond the civilizations that seem to hold them. In the shadows of the Gods are the very Gods themselves, their myths in the midst of what survives because it will not go away.

Borges said in a late poem ("Quince Monedas"):

Solo perduran en el tiempo las cosas
que no fueron del tiempo.

In time, only those things last
which have not been in time.

(*The Gold of the Tigers*, Alastair Reid, tr.)

# Education

It may no longer be possible to learn to live a fully human life by living the experience of life itself. At one time this was certainly the way one entered humanity—through the tribe, or through the folk, the family, the community; through the handing down of tradition. Culture was seemingly natural then. Imagination was alive. People spoke to each other in stories, not logic. The towns were filled with characters, not blank-looking functionaries. Nature was close and kept people close to their own nature. Houses had porches, and people sat there watching other people walk. Children played well into the dark. Life was about birth, life, love, and death. Simple things were exciting. Labor had the mark of craft. But we must be clear about the nostalgia produced by such memories. The longing centers, not on the return to the way things were, but on the need for value. And, where once, presumably, the forms within which life took place inculcated value, all this must now take place on another plane, education.

Talk of educational reform abounds these days—and action too. Everyone knows that there is something seriously wrong. Commissions have studied the problems and made their recommendations. Many good people are working to better education. This is the arena in which the life of culture is at stake. External solutions, however, address only one half of the situation. Strong images of democracy must be recalled as the form of life requiring a particular form of education—the best for all. And it must be recalled that learning can never be imposed from the outside since it belongs to the nature of the human soul as its primary mode of transformation and joy. Anything occurring on the outside must conform to the basic necessities of the soul—and what the soul hungers for is an imagination of the world, an initiation into sensibility, the development of the capacity of reflection, and the ability to stand apart from what it knows, to look at it dispassionately with understanding and insight.

The key, the bridge, the irreplaceable link between the institution of education and the desire of the soul to learn, is the teacher. What unusual creatures are teachers! Buffeted about the institution with its demands, trying desperately to remain true to their calling, their vocation, what they most need is respect, admiration, and support. What they are getting is tests, criticism, and management. Teachers may be the only cultural resource we have. Mistreatment of them will surely mark the end of culture.

The articles in this chapter concern fundamental educational reform which is quite a different thing from restructuring. These reflections go to the roots, reach into the subsoil, recognize that treating the topsoil alone produces frail fruit for but a few seasons. Education cannot be content as the instrument of civilization. It must go down farther than that and confront the fact that it is the source and the manifestation of the human spirit conforming to the cosmos at large, together fulfilling a destiny.

*Robert Sardello*

# The Necessity of a
# Liberal Education

## *Donald Cowan*

From the moment of birth, life is a process of learning. It is the chief obligation of all living things, their chief task and chief joy. Surely it is only an overseriousness of entomologists that denies us an account of young ants at play, like young tigers exuberant in their learning of survival traits. All things rejoice in learning, dolphins and dogs bodily smiling at the task. When the mind is either satiated or anorexic and cannot learn, despair sets in. "Give us this day our daily hunger," says Gaston Bachelard, an avid reader of books. For whatever reason we learn—from desire, from compulsions, from pride, from greed, for use, for pay—we gain joy. . . .

Instructors for life are manifold. Once out of the common womb, an infant is taught by every object, every being, every event that surrounds it. The instructors vary widely in their quality from home to home, and I am not so socially insensitive as to suppose this variation makes no difference nor so genetically innocent as not to recog-

nize prenatal determined capabilities.

As for the first, society must do what it can to alleviate and compensate for environmental differences, keeping in mind that they are statistical and not individual determinants.

The second differentiator, innate abilities, has so small a range on any cosmic scale as to make a concern for it only of second order. . . .

What I touch on here is basic to democratic principle, that throughout required schooling there be one track only for the curriculum. A multitrack system, with children grouped according to their assumed ability to learn, establishes a class structure defined in childhood, a slaughter of the innocents so to say. So, too, does a vocational track in secondary schools. It seems to the privileged members of society a kind and concerned expedient to provide a ready path for sustenance and "a way up" to lesser abilites and limited ambitions, but such an attitude is an unwarranted condescension and an unrecognized intention of preserving the status quo. Vocationalism, however, is a preparation for obsolescence, a harbinger of frustration. The public is ill served, both economically and culturally, by such a separation, and democracy is thereby rendered a virtual impossibility.

The educational process itself benefits from a normal mixture of minds. The concept of "talented and gifted" is a hoax perpetrated by fond parents and bowed to by school administrators embarrassed by the quality of the enterprise they operate. The curriculum is the center of the problem; it must be designed for the best student, not in its complexity but in its imaginative scope and in its possibilities for profundity. The ordinary and even the less able students respond to such material; they may remain less adroit than their brilliant classmates, but they live on the same plane of understanding. And the bright ones learn responsibility and respect for their fellows. . . .

Let me not dispraise the public school. Universal education is a remarkable accomplishment. It has managed to offer twelve years of schooling for everyone, although I think we can grant that only recently have we made it for everyone. It is a great moral achievement, but like most moral gains, it comes when it becomes practical. . . .

Schools developed in the eighteenth century in an industrial pattern, deserting the monastic and cathedral school tradition designed for postulants. As in other modes of industrial work, in the schools there was a work day, with workers turning out a product in a batch process, organized around clock time. And it served fairly well. Society was advanced if not elevated by the strategem. But now that industrialization is approaching its asymptotic limit, and the economic world is undergoing radical changes not yet fully envisioned, it is time to reconsider the pattern of schooling. . . . Liberal education is not defined by its contents; that is, it is not limited to the liberal arts. . . . Liberal education continues to be the preparation of noble minds.

There was a time when such an end needed no justification, when the greatest rascal in the world recognized his rascality by how far short it fell of the noble ideal. No more. A charge of "elitism" rings out against universal liberal education. Somehow it seems undemocratic for a noble mind to presume nobility in others. The equality that democracy demands certainly does not depend on fine manners or elegant speech, on wit or intelligence, on station or circumstance. Humanity is a common thing in which we all share equally, not only before the law, not only in our rights, but in our supralegal concerns for the welfare of all, regardless of circumstances. . . .

Ennoblement of the mind comes through a process of idealization. Those things that stock the imagination are reshaped as they are put there, reshaped from the partial and mutilated forms that reality presents to the pristine form they are "supposed" to have. The actual image is not lost but the idealized one shines through and is a normative reference. What is observed is not thereby artificial; it is real with all its deficiencies apparent, but it is perceived in the aura of its ideal and judged in the light of its aspirations. In truth this action is a natural one. It is an extension of that tendency of the imagination to complete an image, to make it whole under the guidance of a loosely structured intuition.

The basic action of a liberal education, then, as I am describing it is an act of criticism, a term I use in the sense of literary criticism or art criticism, but I imply something much more general, something that acts on physics or philosophy or on any symbolic activity that expresses value in life. I see criticism as the complete dynamism of the act of knowing. . . . There is a part of all people that does indeed stand aside and view their own thought, dispassionately. The part that stands aside governs one's learning ability, and elevates it to the place of understanding. The fruit of that understanding is what one does in life, one's critical comment on existence.

The critical mind seeks truth, seeks it in a fullness of being that is a fusion of the subjective and objective; discerns relationships and establishes coherences, taking what is immediately before it and finding an essence in the particular that has universal implications. This process is the action of learning, something I see as occurring in three stages.

The first is the immediate apprehension of a thing; the second is the unfolding and structuring of it in the mind; the third is a truly creative action, transforming the initial things into something new, which is then given to the shared world of knowledge. . . .

The first moment, as I have said, is the innocent acceptance of, the dwelling with, an experience, its reality taken into the mind as a whole. It comes from a love-at-first-sight experience, a knowing something before rationality sets in, before analysis has torn it apart. Music comes to us in such a fashion and for most persons remains a nonverbal, nonrational experience of satisfaction. . . . What comes to the mind through sight is perceived as meaning, but what comes in through sound is sensed as form. Poems, accordingly, should be read aloud on the first encounter so that the impatient visual perceptors, angelic in their rapidity, can pace themselves to the more human sequences of spoken language. . . . But let my emphasis on the preposition *before* as applying to time be modified a bit. Admittedly the apprehension does not always occur on the first reading or hearing—frequently not until analysis has been considerably advanced. Particularly in a discipline such as physics, wholeness forms in the imagination only after long contemplation through analysis. . . .

When I say that this full-bodied, intuitive act of apprehension cannot be taught I do not mean it is wholly apart from teaching. What a professor seeks in a classroom is the moment the lights come on in the faces before him—when what was before merely argument becomes reality. It happens one by one among students, not seemingly from an adequacy of explanation by the professor but by insight in the student. Students have provided moments of pleasure for their professors by a sudden grasping of a concept which, in his inept fashion, he was trying to demonstrate. Not his own brilliance but their luminosity brightens his day. That is the nature of his calling.

The structuring stage is the arena for theory. This is a kind of mapping, one could say, indicating that there are many different ways to lay out an experience, to chart it so that it may be studied. . . . A mapping is a device for presenting experience to the mind in a manner the mind can handle. It is a communications device as well, for we can assume that if the map is simple everyone is seeing the same thing. Any one mapping should be complete; we test for completeness and accuracy against the model held in the mind.

It is in this structuring stage that the idealization process occurs. A certain exaggeration, or distortion, which is not in conformity with the actual world is necessary for coherence of structure. . . .

A genre theory of literature is an ideal mapping, for instance, requiring some notion of a heightened form—

tragedy, let us say—not to be found in its entirety in either literary examples or in life, but evoked in the imagination *by* poetry and by certain aspects of life. Each discipline has different characteristic mappings and each of us adapts different ways of charting to order experience. The fact that there are many different structurings, all complete, is by no means disturbing. . . . Each structuring that is consistent and complete and represents a serious attempt to chart experience brings out salient features of the real subject under study. . . .

Physics often suffers from an overelegance in mapping. So, too, does philosophy. Logic often checks against itself for consistency rather than against an extra-mental reality. I have never approved of logic as an introductory course for that reason, fearing the student would become so entranced by the map that he never noticed the very real terrain. Logic should come later, in the position of critique. . . . Learning must cause a metamorphosis of the person, not merely elevate him—must make him into something different from what he was before. The evidence for this change comes in the moment of *making*. There must issue from the learner something new, something he has not been taught, that has about it a recognizability of authenticity. Let me illustrate this process by recalling the figure of sound and light I set before you earlier to demonstrate the primacy of nonverbal meaning. I suspect you gave it an immediate validity—that is, you grasped it. Then your mind immediately started rearranging things so that the new concept fit in, that is, a structuring process ensued. My mind did so, and I took hold of the velocity of light being a million times faster than sound so that one receptor was flooded and the other ordered; and I envisioned the little area in the brain where visual images are given quick processing before forwarding to the more interior central unity, whereas sound comes into the larger brain area and is apparently more fully processed. Then out of this sort of quick mapping issued a metaphor, that of impatient angels. Your own structuring was no doubt quite different, characteristic of your own discipline and experience, and what you made of it was yours. But we apprehended the same thing.

For the third, creative, moment to occur, the first moment must have taken place. However intricate and extended the analysis, if the moment of recognition has not come to the thinker, he cannot make a significant addition to what he is studying. The thinker must have apprehended the object whole in his imagination in order to say or do anything important about it. In contrast, the analysis, the second moment, is not an absolute necessity. A work of art can be made out of direct apprehension, but such a work is likely to be primitive or accidental. All three moments must occur for the process to be complete, for an increase in the world's body to

come about. . . . It is this entire process that I call liberal education.

# The Joy of Learning

## Louise Cowan

Learning has been my occupation for some forty years. This is by no means to say that I am learned; quite the contrary. Actually, a learner, in the end, is likely to know very little. He has relinquished things and systems as they yield him insight, has been concerned more to see and love the reality before him than to attempt to possess it. But after one has learned how to learn, authentic works of the imagination, gone over from time to time (in the way some people used to go over the Bible as a constant companion) show one how to teach: how to continue to learn oneself and to share the awakening of learning in others.

For learning requires a mentor— an Athena, a Virgil, a Beatrice—to lead and teach, guide and instruct their young Telemachus and Dante, showing their charges how to learn, stepping back when the pupil begins to see and understand on his own.

Learning, then, is not automatic in study. It is difficult to begin it by oneself, no matter how much one reads—and almost impossible to achieve it with a negligent and inade-quate teacher. (Let me make clear that I am not denying that one can learn by oneself: indeed the great part of our acts of learning occurs in this way. I am saying that without a teacher to show one what learning is, it is highly unlikely that one will discover it for oneself.)

Learning is a rare phenomenon, in fact, though of course it ought not be. It is the least recognized activity in our schools, the least valued of all acquired excellences by the general public. . . .

The one activity of which the human person is capable that does not dim with age nor fail with sickness, persecution, or disgrace is learning. To learn does not mean one has to be brilliant or original, well informed or keenly rational. To learn is to take an aspect of the world into one's mind, to regard it with interest and delight, finding in contemplation its true significance, and allowing it to lead one to a new territory. This process may be brief and minor, or it may extend over a long period, issuing in a major vision. It is an act potentially available to every person, characteristic of the human species. But people must be taught to learn before they can learn, just as they must be taught language before they can speak, even though the potential for speech is present in the human soul.

Many people, as I have been implying, never learn to learn: they amass information, knowledge of systems and processes, which they can recall at will and even recombine to fit new situations and new problems. By living in a world of things and customs and operations they acquire skills—some of them ingenious and some of them extremely pleasurable and satisfying. They may have a feeling of creativity and free play; but in the sense I intend it, they have never had the joy of learning, have no notion of what it means or of its transforming power.

I mean no patronization of the people who, I am saying, do not learn. Indeed, one must recognize among some of them a wisdom that comes from a faithful attention to the rhythms of life, to the variegated faces of objects, the plasticity of earth, and the pathos of creatures, to the necessities of living and dying. . . .

Some of Faulkner's best characters are of this sort, as are Hardy's and D. H. Lawrence's. It is this solid, grounded nonlearner that we all hold in our hearts as some kind of ideal: an image of harmony, humility, wholeness. Is it a memory of the Garden? Or the regions just outside it, where faith and obedience are still more important than individuality and progress; where the cosmic elements and

the human powers have intimate intercourse.

But in our time, when a total reorganization of society is coming about, with the farm mechanized and a major percentage of the population living in cities, with electronic communication taking the place of the transportation of goods, with manufacturing given over to a few designers and innovators, and production increasingly relegated to robots or robot-like human beings, there is little chance of our having any longer a folk—a folk who maintain their own order of existence, in unbroken contact with archetypal forms, religious faith, and a sacred familial structure. The tribal order is irretrievable; even the small-town folk have condominiums, cable television, Dairy Queens, and Walmarts.

And even more to the point, those in charge of the huge systems that control our cities and hence our civilization are, many of them, people who have had neither the formation of character imparted by a traditional society nor the transforming experience of learning. They may acquire the ability to reason to a conclusion and from available facts go on to make judgments. They may invent new systems and improve old processes; they may even by a thorough saturation in the processes of their particular industry make a creative leap—or hire someone to—by designing a new product that will corner the market. It is a mistake, however—and a fatal one for our society—to consider their progression of thought learning.

For learning implies a move to a higher stage of understanding, into a new relation with the world—a distancing of oneself from the personal and at the same time a union with the thing through which learning occurs. Learning implies nothing less than the apprehension of a cosmos, even if that apprehension is partial, brief, and transitory. It is not that one learns something, but that one is changed by the joy of learning. . . .

I should like to try to define joy, in distinction to some of its near-synonyms: ecstasy, beatitude, happiness, pleasure, delight. (My definitions are not meant to be based on etymological roots, or even on standard dictionary definitions, but on a kind of sense of the word itself, as poets and literary people would use and have used the words in their writing.) *Ecstasy*, applicable to the mystical experience, implies being carried out of the body into the love of God, a transitory state; when we speak of the ecstasy of lovers, we are of course being metaphoric. *Beatitude* implies a permanent transformation by divine love; *happiness*, too, suggests a state of permanence: the well-being of the soul in the presence of the good; *pleasure* is a temporary feeling: delectation through senses; *delight*, which is a delectation of the intellect and spirit, is in response to particular events and hence cannot be long-lasting. **Joy**, in contrast to those other states of glad-ness, comes almost entirely from the contemplation of a form discovered, a witnessing of the coming into being of a splendor. . . .

And it is with this joy that has a paradox at its very center that we learn, for learning is seeing a form in matter and ennobling it in the soul. It is a witnessing of the informing of the corporeal by the incorporeal, the darkness by light. . . .

There is an act, which Dante speaks of in his letter to Can Grande della Scala, which gives form to the actual perceived life of the human person and which, hence, may be taken as exemplifying the act of learning if, as I have said, learning implies the apprehension of a form. He speaks of the "allegory of theologians" and the "allegory of poets," and he seems to mean by his first phrase the true way of poetry, whereas the allegory of poets signifies for him a merely literary art of saying one thing in terms of another. . . . By the kind of poetry he was writing he meant a shaping of life, through images, so that understanding and meaning are discerned in what would otherwise seem a flux of sensations, emotions, opinions, and thoughts. . . .

The true way of poetry is described by Jacques Maritain:

> By poetry I mean, not the particular art which consists in writing verses, but a process both more general and more primary; that inter-communication between the inner being of things and the inner being of the human self which is a kind of divination. Poetry in this sense is the secret life

of each and all of the arts, another name for what Plato called mousike.

I want to call this "divination," this communication between the inner human self and the inner being of things *poiesis*, so that it will not be confused with poetry as verse. Poiesis, as I am using it, is a making by seeing.

The high moments of this poiesis have been preserved for us—not only in poetry but in what we call the *liberal arts*. This is, as a matter of fact, what characterizes any study as a liberal art: it is based on the vision of a form. It expresses this vision in a structured art which by the skill, its enticement, can lead the pupil to the vision that lies not only behind a single work but behind the entire discipline and finally, by implication at any rate, behind the entire act of knowing.

For the marvelous power of the liberal arts is to engender in those who follow in their path the essentially *same* action, since theirs is likewise an imaginary or intellectual action, not a reportorial account of personal experience. The particular is raised to contain the general. In Dante's poem, it is the "invisible and hidden" spiritual course that all human beings could undertake that engenders learning, and not the "obvious and external" journey which is its analogue. . . .

Those who read literally, or simply for the pleasure of "the song" intending to follow without discerning the inner meaning, had better turn back; for art taken in such a manner can dangerously mislead. But those few who have learned how to learn, how to take the art as leading to the inner meaning, can "entrust their vessels to the high seas" without fear. . . .

The liberal arts take us by the hand and lead us along the way and, scolding our stupidity and cowardice, praising our timid motions to acquiesce, develop in us the power to make the same spiritual journey as Dante and to gaze upon the same splendid sights. It is not only poems that guide us to this re-enacted journey; philosophy, too, can enable the learner to follow with guidance in the footsteps of Plato and to have the same insights he had; the ordinary college student in physics today, if he is diligent and perseverant, and has a good teacher, can reach the same plane of understanding as an Einstein.

The teacher, then, as I have been saying for some time now is the key to the remedies for the manifold ills ravaging our schools. For learning is the school's very reason for being; its chief occupation should be teaching pupils how to learn. But teachers themselves need to be transformed and to have found for themselves the mind's happiness. And I call the process of discovering it joy.

# The Learning Instinct

## *Robert J. Sardello*

I want to begin with a claim which counters present theories of learning, but nevertheless carries enough force to be cultivated into insight. The claim reads: of all the instincts—reproduction, hunger, aggression, survival—the most characteristically human instinct is learning. While much of education has as its goal the preparation for earning a living, if one starts with the premise of learning as instinct, the goal of education transforms into 'learning a living,' for the instinct continues to awaken all through life. . . .

Who can deny experiencing an impulse for learning, a force welling up from within, a powerful, autonomous urge, satisfied only through release, and when released producing an intense form of pleasure that can only be called joy? My purpose, then, consists of serving the forgotten soul of learning, beginning with a description of its impulsive vitality. . . .

The impulse for learning originates in an alluring display of the things of the world, evoking desire for union with them—an urge toward intimacy with the spirit, soul, vitality, the particular beauty marking each thing as

standing forth from an abyss of holiness. Things draw us to intimate knowledge as if they need us, though in an entirely impersonal manner, for their own completion. The forceful allure of the world to be known draws the soul out of a self-enclosing illusion of mastery through detachment into soul engagement with reality. This innate desire to experience the world pulsing through the body constitutes a drive toward transformation initiating care for all things. Learning compels us to have regard for what is outside and beyond ourselves, and in knowing this to become like them. Thus, the basis of the learning instinct lies in mimesis, an imitation of the action of the things of the world, knowing as entering the manifest mystery of things. In climactic moments of history the inner life of the world bursts forth initiating a flowering of culture. Renaissance begins, though, in the soul, through release of its most natural activity, learning.

The repression of instinctual life prompted the creation of psychoanalysis. Freud uncovered two primary instincts, eros and thanatos—the urge toward life and the urge toward death. The contribution of Jung lay in the rediscovery of the psyche, which, he showed, does not belong singularly to human experience, but to physical things as well. A third instinct, learning, drives us between life and death; it has as its purpose a union with the psyche of the world. An understanding of this instinct requires mythical modes of thought reminiscent of the pre-Socratic philosophers and early storytellers. One such myth, central to learning, concerns genius.

Ancient psychology spoke of genius as mythical beings, daemons of a particular sort, whose work consists of guardianship of the world. The genius within things gives them vitality, continuity between generations, and attractiveness. The spirits of things at the same time, though in a slightly different manner, are guardians of individual human beings; individuals are also accompanied through life by a genius. The relation between individual genius and those of the world, the push and pull between them, seems to me to lie at the heart of the learning instinct. In the act of knowing, to become united with the thing known, is pre-disposed by the presence of the personal genius attracted to its similars in the world—which may be physical things, ideas, books, music, art, language, music—all have their guardians. . . .

Today we equate genius with extraordinary ability, as if it were a possession of a gifted few, a mistake perpetuated in schools through pro-grams for the talented and gifted. The word, genius, however, comes from Roman mythology, equivalent to the daemons of Greek myth. The word derives from 'gignere'—to engender or engenderer; genius names those guardians who engender, give gender, generate life and vitality in our surroundings, assuring that things will be cared for because they are animated by spiritual presences. When things are approached with care, their genius shines forth. Genius also inspires the potency of individual life. In those times when the world was perceived as living, individual genius was honored on the day of one's birth. At the birthday celebration certain foods appropriate to the nature of the genius were offered. Those who indulged their genius were called 'genialis', from which we receive the word 'genial'. The person who refused indulgence was called 'aridus', dry.

The coordination between world-centered and individual-centered genius has its own specific mythological rendering in astrology; one's astrological chart depicts the attractions between individual and world. The latin word *natale* means 'companion', and from this word comes the term 'natal chart'. The chart gives images of the particular sectors of the world with which one's genius is congenial. We now call this attraction talent or ability and try to measure it with intelligence tests; and in so doing, the necessary contribution of the genius of the world is obscured. . . .

The central task of learning consists

of learning to learn, a yielding to one's genius, allowing the instinct to be released. Those who more fully allow themselves to be inhabited by their daemon, who no longer seek to control and keep it repressed are true teachers. They are teachers because they cannot stop learning themselves. When education recognizes this force, the spiritual/cultural necessity of learning will take its rightful precedence over practical and social concerns. The purpose of learning, its goal, is to be a means without an end. Indulging the appetites of one's genius leads to voracious seeking after the pleasures of knowledge. Learning is to the soul what food is to the body. Bad soul food consists of undigested facts, raw information, half-baked ideas, cafeteria curricula. Good soul food is prepared with imagination, warmed with the heart, served as a feast of ideas. Then learning can get into the blood, circulate, enter the materiality of the body, transform it, and be released into the body of the world.

While the specific effects of learning thus understood are unpredictable, the locus of those effects can be specified. If learning were free to work in the world it would produce a ferment of conversation, writing, performance, speculation, investigation, and the making of images—in art, music, poetry, drama, music. I am not suggesting that the arts would flourish, for the arts would no longer be separated, specialized realms. Culture would flourish, bringing about a synthesis of imagination such as we have

not seen since the Renaissance. The manic world of economics, production, consumption, would cease, replaced by the living materiality of world-filled imagination. . . .

In a recent film, "Teachers," a call is put in for a substitute teacher for a high school history class. Unknown to the recruiter, the man who answers the phone is not the substitute but an inmate of a mental institution, who happily responds to the opportunity for early release by walking out of the asylum and entering the teaching profession. He takes well to the task of the classroom by costuming himself as the historical figures who are the subject of the lessons—as Lincoln, as Washington, as Custer—and enacting scenes of importance, engaging the students in the lessons. This teacher was not utilizing a ploy, a trick, a kind of audio-visual aid to illustrate history. He became inhabited by those figures. When he is finally discovered as a lunatic, the men with the white coats are called in and he is hauled away, rather brutally. As the attendants drag him down the corridor, the teacher exhorts them to take their hands off him and treat him with respect, for, he says, "I am a Teacher." Now, in the whole high school, it seems to me, this person was in fact the only teacher. The hero of the film is supposed to be the real teacher because he is so involved in the lives of the students; actually, he is more of a social worker, concerned with making school 'relevant.' Others are involved in school politics, or concerned with how to keep discipline, or lobbying for a union for pay increases, or satisfying the superintendant. But only this one madman is hospitable to the spirits; the madman is a genius.

The qualities of learning I have been attempting to evoke cannot be institutionalized. But the educational institution might be revisioned, seen as the structure whose task is to protect the inviolate space of the classroom, whose duty is to arrange a situation in which teachers are allowed to teach. With such protection, teachers could follow the demands of their genius, awakening the genius of their students. The genius of teaching makes the following demands: to at all times engage in living thinking—the recognition that ideas are living entities; to be devoted to the pleasures of truth and knowledge; to teach out of a deeply rooted feeling that there is something higher than ourselves; to take 'outer' things and allow them to re-echo in the soul by exercising the faculties of imagination, inspiration and intuition.

# The Essential Elements for a New Educational System

## Mortimer Adler

We are on the verge of a new era in our national life. When the potential in its human resources is fully exploited, America, the slumbering giant, will realize its potential to the full. A revolution in education will usher in the dawn of a new day. As the century draws to a close, we are about to see that revolution take place. . . .

But the democratic pledge of equal educational opportunity, half fulfilled, is much worse than a promise broken. It is an ideal betrayed. Equality of educational opportunity is grievously misunderstood if it means no more than taking all the children into the public schools for the same number of hours, days, years. If they are divided there into the sheep and the goats, into those destined for economic and political leadership and for a quality of life that all should enjoy, then the democratic ideal has been sorely traduced by an inadequate system of public schooling.

Inadequate because it has achieved only the same quantity of public schooling for all, not the same quality for all. Worse than inadequate, the failure to achieve the same quality for all is a downright violation of our democratic principles. . . .

The curriculum, which shall be the same for all, is divided into three main columns running through the twelve years as follows:

a.  One is the study of three basic areas of subject matter (mathematics, natural science, and history), in which knowledge is acquired through didactic instruction.

b.  Another is the acquirement of all the skills of learning involving the use of the English language primarily and a foreign language secondarily, as well as other symbolic devices, such as those of calculators and computers and other scientific instruments; and here the instruction must be by methods akin to athletic coaching, rather than didactic.

c.  The third column in this tripartite curriculum consists of the discussion of ideas to be found in books of all sorts and other individual objects, such as pieces of music, visual works of art, film, etc. The method of instruction here should be neither didactic, nor that of coaching, but rather maieutic or interrogative. In addition, students shall participate in artistic production and performance. . . .

The curriculum shall also include (for twelve years) physical training; and (for some portion of the time) training in such manual arts as carpentry, cooking, and sewing (for all regardless of gender); and (for the last year) an introduction to the world of work, i.e., a comprehensive view of the variety of particular vocations by which a living can be earned and a career or occupation engaged in.

The liberal and general character of the curriculum is regarded as pragmatically useful to all in that it provides preparation for a flexible adjustment to the world of work as well as to further study at optional advanced levels of schooling, where specialization can take place, though it is recommended that some continuation of general, liberal learning accompany such specialization at these higher levels of advanced schooling. . . .

The preparation of the teaching personnel to staff basic schooling shall involve advanced schooling that is largely liberal and general in character and is accompanied by specialized training in teaching itself that is like a clinical internship in medicine. Teachers, in addition, should all be engaged actively in learning. In the

organization of the school, at either the elementary or the secondary level of basic schooling, the principal must play the role of principal teacher, not just that of chief administrator. . . .

The required course of study set forth in the preceding pages is as important for what it displaces as for what it insists upon and introduces.

It displaces a multitude of elective courses, now offered in the last four years of basic schooling, which have no place there at all, for they make little or no contribution to general, liberal education.

It eliminates all narrowly specialized training for particular jobs.

It throws out of the curriculum and into the category of optional extra-curricular activities a variety of activities that have little or no educational value.

If it did not call for all these displacements and eliminations, there would not be enough time in the school day or the school year to accomplish everything that is essential to the general, liberal learning that must be the content of basic schooling.

Something like what is here proposed has been done in other countries. Something like what is here proposed has been done in our own country in a few exceptional schools, public as well as private.

Those who think it cannot be done for all as well as for the few fail to realize that most of the students for whom it is not now done have never had their minds challenged by re-

quirements such as these. They will
rise to higher expectations when those
expectations are set before them and
their minds are challenged by teachers
able to give the different types of instruction called for by the three basic
columns in the required curriculum.

Not only ignorance, lack of discipline, deficiency in rudimentary skills,
and minds lacking in requisite understanding result from most of the existing programs of instruction in our
public schools.

What is worse, the absence of intellectual stimulation, the failure to
challenge students by expecting the
most of them, turns students off rather
than on, and leads to boredom that
breeds juvenile delinquency, intramural
violence, and other forms of destructive conduct. Unless the overflowing
energies of the young are fully
employed constructively, they will spill
over into all forms of destructive activity.

They can be fully employed constructively only by a program of
studies that engages their minds, that
solicits and supports their active participation in learning, and that pushes
and helps each student to reach up for
as much as he can get out of school.

# The Inner Urge to Learn

## *Donald Cowan*

Human beings share with all living things certain life-sustaining instincts, reactions that apparently need not be learned. Other advantageous traits rise out of innate powers whose realization comes from self-instruction . . . sometimes with the help of situations contrived by parents, as birds learn to fly.

That much of this development occurs in play is evidence of a peculiar characteristic that seems to be truly instinctive, at least with animal creatures, and that is a joy in learning. Whether or not flowers rejoice it is hard to say, but puppies and kittens and children observably delight in the mimicry of the learning situation. As the process changes from mimicry to mimesis (becoming an imitation of principle and not of mere appearances), going on then to mastery, insight, innovation, and finally creation, the constant mark of the process is that delight. By joy I do not mean fun and games, divertissement, amusement. Nor do I mean a feeling of superiority over others. I mean a deep internal sense of satisfaction that comes with an awareness of having increased one's grasp on reality. No other incentive is needed

for learning, and indeed none other is very effective. Yet it is that particular quality that is most diminished by the institutionalization of learning in schools.

By no means do I denounce schools. I sing their praises. Schools are one of civilization's greatest inventions. The American school in particular has been a history-shattering idea—universal education, not for the security of the state, nor for the service of the economy, but for the enhancement of the person as independent citizen of a democracy. No criticism that we might pour upon the public school system can diminish its accomplishments. It is a remarkable institution. But institutions quite generally oversystematize in a legitimate search for efficiency; they rigidify in a practical setting of standards; they trivialize in a commendable seeking of breadth. When efforts at reform of schools are directed toward excellence, too frequently they result in a grim approach to study, and almost invariably they divide the students into a small group that benefits and a much larger group that quickly loses interest—and the general situation is worsened. These deviations are all institutionally engendered. And all of them destroy, for most students, the joy of learning.

I believe I can safely suppose that all of us gathered in this assembly have a deeply rooted concern for learning, consider it fundamental to the enjoyment of life for the individual person and essential to the happy operation of society. . . .

Obviously I am endorsing the idea of the common school as prerequisite for a fully realized democracy. Ours is essentially a classless society. Though there no doubt are ranges of intellect as well as of affluence in the population, there is surely some base of adequacy for both learning and earning on which a free society rests. But for the present moment my concern is educational, not political. And the common school properly conceived is an educational asset for everyone. The learning of an individual is greatly enhanced by an enveloping coherent culture. In my own experience as president of a young university I witnessed an immense gain in learning efficiency upon the initiation of a carefully chosen common core curriculum for the entire campus. Courses were no longer separated segments always starting from scratch but were built one on another . . . not so much by design as by a natural use of a set of references and fund of metaphors that everyone understood. Not only in class but outside, conversation reinforced learning. Even the jokes arose

from that shared intellectual experience. And originality, creativity, seemed to blossom in that environment. This sort of synergy could apply on a much larger scale. What if a whole community, a whole country had the same rich basic schooling? . . .

Certainly we have no desire to emulate Russia, where every child in a certain grade all over the land is studying exactly the same thing at exactly the same hour, week after week. . . .

Consequently, if we are to have in this country a common schooling of high quality, it must be approached district by district, and I should say in a less formal sense school by school. That task is immense but it is a very American sort of undertaking. This is to say that we the people must want it, must have it for the good of every child.

Let me warn you that the burden of any reform of schooling will fall on teachers. They are the ones who must spend long hours of study, of meeting together in seminars instructing each other—not in methods and techniques but in real learning. But that is the task to which they have already dedicated their lives; only by themselves learning and loving to learn can they be guides and models for the young. And only by so being can they restore to every child in school the joy of learning.

# The Teacher

## *Louise Cowan*

The teacher is central to the educational enterprise, its humanizing element. And I should say that teaching is all one thing, whatever the subject, however diverse the students. It is based on an act of generosity—the giving of self for the good of others, and is in no sense a mere hired function for which there is adequate remuneration. A teacher's salary is meant to be a living; it is not pay for a certain number of hours on duty or recompense for a certain amount of work completed. Granted, it is a modest living provided for a position freely held, a vocation that can be ill or well served, according to conscience—a ministration which is necessary to society but for which there is no adequate measure. As teachers, we are all too well aware that we do not always live up to our calling; but despite any shortcomings we should be unreserved in considering that calling noble almost beyond compare. For teachers attempt to impart to others not mere skills or information—but a wisdom and judgment about the human *use* of skills and information.

To write an effective sentence, to balance a column of figures, to reason toward an end, to read a poem, to cut a piece of wood smoothly—these are acts that must be taught, arts that generations of people would be hard pressed to discover for themselves without instruction, accomplishments that are not merely self-expression but acquired habits for which one must learn respect. The teacher is the channel for this learning, the guide, the mentor, the companion who has as his motive the passing on of things worth doing to the novices who will someday become free and creative in their performance of the human skills.

A part of the teacher's task, then, is to be true to the things he has himself learned (the arts of thinking and doing), to guard them from debasement, to refuse to engage in the "make-believe" of which Professor Barzun spoke, and to bring others to a mastery of them and a respect for them. The teacher loves the things he teaches, even when the proficiency he cultivates is something quite mechanical-seeming, like punctuation or logic. It is the love of a thing that should be well done in itself that motivates teaching, and schools enable the practice of this instruction to be carried on in a leisurely setting, apart from the busy economic world and its pressing demands.

But a teacher is not a mere guide in crafts or techniques, not even simply a stimulator of thought, important as those functions may be. The teacher is a mediator, a conductor, between one world and another, between ignorance and comprehension, in the way that Athena guides Odysseus and Vergil guides Dante. Yet the teacher is no rarified, unearthly being. He is quite ordinary and commonplace. Students need their own teacher—not simply a performance by a master teacher. We have enough good teachers now in our school system to provide a high quality of education. *If we say that all students can learn, then we must also say that all teachers can teach.* Some do not really try to do so, either out of discouragement or cynicism; and some allow the naturally human art of in-struction to be obscured in themselves through misguided theories or notions. But by and large the person who chooses teaching as a vocation wants to teach and is intelligent enough to fulfill that role, capable enough to do so well. But he becomes part of a Leviathan, an enormous, almost monstrous organization, of which the teacher is the lowest, least important member, paid the smallest salary, ac-corded the least respect. And yet the teacher is not only central to the en-tire process but the one irreplaceable element in it. . . .

And there is not an inexhaustible supply of teachers, as we are finding

out. And to lose even one dedicated teacher is an irreparable waste. Worse, to embitter teachers or cause them to lose heart is to damage the instrument right at its cutting edge, where the enterprise can either achieve or fail to achieve its purpose. Nothing short of a changed attitude toward teachers will restore our public school system or keep it from moving ever more rapid-ly into a disintegration which we have good reason to fear. It has been teachers in the past, not educational managers, that gave the American school system whatever success it has achieved.

Perhaps I can go on to say, then, without fear of seeming self-serving, that the teacher is not only central to the educational process—and irreplace-able—but in a sense *is* the process. Everything else in the schools exists so that the teacher can teach. He cannot be supplanted by anything inanimate; video tapes and other visual aids, com-puter instruction, and the entire panoply of technological devices, help-ful though they may be, pale before the power and effectiveness of the teacher. It is to the teacher that the school students are all drawn—not to the buildings or the equipment or the films or the administrative officers. These all exist to aid the teacher do his work better, to provide a structure to support the transforming work that takes place in the classroom. . . .

The schools exist to implant within the young the most valued knowledge of a culture, its treasured ideals. These cannot be transmitted by indoctrina-

tion but only by that magical power
—liberal education—which preserves
individual freedom as it leads a student
onward. This motive must permeate
all learning; but the only way it can
do so is through the teacher—the
teacher protected by the *school system*
that respects learning and sets it above
all other aims, unburdening itself from
those special tasks that have been
placed upon it by society; the teacher
encouraged by an *administration* that
can recognize when learning occurs;
the teacher reinforced by a *curriculum*
that makes available to the student the
accumulated wisdom of civilization.

I am saying, then, that what is
needed to reform our schools is not
money, not law, but that most powerful of forces—a change of heart. It
would not take thirty years or twenty
years; it would not take thirty days—
Dallas could do it *now*.

# The Technological Threat to Education

*Robert Sardello*

I am going to talk about computers and the promised revolution in education attendant upon the arrival of a promised computer culture. I want to expose the utopian fantasies inherent in all talk of computers revolutionizing education, and right at the start, let me say that I am firmly opposed to the introduction of the computer as a technological device oriented toward changing the very tradition of education. . . .

First, let us establish the particular kind of computer education that is a threat to the whole of western culture. Computers used as technical devices to perform operations that are themselves technical are not included as threatening to culture. Pocket calculators, word processing, and all the variety of programs that are ready-made for use in personal computers do not pose a threat to the very meaning of education. These technical devices can free the imagination for the consideration of matters involving mathematics, accounting, economics, or business. Or, in the case of word processing, the imagination is set free to focus on the craft of writing itself.

What is called "computer assisted instruction" also does not pose a real threat to culture. Teaching machines or programmed instruction have already shown themselves to be dismal failures, precisely because they turn the learner into a mechanism, who duly responds with frustration and boredom.

The technological threat to education is to be found in the claim that teaching the child to program the computer can be done in such a manner that programming teaches the processes of thinking itself and thus removes the necessity of formal classroom instruction. Such a claim has been put forth by Seymour Papert, professor of education at MIT, inventor of the system of programming called LOGO which is rapidly finding its way into educational settings. . . .

Teaching children to program computers in school does not have as its aim the introduction of a new subject matter into education. Computer programming as outlined in the LOGO system is not subject-centered but child-centered. It is the ultimate extension of the methods course now so prevalent in teacher education, for, in a significant way, it eliminates content altogether and reduces all education to method. . . .

The computer looms before us as far more than a device for presenting in programmed style traditional subject matter to be learned. The claim that we are entering into a computer culture must be clearly understood and taken quite seriously, in spite of all of its falseness. Culture is never a progressive affair. Culture always comes about by looking backward, by recovering the past, by relating the present to permanent patterns of the soul, by remembering the dead, by reflecting on values.

We must realize, however, that the claims of programming carry any persuasive power at all because true, living culture is itself nearly dead. Education has not done its job, the primary job of schooling, which is the initiation of the young into the life of culture. As Donald Cowan pointed out in his lecture on the economics of taste last summer, the techno-economic sphere of society has already invaded the cultural enterprise of education. Education models itself on the pattern of corporate mentality. Administrators are not the intellectual leaders of the school but the managers of a system. And teachers are not considered to have the inner authority of those who follow a calling in life, a vocation, but are considered to be staff. The technological conception of education took over the schools quite

some time ago. Moving in the devices cannot be seen as an innovation, but rather brings a technical vision to completion. Computers would not have a place in schools not already become possessed by the technical imagination.

How will computer programming eliminate curriculum in the schools? Programming as a method of learning has entered the school through the introduction of what Papert calls "the LOGO environment." The aim of this computer environment is to replace curriculum. For example, one of the subjects currently studied in schools is English grammar; it is part of the curriculum. But grammar is not a subject that interests students very much. And, for most teachers, it is probably a pretty deadly subject. Because teachers themselves do not find life in such a subject, students find it totally unrelated to life. Teacher education courses have devised methods courses for the teaching of grammar, but with the concentration on method—on how to make the subject lively and interesting for the student—more and more life is drained from the thing itself. It is an instance of the now universal occurrence where teachers themselves do not learn to love grammar and in so doing find the life within the thing, but instead learn all kinds of techniques for infantilizing grammar to make it suitable to the psychology of the child. The attempt is to care for the child more than the thing, which is really a terrible kind of psychology because real learning is possible only by becoming the thing, not by turning the thing into a subjective child-centered psychological process. . . .

The LOGO approach to the teaching of grammar through computer programming is that grammar is not studied at all. Grammar is eliminated from the curriculum. The subject would be replaced by the programming of a general structure, for example, the structure of a poem, within which words are selected from a random list to fill in that structure. The student plays around inserting various words into the general structure until an error-free poem is produced—that is, one in which each part of grammar is perfect. The aim is to bypass grammar because grammar is not interesting; but a child can feel like a poet by writing a poem, and incidentally, effortlessly learns the parts of speech and what they do while constructing a poem.

The argument in fact is quite persuasive. When we learned to talk in our early years, none of us did so by studying vocabulary and the parts of speech. We would say something and perhaps be told that we had used an incorrect word or a word in the wrong place. Gradually, we learned to speak more or less correctly. Now, what is the difference between that kind of learning and the learning proposed here? Most obviously, learning how to talk occurs in the context of a family, a community, through the mediation of all of the senses,

through the breath and the heart of those with whom we are most intimately connected. Remove any such community or put them aside from the actual act of learning and into the role of cheerleaders and what do you have? . . .

It is just here that the psychopathic character of programming as a method of learning begins to show its disguised ugliness, how education has gone from the order of the heart to the order of calculative manipulation. In order to highlight this psychopathy it is necessary for a moment to describe this psychological illness in some detail. I am neither leaving the subject of computer learning nor imposing a psychological category onto programming but rather merely describing the inherent psychology within programming as a method of learning.

Psychopathy is actually a kind of programming in life, learning how to "de-bug" life. The psychopath does everything effortlessly, freely, without any sense of inhibition, restraint, or suppression. Nothing of the world makes a claim on the soul of the psychopath. Cheating, lying, saying one thing and doing just the opposite without the least concern; changing a position from one moment to the next in order to satisfy the situation, the psychopath is always a winner. Appearing better than one actually is, successfully gliding along the surface, intelligently, but without feelings of the heart, only programmed feelings to suit the situation, psychopathy constantly assures that everything works smoothly, efficiently, always to one's advantage. Everything is a game—feelings, emotions, courtesy, love, sympathy for others, expressions of care. The psychopath can imitate any form of behavior without its going through the heart. . . .

The psychopath lacks any erotic connections with the world. The illness is one of constant manipulation of one's own psychic processes for the satisfaction of the moment. The center of gravity is totally on the side of oneself. Is this not like the child looking at the computer screen, and what is displayed there is not a content, a curriculum that one must become in order to learn; rather, one sees only one's own psychological processes as they are happening at each moment, and is given the task of manipulating them. And of course, it is fascinating, absolutely capturing to stare at oneself displayed on a screen for hours on end. Of course it is intriguing to control one's own processes, making them do whatever is necessary to receive a result. Of course, this is exciting. But it has no heart. . . .

The object of computer learning is to remove the child from the actual world and to insert him into his own subjective processes where an imitation world is invented. A recent NOVA television program devoted to the work of Seymour Papert provides a series of striking images of children learning to turn away from the world . . .

A first scene. A group of children

stand out in an open field. The field is beautiful—tall green grass, purple and yellow flowers beneath a deep blue sky. The children are not playing in this field; in fact, they are quite oblivious to their wonderful surroundings. It is quite an extraordinary image. Imagine standing outside on a cool autumn morning: there is dew in the grass; the clouds play coy games, making themselves into shapes of monsters, old men with flowing white beards, beautiful princesses. The air, pure and cool, draws deep breaths. The coolness says in a short time this grass will go to sleep for the winter; this may be the last time for six long months to romp and play, turn somersaults. Even an adult could not resist being moved to play, or at the very least to walk and contemplate the change of seasons. But these children, unmoved by such beautiful things, walk off geometric shapes through the grass. One little girl takes ten steps forward, turns left, then another ten steps straight ahead, another left turn, ten more steps, and a final sharp left turn. The girl is blind to the world. And so are the rest of the children, who are all calculating the movements necessary to make a square. When they have completed the motions, they all go inside and sit in front of the computer and program the shape of a square. This scene is paradigmatic of computer learning. It is an abstraction. Learning here does not celebrate the actual things of the world, but turns away from the world in order to program an imitation world.

Another scene. Two small girls dressed in black leotards sit cross-legged on a stage, facing each other. Music starts. The girls spin around on their bottoms several times, rise from the floor, twirl several times past each other and then cartwheel back, crossing each other again. It is all perfectly executed. It looks like a dance. It is a perfect imitation of a dance. Yet, it is not a dance. Absolutely no tension shows on the faces of the girls; and there is no tension in their bodies, and no tension between their bodies, in the space between their movements. It is a perfect series of movements, but it is not interesting to watch. The viewer is not moved by the dance. There is no edge to it, no fearful, exciting feeling that the girls are right on the line between an earthly form, the natural movements of the body, and the transformation of the body into the world of the dance. The girls had programmed the entire sequence of movements on the computer, analyzing each movement necessary, and then followed this program to execute the motions. It is a new ballet—the dance of the psychopaths. . . .

These actions seem to be instances of learning, rather remarkable accomplishments. And even if they lack the central dimension of heart, even if children are numbed, anesthetized to the world, are not the accomplishments the true measure of learning? Are not these children being prepared to enter the world fully capable of mastering any task quickly, efficiently, and perfectly? Is not the absence of heart that is so apparent in the actions of these children nothing more than a sentimental attachment to a world that no longer exists anyway? I can only answer by saying yes indeed, this method of learning suits the culture we have constructed. The age of psychopathy is in its prime. But, there are two reasons why this world, dominated by the technical imagination, is unacceptable and must be reversed. Lurking within every psychopath is suicide, depression and violence. Here is the price that we shall have to pay for quickly won perfection lacking the beauty of the heart. A massive bomb is in the making, and while we have made the bomb, it is our children who will explode it at the very moment when life, as it always does, gets its way and manipulative calculation does not work. We see it already brewing in our children. The moment their calculations in life do not achieve the desired result, they are quick to violent anger.

The second reason is, however, far more important. If, for a moment, it is possible to realize that education is really not for the sake of persons at all, but rather for the sake of the world, it suddenly becomes clear that child-centered learning is a preparation for the destruction of the world. My thought is simply this: How could it ever be that the world could matter so little that it becomes a garbage heap in the midst of incredible technical achievement?

# On the Purposes of Public Education

## *Leo Paul de Alvarez*

A passage from Alexis de Tocqueville's *Democracy in America* reminds us of the origins of public education in America:

> But it is the provisions for public education which, from the very first, throw into clearest relief the originality of American civilization.
>
> The [Massachusetts] Code states: "It being one chief project of the old deluder, Satan, to keep men from the knowledge of the scriptures, as in former times, keeping them in an unknown tongue, so in these latter times, by persuading them from the use of tongues, so that at least, the true sense and meaning of the original might be clouded with false glosses of saint seeming deceivers; and that learning may not be buried in the grave of our forefathers in church and commonwealth, the Lord assisting our endeavors. . . ." Provisions follow establishing schools in all townships, and obliging the inhabitants under penalty of heavy fines, to maintain them. . . .

One finds no doubts in the Massachusetts Code as to what the purpose is of the community and therefore of education. I always like to remind students of the origins of public schooling, for we have moved so very far from the origins and have indeed forgotten them. The purpose of education is of course always the same as the purpose of the community, and we must ask ourselves, what is "public" today about public education? That is, what is public or common among us, what purposes do we in fact agree upon or share? Tocqueville remarks on the Massachusetts Code, "No doubt the reader has noticed the preamble to these regulations; in America it is religion which leads to enlightenment and the observance of divine laws which leads men to liberty." But we can no longer make such a remark.

What was established in New England was the common school, which has received its paradigmatic incarnation in the little red schoolhouse. Lawrence A. Cremin has pointed out that, "Common school in its classic form was a Northern and Western phenomenon and reached its apotheosis in rural and small-town America west of the Alleghenies. It thrived best where there was already a reasonable homogeneity of race, class, and religion, and communities were not so large as to permit the development of substantially dissimilar ghettos."

The New England school depended then for its success on a homogeneous community. Where that homogeneity did not exist, the common school either did not exist or did not flourish. In the South, blacks were excluded from the common schools. In the urban areas of the East, private schools were established or by residential segregation public schools were in fact not common, and, further, Roman Catholics constructed their own school system. Thus the public schools were common where there existed homogeneous communities, and where there were none then some form of segregation took place, either by class, religion, or race.

The task of the public schools has of course been fundamentally changed since colonial Massachusetts. Instead of a religious purpose, the task of education was restated by Thomas Jefferson as an education for democratic citizenship, combined with a practical concern with the sciences and arts and widespread popular learning. We should remember, however, that Jefferson spoke of the need to select out the best from the annual trash, in order that they might perform the tasks of a natural *aristoi* for society.

That Jeffersonian understanding remains at the core of public education, most notably in Horace Mann and John Dewey, perhaps the two most influential figures in shaping our modern system. Mann professionalized teaching and introduced the Prussian system of education to the United States. John Dewey wished to make education and everyday life one, so that schooling and society would not be separated one from another. Both acted upon the premise of a common culture or tradition which ought to be part of the heritage of everyone. We have had today however a practical abandonment of the aims of Mann and Dewey, for we have in fact established various structures of special education for different groups.

We note in passing that with Mortimer Adler's Paideia Project we have an attempt at a return to the Deweyite purpose of a common education for the sake of democratic citizenship and the development therefore of free human beings.

The question which seems to me to remain unanswered is what is the substance of this common democratic culture? In one of the sessions of education sponsored by The Dallas Institute, I heard a prominent administrator of the Dallas Independent School District denounce Western civilization as imperialist and racist and who then suggested an education in Hispanic and Muslim civilizations. It quickly became apparent that what was meant by Hispanic civilization was not *Spanish* (which was of course part of the wicked West) but rather Mexican-Indian. But Muslim civilization is one of the great slave civilizations, and remains so, and one wonders about the extent to which liberty and equality were operative principles in either the Amerindian or Muslim cultures. I mention this incident as an illustration of the current opinions with which one must deal. What it indicates is not only a lack of agreement amongst us as to what traditions we share as a community, but also what one has to call an ideological blindness to what should be simple truths, one of which is that only in Western civilization have liberty and equality become ruling principles.

Among the burdens now placed on the schools is that of constituting a new culture, a task which Dewey first outlined in 1916 in his book *Democracy and Education*. To paraphrase his argument: Industrialism is destroying the traditional home, shop, neighborhood, and church; they are no longer performing their educational functions; some other institution must take on these functions; the school must do so. The schools are to be nothing less than the instrument of a new civilization. From the clarity of battling against the "old seducer" we have moved to conflicting and often misconceived notions as to what a democratic or popular culture ought to be.

Our incoherence in these matters is especially revealed, as Charles E. Silberman remarks (*Crisis in the Classroom*, 1970), in the multiplicity of proposed curricular reforms all of which make the fatal error of not asking the questions: What is education for? What kind of human beings and what kind of society do we want to produce? It is also revealed in the experience of the classroom teacher who discovers that he cannot rely upon a common fund of knowledge which comes from reading a common set of books.

Let me add to this incoherence by speaking of what Professor George Anastaplo has called the Babylonian captivity of the public schools. That Babylonian captivity has echoes which are both biblical and classical, and it signifies both a subjugation to an imperial power and to become like that imperial power, to become like Babylon. In the first case, it means that education has become Babylonian in that it has become the custodial care or rather the imprisonment of children. Silberman so describes the condition of the classroom:

> I am indignant at the failures of the public schools themselves. "The most deadly of all possible sins," Erik Eriksson suggests, "is the mutilation of a child's spirit." It is not possible to spend any prolonged period visiting public school classrooms without being appalled by the mutilation visible everywhere—mutilation of spontaneity of joy in learning. . . . The public schools—those "killers of the dream," to appropriate a phrase of Lillian Smith's—are the kind of institution one cannot really dislike until one gets to know them well. Because adults take the schools so much for granted, they fail to appreciate what grim, joyless places most American schools are, how oppressive and petty are the rules by which they are governed, how intellectually sterile and esthetically barren the atmosphere, what an appalling lack of civility obtains on the part of teachers and principals, what contempt they unconsciously display for children as children.

The failure of other institutions in society has worsened the situation, for what has happened as everyone knows is that extraneous demands have been placed upon the schools. They now serve, as Dewey suggested, as surrogates for other institutions. It has meant that alien ways have come to dominate the schools.

What has made public schools most like Babylon, however, is their size. We must wonder why we have chosen to make our schools so big. Undoubtedly, questions of economy, our mass society, our tendency to systematize and technologize everything— all of these have something to do with it. But how then are our schools to become true communities? Must we not then perforce resort to bureaucratic methods and rigid rules to govern such institutions? "Thus," Professor Anastaplo concludes, "the urban public school system has both been taken over by Babylon (by alien concerns) and become like Babylon (an unwieldy leviathan), unable to get a grip on itself."

What is the appropriate size? Anastaplo suggests that it should be about 200 in the elementary schools and 500 in the high schools. Such a size would certainly be conducive to less bureaucracy and to the formation of true communities of students and teachers.

Our civilization, I have been saying, no longer exists as a whole, and our education clearly and visibly externalizes this schism. We are in the midst of a great civil war which is at once spiritual, intellectual, and material. The souls of men are the spoils of this war, and education, especially higher education, is the principal battleground.

Let us remind ourselves of the tradi-

tional biblical and classical morality to indicate what is at issue. I quote from an essay by Professor Leo Strauss:

> Greek philosophy and the Bible agree as to this, that the proper framework of morality is the patriarchal family, which is, or tends to be, monogamous, and which forms the cell of a society in which the free adult males, and especially the old ones predominate. . . . Consisting of free men, the society praised by the Bible and Greek philosophy refuses to worship any human being. . . . The highest place among the virtues is assigned not to courage or manliness but to justice. And by justice is primarily meant obedience to the law. The divine law is the basis of all law and the divine law is the common ground between the Bible and Greek philosophy.

How much do we accept of this traditional morality? These are the crucial issues, and one may praise such a group as the Moral Majority for at least understanding that point.

We disagree, do we not, on the most fundamental things? That is, we disagree about what is a human being, about *when* a human being is a human being. What used to be settled in terms of the sacred—the matters of life and death—are now matters of controversy and we have even made it a rule to let everyone decide for himself. One might add that once the sense of the sacred governing these things is lost, then no amount of legislation or controversy will ever settle the issues.

Instead of the sacred or the divine law, we moderns have become anthropocentric. We are no longer theocentric or cosmocentric. The moral orientation has therefore radically changed. Rights have become primary, passions have

become emancipated, freedom has become *the* virtue, the self has replaced
soul. Man does not have a nature but
human nature is rather a product of
human activity or work. And finally
we have had the radical emancipation
of the human from the divine.

Is there an education connected with
this new morality? I do not think so,
for there is no soul to be formed. What
we have instead is either freedom, i.e.,
self-realization, or revolution, which
concludes in the transformation of social and economic structures. We have
then not education but the project for
the radical reconstruction of self and
society. The only question which is still
at issue is which is to be dominant
—the reconstruction of the self or that
of society?

# The Body in Learning

## William Burford

I want to begin by talking about the rhythmical sense without which, I do not think, anything can be done in human relations, in writing, or in teaching.

In the midst of various kinds of rhythms what we call education is located. We are surrounded all the time by varying rates of speeds and varying rhythms that influence all of our lives. That has always been so. Different ages have had different kinds of rhythms to them. The seventeenth century doesn't have the same kind of mental rhythm that the eighteenth century has—and throughout history. I do not think that anything can get done in education—curricula cannot be planned, teachers cannot be improved, nothing can be done—unless we take into account the kinds of rhythms we are dealing with.

What we call studying would seem to be a surcease from frenetic activity, a turning on of a rhythm that is deeply quiet in contrast to all that surrounds it. The very notion of teaching and study would seem to involve a calming of our impetuous and always pressing muscular life which each one of us has. . . .

Now, I think that the whole effort of education—physical education or mental education—is based on the balances of the body, upon the balances and rhythms within that body and its movement into the world. There is no "out there" and "in here." The body—in its stepping, walking, thinking—is at the very core of education.

At the present time in Texas we are engaged in an argument over intellectual education and physical education. But there is no difference between them if they are properly done. Of course both of them—the intellectual and the physical—have gotten into fantastic distortions and perversions of their true nature. It is very strange, but very understandable, that in modern American life we should play football dressed in these enormous, bulging outfits. If Mr. Perot wants to work a change, some kind of marvelous revolution in education, he should drop his attack on physical education and think about what *is* physical education and how it should truly be done. It may well be that modern sports do not have the true rhythms built into our bodies. Of course, over the years the body can be taught to jerk and thump and to bang and to bounce. But in a true education there would be no difference between the feeling of physical education and what is done in the classroom where you were studying a poem. No poet can do anything without a sense of the balance of his human body. At the present time, there is an extremely distorted intellectual vice in poetry. There is very little sense of rhythmical power in modern American poetry. It is a kind of intellectual, argumentative power that has taken over poetry. And that is as distorted as the kinds of games that the body has fallen into. They should both be mirrors of each other.

Let me give a very famous example of a rhythmical clash, because I want to talk tonight about rhythms that do not suit each other. There is the famous scene in Plato's *Symposium* when they are all talking and the banquet is begun and then halfway through the banquet—an arena of discussion and great charm—Alcibiades, drunk, comes charging in and introduces an entirely different rhythm into the whole proceedings. He butts his way in and breaks up the banquet and has no sense of the rhythmic structure of the minds that are around him or even of the bodies—he insists on rearranging the room to suit himself. He completely changes, momentarily, what Socrates and the other guests are trying to accomplish in their discussion.

Socrates, very slowly, tries to stop Alcibiades and to bring him into the rhythm of their discussion that evening in that room, where they are eating and listening to music and talking. And it is almost impossible for him to do this because the rhythm of Alcibiades' life is completely different from the rhythm of Socrates' life. I'm not saying which is better. I'm speaking of a problem of the rhythmical sense. We know that Alcibiades, throughout his whole life, kept charging forward in every way. He could not, at any moment, enter into the repose of study.

These contrary movements have to be dealt with if we are going to talk intelligently about poetry or education or any of those matters. There is a physical movement that surrounds us in the world, a rhythmic texture that is everywhere around us. We have in our own interior, rhythms and movements that force us this and that way. All the time we are trying to create the whole, balanced body.

One of the most rhythmically gifted people in the modern world was Garcia Lorca, the Spanish poet. He always performed his poetry to the guitar, to music. In a book of Lorca's called *Deep Song*, he speaks about singing: "What you must search for and find is the black torso of the Pharoah."

When you are singing, when you are writing poetry what you must search for and find is the black torso of the Pharoah. Now, I think that in writing, teaching, and poetry we are searching for a creation or a restitution of the essential wholeness and totality and sanity of the human body.

There has been a very long argument in the history of culture which also took place in Greece—a division between the idea of teaching the body and teaching the mind. I want to give some examples of that. Here is a quote from *Charmides*, a dialogue of Plato's. Plato is introducing Charmides into the dialogue and noticing him as he enters into the view of people. "Everybody was looking at him as though he was a statue. 'What a handsome face he has,' cries Socrates. 'But if he was naked, he would seem to you to have no face. He is so beautiful in every way.'"

Now the face, of course, when he is entirely naked, means that the totality of the body is unbroken by any contrary thoughts or even any disruptions from the soul. The body is an entire value in itself, not to be interrupted or to be disturbed by dark passages of thought, or argument or misunderstanding.

Now it was Socrates who questioned this will to absolute beauty and in a way undermined that will by his questions on the very edge of the wrestling ring. In Greece the aristocratic classes absolutely believed in the bodily education, and the intellect was something contrary and even disruptive of that. . . . Education fell into the hands of an intellectual kind of class or type that was not at all the original

aim of Greek education. . . . In the division of the body and the mind or the spirit or the faculty of learning—when that takes place and the body is left behind because of the demands of the mind—a kind of fatigue overcomes the whole system.

In the classrooms today, it is clear that there is a double rhythmic failure. One is in the direction of an incredible restlessness and the other in the direction of fatigue. Both fatigue and restlessness are rampant in the halls and in the classrooms of our schools. It is even in the architecture of the schools. It allows nothing to move correctly. The art of architecture is the art of bodily movement made into an architectural plan. It is extremely difficult to break those deeply ingrained bad rhythms.

True study is impossible in the schools. True study is a kind of condition. Study is not simply the study of this course or that course. It is not the study of mathematics, English, science. You can do all the tinkering with the curricula you want and it will not help at all. All you have to do is to be in those classrooms day after day to see that it is not the particular study that they are dealing with, but it is a question of the whole formation of the sense of study.

There was a French woman who died in England in 1943, Simone Weil. Shortly before dying, she wrote a work called "Reflections on the Right Use of School Studies with a View to the Love of God." It is a marvelous presentation of a state of suspended rhythm in which all the faculties slow down and yet remain extremely acute:

> Although people seem to be unaware of it today, the development of the faculty of attention forms the real object and almost the sole interest of studies. In order to really pay attention, it is necessary to know how to set about it. Often, attention is confused with a kind of muscular effort. If one says to one's pupils—"Now, you must pay attention," one sees them contracting their brows, controlling their breath, stiffening their muscles. If after two minutes they are asked what they have been paying attention to, they can't reply. They have not been paying attention. They have been controlling their muscles. We often expend this kind of muscular effort in our studies. Since it ends by making us tired, we have the impression that we have been working. That is an illusion. This kind of muscular effort is entirely barren.

Now, the major image of thinking or studying in the twentieth century is Rodin's statue "The Thinker." That statue is a statue of non-thinking. Rodin's statue is in a terrible position of tension. The whole body is twisted. The head is sunk on the knuckles of the hand. The body looks paralyzed and stupefied and not getting anywhere—in an absolute muscular bind. Actually, Rodin made that statue for a great gateway called "The Gates of Hell." Originally, it was to be Ugolino, who appears in the Inferno in the thirty-third canto of *The Divine Comedy*. It is a statue of muscular stupor. It is not a statue that contributes to any kind of rhythm of thinking. . . .

I think that the first reform in education would be to try to determine either architecturally or physically how to put the enormous powers of the body in repose or at the service of learning or attention. . . . The condition of reposeful alertness not only should be the position of intelligence but it also moves over into the position of the soul. . . .

# Education and Its Double

## *Louise Cowan*

I want to talk with you about two things: first the heritage of civilization that we hold in common and are committed to preserve, extend, and transmit; and second, a phenomenon that I want to call the "double." The double is a hollow imitation of something real—a quality, an ideal, an idea, a virtue. It seduces us into accepting it as the entity it mimics, satisfies our sense of responsibility to the good, consumes our energy, and can misdirect not only our own lives but those of our children and of generations to come.

When I speak of a civilized heritage that is our chief cultural treasure and of our duty to preserve, extend, and transmit it, I am speaking primarily of education—that process of implanting into each member of our society a sacred deposit of value, like a seed, one might say—a seed that will grow in its own soil in each individual person. We mistake the purpose of education when we think of it as the acquisition of mental ingenuity, information, or practical skills. We mistake it even more seriously when we consider it to be the encouragement of each person to "develop his own opinions."

I am of course aware that everyone must think for himself to be fully a person at all: I know that our American tradition is based on a healthy diversity and that we must not only allow but encourage the eccentric, the innovator, the dissenter, the startling new mind, and the minority voice. But this is not the purpose of education. Its primary purpose is to make a civilized member of society out of otherwise raw material—to inculcate the chief ideals and ideas which a common language and a common political tradition require us to pass on to others. Education has other purposes, of course—the awakening of the students' souls, so that they may be able to pursue truth, beauty, and goodness throughout their lives; acquainting them with the world in which they are to live, and, on a more advanced level, educating them in particular disciplines, trades, and professions through the practice of which they may become useful and productive members of society; and finally, actually contributing to new thought, new research, and new insights. But none of these is the primary purpose of education, which, as I have said, is to transmit a common core, a deposit—a minimum requirement for being a civilized person which, after implantation, can grow within that person and bear its own variegated fruits. Far from depriving one of freedom, it endows one with an essential liberty. (Freedom is not the product of barbarism, but of civilization.)

Now: this process of implanting a core, a seed, within a person is accomplished not primarily by skill in teaching but by what is taught. Not by methods but by content—the knowledge of what it is important to teach. What does that core consist of? Ask yourself truthfully what you would choose for your children if you were given absolute control of their destiny:

1. economic security, without regard to virtue or decency; or
2. character and virtue, without regard to economic or political status.

I am not implying that these objectives are necessarily in conflict. I am speaking here of priority. Which would you put first? I think there is hardly anyone here who would not, if you had to choose, opt for character and virtue. We quite simply do not admire cowardice, selfishness, or deceit. We know that the public virtues —such as courage, honor, generosity, justice, and mercy—are necessary if a city is to thrive and life within it is to be of a high quality. What we have forgotten is that these virtues do not occur on their own; they must be taught. If we leave young people to grow up any old way, and to be taught any old thing, then some of them, no doubt, out of whatever inbuilt gift or mysterious influence, will develop on their own some of these qualities necessary for the survival of civilization. But society cannot exist on a civilized basis without everyone honoring these public virtues, whatever one's innermost heart. Civilized society, as Allen Tate has said, is an agreement not to look into the abyss. Poets and any real thinkers are obligated, of course, to do so; but they unearth the dark side with a concern for form and truth. And we all must look into the abyss at times in our private lives. But publicly, as soon as we start accepting the nonexistence of virtue as an axiom—the cynical belief that everyone is out for himself, that all people are envious, or the "economic myth" that everyone is motivated primarily by gain—then we assist in the downfall of society.

It is not of course only virtues that make up the core of what must be taught. There are intellectual principles likewise that make up part of this shared deposit; ideas worked out from the time of the classical, medieval, and Renaissance world. I am not advocating a simple return; I am speaking of the crucial need for serious consideration of what makes a real curriculum in our day: how do we preserve our civilized heritage and fit a young person for a place in the modern world?

Nothing in our society is of more importance than the recovery of a belief that a humanizing course of studies should be taught to all. Without its civilizing effect, our society quite literally will sink into barbarism, with a few in charge of a horde that can be controlled only by force. "You start with unlimited freedom and end with unlimited despotism," Shigalov says prophetically in Dostoevksy's *The Possessed*.

The lamentable quality of our public educational system can no longer be concealed; it is out in the open, not only with the commission's recent report, "A Nation at Risk," but with concrete examples in almost every home of young people who have been cheated of their heritage. We know it, we see it—what are we going to do about it?

And this is where my second topic comes in: the double. The double is a shared illusion that grows up among people concerning current questions of public policy. Most protest movements follow the double of an ideal; many causes are based on the mere appearance of the authentic. But even more strongly does the double have its effect among leaders of a city as enlightened public opinion: others take it on; it is a way for us, when we do not wish to think deeply or give much energy to an issue, to think and speak without taking any risk and yet to have the feeling of being for the good. We support the double, give our moral energy to it, and the genuine idea is defeated then by an ersatz good, by an imitation of reality, not by evil. (Real justice is complicated; really righting a wrong requires thought and sacrifice.)

One of the marks of the double is that people who espouse it cannot be argued with; it has the feeling of being self-evident.

On the question of our schools, the double is a false notion of what education is all about. It manifests itself in those sayings that we are beginning to hear over and over again: "We must get back to basics." "Teachers are not teaching basics." "Teachers are to blame for the low quality of our schools." "Teachers are as incompetent as they are because only the lower fourth of a college class is attracted into teaching." "This situation exists because teacher pay is so low. (What can you expect?)"

Consequently, the story goes, raise the pay, award merit bonuses, establish master teachers, call in experts to show teachers how to teach, use visual aids and computers, but above all, by whatever prestidigitation is required, teach people how to read, write, and figure a little. It doesn't matter what they read or write or figure.

The genuine reforms would come about by restoring to teachers their authority as people with vocations; by reinstating the curriculum as an image of life, not allowing it to be a mere conglomeration of skills. We shall have to recognize that the problem does not lie simply with the public schools alone but that a crisis of sufficient proportion to destroy us exists in our entire educational system—our colleges and universities as well. They too, for the most part, have lost the idea of what a curriculum is, and there too "the hungry sheep look up and are not fed." The issue cannot be decided by a simple question: how would you do it? The question is not how, but what and why. Once a people have decided what is right and have begun to think seriously about a problem, they can proceed to plans for achieving their purposes.

To me it has long seemed apparent that Dallas could lead the nation in education; this city need not participate in the general decline; it has the resources here to construct an educational system that could be the model for the entire country, from the lower grades to universities and graduate institutes. But such achievement would involve a body of concerned citizens who would take the trouble to learn— what everyone took for granted up to a century ago—the principles and purposes of education: what it is about and what it is for.

# Architecture and Design

If, when we enter a city, we ask it to speak to us, to reveal to us what it most wants us to know—its essence, its genius, its soul—what would cry out for our attention? What language would it use to have us know it fully?

The voice of the city can be heard coming from unexpected sources, other than from its own people. It is housed in its buildings, in its streets, roadways and freeways, in the detail of its spaces which, when cared for, become places, in fountains, benches, flowers, bells, trees, lights, clear glass windows, food vendors, street corner musicians. It can be heard in the click of heels on the sidewalks—the rhythm of the daytime pace of the city—and in the steady, low rumbling of the automobiles—the early morning and late afternoon ritual pulsations of entering and leaving.

The architecture and design of a city cohere to form a living language—a comprehensible pattern of phenomena sequestered within a given region which tells the story of its soul.

Civilizations can be defined by their architecture. The image of a people and their culture resides in the things they build—their shelters, their holy places, their public squares, their centers of commerce and festival pavilions. Where the built things *are* in the city, their height and dimension, the relationship to each other, their regularity or 'naughtiness', all together weave a syntax of form.

The architecture of the city tells how things *are* there. It sings of an indefatigable spirit or whispers softly of times past. It reveals how the city uses its money, whether as an enabler —allowing ideas a visible expression—or as a scam—promising ever more opportunities for money-making deals. Architecture discloses a city's investment in education and even tells us what kind of education is going on—learning or job training. By the design of its parks and gardens, the city speaks of its need for repose, contemplation, fantasy, and reverie. The design of the city answers questions concerning its vitality. Where is the new, young life; the hot spots for the night crowd? Does it spring up spontaneously or is it a planned development? Do poets live in the city? Do artists? Are their works visible, and if so, are they noticed? Do young people go to the theatre? Dare old people walk in the street? Does a corporate office park have a bench carefully placed under a tree? If an "undesirable" rests there, is he or she asked to move on? Is the interior of an office or home crafted so that a human person can be human in it, with a need for sanctuary and day-dreaming as well as the opportunity to be efficient and productive?

It is my theory that cities want us to know them intimately. They want to know us so that they can care for us. They want to share their secrets with us, and will if we approach them in a certain way—as prospective lovers, perhaps. Certainly, the architecture of a city wants to be seen. It wants to be paid attention to. There is little difference in this need to be seen and understood between the big, shiny building and the small, older, insignificant one. Both want attention; both want our care and understanding.

The following essays are a way of paying attention to the city, to its architecture and to its design. They represent our attempt to truly love the city.

*Gail Thomas*

# Looking for an American Architecture

## *Charles W. Moore*

• Buildings speak, and in order to say something helpful and interesting to us, they need to be given some kind of freedom of speech, of the sort that most modern architectural theory does not allow.

• Every building does not have to be the most important building in the world (otherwise we wind up with a world made of branch savings and loans).

• It is all right for buildings to be bombastic or shy or funny or even frivolous if that is their purpose, and there is no need for all buildings to talk in the same sonorous tones.

• I am excited about the role of memory in architecture after the lobotomized theoretical framework that I and others in my generation were brought up in that believed the past was full of cobwebs and other unseemly things and that we had to start anew with originality and a certain amount of verve to make our cities and to make our world.

• It seems to me more and more that such a world made of new and exciting pieces is not easy to exhibit.

• The major quality of buildings or cities that we care anything about is care itself, or we might say, love. Buildings that get a generous helping of care have a capacity to absorb our care or our love, and then when they get enough of it, to give it back to us.

• After half a century of making macho erections, or making original and exciting buildings, we have been expecting that somehow they were all going to come together and make a city. Perhaps it is now time to have a half century of "yin" if that was "yang," to be receptive to finding the rhythms that surround us, to make our world out of the familiar but with important parts of ourselves added to achieve that surprise which is a necessary element of familiar things.

• Originality, the hobgoblin of architectural minds of this century, must lose some of the absurd importance that it has been given.

• It is all right, even necessary, to look at architecture as a performing art, in the same way that when a quartet plays a Beethoven piece their own presence is not diminished by playing an already known Beethoven instead of making something just for the occasion. They are making up enough. They are putting enough of themselves into the presentation to make it real and to make us connected to it. In fact, having that real thing (that which is already familiar) as a base for what they are doing, provides another level of bonding.

• For too long, we have seen architecture as something that doesn't need that connection with familiarity, with what we are used to, with what we think about, with what our world is made of. We need that connection now.

• In order to believe this you have to believe as I do that the world is full of beautiful things, that there are wonderful places in abundance in the world, many of them threatened and many of them gone, but lots left to give us a model of what kind of world we want.

• J. B. Jackson, a landscape man in Santa Fe who is as powerful a voice for good things as there is on the planet, has a theory that far from being the root-seeking people that Americans are supposed to be, most people value mobility and freedom, and think of themselves as being able to go where they want. The sense of place that is valued in a structure that we architects single out for praise is not a typical American feeling.

• It seems to me that Americans from the beginning have been wanderers; people who take seriously the freedom of the open horizon. Perhaps for people who want, need, and seek roots, and who are much of the time

far from home and unable to remember home, the presence of that base, the wonder of it, gets to be a literary matter—books we've read for example that remind us of our ancestors. The whole business of making connections through the written word is a way of finding and centering.

• Robert Stern has talked about our special qualities as a nation of distinguishing the past and creating ones for ourselves when there were no connections.

• The literature of modern architecture from 1915 on is, in our American sense, very European. It notes that what is in existence is very unsatisfactory and that it has to be fixed and puts forth a prescription for fixing it so that things are more comprehensible.

• What has gone wrong with twentieth-century city planning is the widespread use of Zipatone—a little ivory piece that planners spread onto the paper with some sticky goo. Zipatone is very difficult to cut. It is convenient to cut it along streets when you are making a map because streets are in straight lines.

• We know by looking that streets unite things. What happens on one side of the street is likely to be related to what happens on the other side of the street. With Zipatone as a medium you don't allow that to happen because the paper-colored street is what separates one block of Zipatone—one land-use—from another.

• I keep thinking how exciting our cities would be if our city planners,

instead of being bound to their Zipatone, had been aficianados of, say,
Bargello stitchery, in which mixed-use
communities were a natural outgrowth
of the way they wove the maps.
• (I have never persuaded any city
planning department to use Bargello
stitchery as a technique but I'd like to
keep trying!)
• In the recent past we in the Western world have become dissatisfied
with the manifesto that says something
is wrong and therefore THIS is right.
We have some to consider the
Chinese philosophy of Yin and
Yang—the notion that opposites are
required and, held in some tension,
make for a balance and eventually a
cosmic harmony. This way of seeing
seems beyond us in the West most of
the time.
• I am trying to take the Yin/Yang
philosophy and apply it to one of our
most favorite Western fairytales—the
story of the Three Bears. I have been
collecting as many Three Bears stories
as I could find. My query has been
marred some by the frequent portrayal
of Goldilocks as a naughty little consumer who breaks perfectly good
chairs and eats up porridges not belonging to her and who does other
nonsocial acts. If we take the notion
that if something is too hot, and the
opposite is too cold, then we can
wind up in the middle saying, "Ah,
this is just right!"
• This Taoist mystery and magic of
the Yin and the Yang comes close to
being homely enough to be of some
use to us so that we pragmatic Ameri-

cans might make cities that are not
Too Big or Too Small or Too Hot or
Too Cold, or Too Dull or Too Innovative, but can end up somewhere
in the middle as Just Right. A good
note to end on!

# The Integrity of Place

## *Lyle Novinski*

This is the story of the refounding of a community, the coming of age of a community and of those touched by it. It is the account of a small design effort as measured against the immense scale of most of our images of urban design. But I am sure it is a tale worth telling, for it provides a recall to the authentic and speaks about the real economics of taste, about the making of a community through the recreation of its place. . . . I did not begin this work as though it were to end in a lecture, or even a lesson. I began it as a friendly favor to my good friend, Father Tim Gollub, pastor of Holy Cross on Bonnie View, in Dallas. Father Tim had badgered me for some time about the need of his parish for a more decorous place of worship. So the project began as an attempt to help a friend with some reshaping that might make his place, and the liturgy celebrated there, a more fitting union, that is, that might make the life lived there be lived more fully. . . .

The important ingredient in the plan was my conviction, continually affirmed by my growing knowledge of the spirit of the people, that we could do this together. . . . I realized that we were blessed in not being able to redo the whole complex, and thus destroy it, change it into something else. This was no clean slate. The economics of this situation in the parish dictated that an artfulness enfold the memories of the old parish place and replace them into the life of the new one, creating, in fact, a new and richer community while we created a richer place.

And so we began, just after the June weddings, early in July, tearing out the old steel framed doorway and the long brick wall. We cleaned the bricks one by one, hundreds, thousands of them. Everyone cleaned bricks, people of all ages, elderly ladies sitting in folding chairs, while children brought and took away the cleaned bricks. As soon as we had enough, Rick began to lay up the new piers, to match the old, and to close off the hallways, setting in place across them the old steel frame, keying it in with the new bricks so it would match . . . almost. The lumber from the platform was salvaged; every stick of it went into the framing of the new wall.

In this project we have sought to

bypass the ordinary sense of economic exchange in our building scheme and replace it with rather a system based on quality. . . . We have in this task little surplus in the sense of a mass of unused or borrowed dollars. We do however have a surplus of labor, of feeling, of knowing, understanding, and of time which we committed as our surplus for the good of our fellow man. . . .

Think then upon the request to bring two by fours to church. Father Tim said everyone has a two by four or two around, a short one, a long one, or several you have been saving to do something with. Bring them to church. And they did. . . . So that pile became the altar platform. . . . The carpet on top was the old carpet, which was perfectly serviceable, and on one Sunday a carpetlayer with the community reattached it on the platform. We trimmed the step riser with salvaged prefinished oak trim from the old chancel, and continued the renewal in this fashion. . . .

Taste could not be applied to this structure. In that I mean there could be no added ornament, or any pretense of resurfacing, and covering up older surfaces, as though we disagreed with the taste of the given forms; rather we simply wanted to make the spaces work and to reshape them inside of the grammar of the older structure. . . . It is simply economic sense not to disturb too much. . . . The level of taste was then to do things right, in a way that did not call attention to itself, but to

the integrity of the old fabric. . . .

The restoration of integrity required that the place be a permanent home. . . . A room that asks you to enter the corner, turn 180 degrees and face a platform behind a folding door is a temporary space, even if it is used for 25 years. A room that you enter on axis, center aisled, with all evidence that the room can be rearranged for dinners, dances, or any other community function is still a permanent space, and proclaims itself that way. . . . I insisted that alterations would be laid up in brick. If there is to be a wall, it will be brick, and not a sheetrock renovation. If there is to be an end to the altar sanctuary area, let it be a brick column. When we move doors, let's key in the brick so the demarcations are invisible; when we get to the floor, let us bypass the efficient green tile and go to oak parquet; let us make a new set of matching furniture, altar, lectern, tables, shelves, all that match, and banish some of the well-meaning collected pieces, to honor the new scale of the room. . . .

A place that constantly is at odds with the practical function within causes damage to the activity, and to the myth that supports it. My function was to restore an integrity to this place, to make it worthy as a place of worship, and to do so within the parameters of the community that worshipped there. The result is that during the construction the activity engendered by the project, the increased expectations, and the satisfactions, the bonding, has greatly strengthened the community. . . .

To maintain the wholeness is the question. Setting aside the nagging concern formed of shapes in disunity, we try to make things the same. Comfort is in that, the comfort of seeing sameness within things, not the alikeness of all parts, not the matching repetition which rules out order of any kind save the lockstepped identity of uniformity. I speak of the comfort of knowing inside that something is the same. Sameness as a quality within things is the unity that allows the petals of a rose to be samed to the reaching stalk, and the glossy leaf. Alike they are not, even similar they are not, yet there is a perceived quality within them that says they are linked in sameness. . . .

I am fascinated by the memory of things that is buried in all forms, and within all construction. There are stories among the workers on any project that they alone share, that make the building somehow theirs. I have built portions of my own house, and I know the feel of making things. I know the fun of a good fit, and the discipline of redoing something that is not right. I know the day I decided that that is as good as it was going to get. Buried in all structures are those feelings, and they are stripped away from the worker with the sale of the place. There are unexorcized spirits abounding in all structures. Occasionally they can be felt and seen to the perceivable eye, but largely they are

unseen, and are often long dead before we inhabit the place. As we move into more and more distance from the hand at work, the premade parts of many structures have their spirits long distanced from the job—around somewhere in the slag heaps and dross of a foundry. The living feelings of the structure have been sent away, made to feel a distance from the structure. And we feel their loss and their distance in the harshness of many structures.

In our building the spirits and the people are at rest. They have not been bought off, for the labor was not purchased, nor are there new alien spirits about accompanying new bundles of materials. These bricks, joists, and walls speak of several years of labor. They join their old placement with the new, and we are the richer for it. We remember the day we chipped the brick, we remember the gang that argued about the straightness of the rows of the parquet, and we remember fighting through the bankruptcy of a cabinet works that threatened to trap our millwork inside. Our project is the same as we are, the spirit of the same is with us. We are a bit reordered, but then that is a good metaphor for a church building, and the space serves us better. There are baptisms here, younger lives beginning within the community that will not remember any older structure, but we will.

# A Note on Old and New Buildings

## Robert Sardello

It is difficult to argue for historic preservation on economic grounds—in
neighborhoods, perhaps, but not
downtown, unless there is a feeling of
downtown as part of the people of the
city and not merely the workplace.
Tax benefits help somewhat, but the
appeal of the increase in income and
the increased tax base to the city from
a fifty-story skyscraper where there
previously stood a five-story brown-
stone is hard to counter. The argument is first of all an argument concerning quality—and it is an argument
between the upstarts and the elders.
We upstarts think that we can make
the city on our own. Like rebellious
adolescents, we cannot see that the
strength of life comes from a continuity of tradition, from something to
refer back to as an orientation for the
present. Without the visible past,
whatever we make stands nowhere,
and standing nowhere, it cannot possibly serve as a basis for the future.
Can we expect that what we are now
building will be respected in the future
when what we now build is not made
with a respectful eye to the past from
which it derives its spirit? Historic

preservation needs to be recognized as
an essential act of sacrifice, an act of
putting the fruits of the modern world
—its materials, its gifts—in service to
the ancestors. Historic preservation is
not a very good word for honoring
those who have lived here before us—
it sounds like pickling the past or
holding on to what was, unable to accept the inevitability of growth and
change. I have not thought of a better
way to describe the importance of the
city honoring a visible past, but we
must first come to perceive the architecture of the past as vital to the present life of the city. Preservation and
redevelopment as essential qualities of
life of the city recognize the necessity
of images of the past for the liveliness
of the present.

The particular quality that quickens
with the reanimation of the past in the
city is the quality of beauty—not
quaintness, not nostalgia, but beauty.
In our time, the idea of the beautiful
has been replaced by the idea of
energy. The new city is full of energy
but decidedly lacking in beauty.
Modern throwaway buildings of shiny
glass surfaces may momentarily dazzle

the eye but do not mirror any reality other than themselves and their isolated counterparts across the street. Glitter and dazzle have little to do with beauty. Beauty requires detail that is interesting to the eye, curves, a rich interplay of light and shadow, depth, textured materials, human scale. Glass buildings can have these kinds of provocative details. They tend to do so only when there are older buildings around them that have been restored because then the new buildings have to respond to them. Then, it is possible to have glass buildings full of delightful surprises—indentations, juttings, layerings. Still, one wonders about the future of what we are building. The future redevelopment of our buildings is questionable because they are built in ignorance of the processes of aging, appearing ever youthful. They are so completely an interpretation of the present and detached from the past that they may be unable to adapt to future, unknown conditions.

The enemies of historic buildings in the city are the arsonist and the bulldozer. We imagine itinerant bums finding their way into an abandoned building to find shelter for the night, carelessly stoking campfires; angered with their own rootlessness, they perform this act of aggression against the city. The developers' bulldozer can be the brother to the itinerant arsonist, similarly angered with their own rootlessness, turning it into economic power, justifying the urge to destroy by claiming the power to build. The

aggression we feel toward our elders is all contained in the force of that one word—bulldozer! Burn them up, tear them down—we can do better with them out of the way! A way of resolving this conflict is in realizing that what we are building today is not better, only different. If we think that what we are building is better, then it follows that the past needs to be torn down and redone. If we can recognize that it is merely different, then it can stand alongside the past, joyously proclaiming this difference through the beauty, the texture, the harmony, the interplay between past and present.

Now, let us move downtown, right into the center of the city and into those glass towers. What do they bring to the life of the city? These structures achieve an almost complete separation from the earth. Cellophane-wrapped skeletons of steel dominate our imagination of the city. The eyes slide over them quickly, dazzled by their sparkle, but can find no detail, no interesting differences, no relation between window and brick, no portions that have been added on, scrollwork, intriguing columns on which the eye can rest. These glass buildings are greasy to the eye, slick. And they go up, up, up, and just end, flat-topped without a roof. A roof, sloping down, acknowledges the relation between earth and sky—no top, no stop; the sky's the limit—seventy stories, well, why not do eighty? Now, when you do put a sloping roof on a sixty-

or seventy-story building, it is really not a roof at all. Why not? Because a roof embraces a building and refers it back to the earth. A point on a sixty-story building does not return the building to the earth; it merely sticks upward in defiance of its ground.

Well, these things, these citadels of power, are here; my mocking them will not make them go away. Better we understand what they do, how they work, what they give, and what they take away, how to work with them for the good of the quality of the city.

Le Corbusier is regarded as the father architect of the right-angled sky-scraper. He called it a "bone-struc-ture" and was proud of the fact that he freed the design of the tower from the image of the house. He was, in fact, proud that this type of structure was free from any image whatsoever because that freedom left the building completely available for one quality only—function. Unbound from mem-ory, decoration, adornment, landscape, site, earth, detail, this sort of building is free to be only what it does—this is what is meant by the architecture of functionalism. And by specializing in that one quality, enormous power is achieved. The building is free to do one thing—function, and function un-incumbered, thus, with the greatest ef-ficiency. Of course, that makes the millions of people who inhabit these buildings eight hours a day, five days a week, into functionaries. Don't ask me which came first—the functionaries or

the building style to hold them. They simply go together. The dominance of this style of architecture goes together with the dominance of this style of life of the city.

A glass-box building, or its many variations with bits of stone plastered between endless windows of sameness, is a pure medium. A good example of a medium is the light bulb. The light bulb is almost nothing in itself. It is what it does. And what it does is transform energy into light. What is inside the light bulb is almost of no value in itself. Its value lies in what it does. And when it no longer does that, it is disposable. No one cares or saves or cherishes burnt-out light bulbs. Furthermore, we measure the value of what it does through its effi-ciency. Pure function goes together with efficiency. Now, I want to recog-nize function and efficiency as qualities —as important qualities of the life of the city. But you see, when this one set of qualities dominates our imagina-tion, then we begin to think that quality *is* efficiency. The better a thing works and the more efficiently it works, we think, the better the quality of the job. All senses of quality, then, begin to be measured by the standards of functionality and efficiency. Look inside these light bulb buildings. More and more of the complexities of life are removed. Individual offices are not as efficient as stalls. Without offices there is no longer any place to bring in a bit of the outside world—pictures of the family to remind you that you are more than what you do at work; an apple to munch on in the middle of the afternoon so that you can pause and bring a bit of imagination to your work; a place for private conversations, gossip—why, maybe even touching.

I was writing this portion of the paper last week in the new Central Library in Dallas. I sat for several hours and wrote maybe half a page. I noticed that every time I would take a break and go outside on the terrace, all kinds of images would come. I would run inside to write them down, and they were gone. I finally realized what was going on and took my pad outside where things flowed. One thing sure about these efficient buildings, they are not made for the functioning of the imagination. You can perform well in them only if you have a specific task to do—assigned work to get out, a directed function to execute. Imagination and creativity, dreaming, if you like, require their own kind of environment for their kind of functioning. Maybe there is no Department of the Quality of Life among the twenty-five or so departments in City Hall because it could not function there.

We do not have to tear down all of these glass buildings to make the city whole. We do need to recognize that they bring the qualities of function and efficiency and task-oriented productivity and take away nearly everything else. So as we make these kinds of buildings, we need to insist, de-

mand, that there are places, immediately available places, for everything that has been taken away from our lives in order to serve productivity. If we do not, we will all burn out in these buildings and be thrown aside like old light bulbs.

# The Importance of Contrast of Scale in Urban Design

*Robert Venturi*

The duality of growth and undergrowth—that which is planned and that which is cultivated—is manifest in two ways: one in terms of the forms of the city, and one in terms of the activities of the city. As an architect, I will speak more of the forms of the city, realizing that form and activity are interconnected, and that much of the latter can derive from and be stimulated by the former. The forms have to be such that they can allow the cultivation to happen. . . .

I want to emphasize two simple ideas. First, we must not make the mistake, as architects tend to, of trying to plan too explicitly for undergrowth. I refer to the kind of urban design scheme where the architect has the café with all the happy people drinking iced tea in the foreground; or where the children are playing with toy boats in the pond. It's all too explicit. Places have to be planned with the possibility of things happening, but those things cannot be planned too explicitly. . . .

The second point, a simple one too, is the appropriateness of the contrast of big and little scale in architectural complexes. Middle scale is generally inappropriate. Generally, architects and urban designers today plan for middle scale only; they do not accommodate the little scale, which is often manifest in the undergrowth aspect. And often, there is not enough concern or ability to deal with the question of the whole —of seeing the whole in the parts and the satisfaction deriving from unity. . . .

I want to give some examples of this wonderful contrast of large and small scale, ending with some examples of our own work which follow this pattern:

1. The Italian palace, the archetypal civic building, very often had a place built into the base of it for different kinds of uses different from those of the spaces above; these were generally commercial uses. Also these buildings as a whole could and do adapt very easily to different uses. These palaces

have the quality of monumentality, of great scale, of civic dignity, and at the same time this other layer of opportunity on the ground level for vitality.

. . .

2. In the apse of Saint Peter's on the outside, there is the beautiful, repetitive, rhythmic quality of the architecture as a whole, but when you get close, there is much there to interest you as an individual. That is, there is a combination of two scales in these buildings. From a distance, the rhythms of the giant order are emphasized. When you get close, you see the intricate details of the mouldings

. . .

3. The grid plan, which is perhaps most characteristic of the American city can also demonstrate this contrast of large and small scale. You have a sense of the whole, deriving from the grid pattern which dominates and to which all buildings conform—until the advent of the automobile; and then, within that grid there is room for varied undergrowth—there can be a kind of formal chaos within this pattern. On one block there can be a city hall and across the street from it a service station. There can be a juxtaposition of elements that are annoyingly illogical or unrelated, but there can also be a richness in this form and process and a beautiful opportunity for undergrowth and a freedom of development for infill, for sequential development that is always within the grid. The grid is another example of the combination of big and little, of incremental and

whole. Several decades ago architects and planners did everything they could to demolish this pattern. They encircled it with great freeways, made super-blocks, made shops turn inwards to themselves; there was no street life. . . .

4. Even in the "strip" there are lessons. There is an order to a lot of it. Advertising signs can give visual richness to a city. A billboard can be thought of, in our desperation in the kind of landscapes we have, as an element of relief, to promote interest and achieve the sense of small scale we need. . . .

And now, let me provide an example of this sense of contrast in some of our own work. We were asked by the developer George Klein to design something formal and symbolic for the Times Square triangular block in New York City. This place is considered the center of New York, its heart; it is the area where George Klein has planned an enormous complex of office buildings designed by Philip Johnson. After these buildings were designed, there was a great deal of criticism because people became sentimental about Times Square. . . . George Klein thought he should come to us as people who understood Las Vegas, to design something that would kind of save the situation. We tried lots of ideas that involved an instant reinstitution of signs and glitter, but this did not work; the beauty of Times Square is in its incremental quality. What was needed was something sculptural, so we designed a kind of Klaus Oldenberg apple. We wanted this element to be imageful, to make a memorable place, so we suggested this big apple which is ninety feet in diameter. In this context you need big scale as well as the repetitive small scale of the office buildings. The base of the apple derives from Philip Johnson's architecture, a continuation of the bases of his buildings. . . .

Many of our American grid cities do not contain big civic gestures. Maybe it is just as well; if such elements are bad, they're monstrous. But we thought this was something that would have impact and wit—our monumentality today cannot be only serious. . . .

What I have been suggesting is the necessity of plans which are grand and consistent in their overall impact, full of memorability and image, and then within these great systems there is the opportunity for variety of undergrowth and cultivation that evolves as places are used.

# Interiors in the Design of the City: The Ceiling

*James Hillman*

I am a psychological analyst. I speak to the private issues that lie inside the public forum, in the *soul* of the city. I am less a developer than an underminer, following the leaks of gas that cloud and poison our personal relations, the drain of strength in insomnia, impotence, addiction, the little mice of impulses nibbling away in the corners of our interior space, the power failures of despair. This interior city is private and unspeakable in the forum. Yet, we can connect this interiority, our soul-life, with the interiority of our public life; in fact, we may discover a correspondence between two kinds of interior. The conditions of our psyches, I will suggest, reflect the interior of our rooms. There are relations between our habits and our habitations. And that is my theme and my method now: the relation between the inside interior of our lives and the interior inside our living places.

Most city *talk* is about major buildings, planned public spaces, tran-sit. In the mind's eye the word "city" conjures a panoramic shot like the opening of "Dallas" coming in from Southfork Ranch, the city through a car windshield, on a TV screen. Glass, of course. This is all seen from the outside, the exterior city: skyline, sky-scrapers, windy squares. That city has more to do with planning boards, tourists, and TV shows than with its actual nine-to-five inhabitants.

Actual city *life* is interior. Inside rooms, sitting on chairs. We push through doorways, go down passages. We wait at elevators, rummage in drawers, stare at walls. Much of the time we are in fact looking down at something on a desk, focused on an electronic device, a piece of paper, or across at another face. No matter how tall the building, or magnificent its skin and front plaza, inside, that soaring feeling reduces to individual rooms, corridors, compartments, cubbyholes with an eight-foot ceiling. You step out of the elevator on the forty-eighth floor into a corridor whose ceiling you can almost touch with your fingertips: we are still in the same tunnel like the underground garage. Let's turn our attention to those ceilings. Let's look up, for I want to encapsulate all I have to say about the psychology of interior design and the design of it upon human interiority by a brief psychoanalysis of the ceiling.

## Looking Up

But before we look up: Consider this curious psychological fact. There is no visible top to our heads. What we see of ourselves upwards are perhaps our eyebrows, a lock of hair in some fortunate cases. There is no limit upward to our self-experience of the head. As the bottoms of our feet touch the ground, the tops of our heads enter the sky. The ceremonial tonsure of monks and priests that open the scalp to heaven remembers this fact; so does the cranial position of the thousand-petaled lotus of awareness in Hindu mysticism; so does the Platonic reading of the newborn baby's still unclosed skull—it is still open to the upper world whence it supposedly comes. So, too, the Jewish and Islamic custom of keeping the head covered at all times, in prayer, and indoors. Because there is no natural separation upward between human and heavenly, the ceiling of a hat remembers the distinction and is a sign of human humility. We have to have ceilings—not just for practical, but for psychological reasons. The atrium opening straight up extends our heads into

hubris and inflation, no cap to the skull, inspiration gone manic, the sky's the limit.

Now what *does* meet the eye looking up? Usually, today, this basic human gesture, that also raises the head and lifts the person, has become so acutely unpleasant that our glance instinctively retreats. We lower our sight. What's up there is tacky, unarranged; scattered islands of air-vents, smoke detectors, sprinkler spigots, loudspeakers, perhaps a red exit sign tucked up high, perhaps a TV monitor eye, and the ubiquitous tracklights pointing every which way, or recessed cans, or fluorescent tubes in mesh cages. The material itself is often acoustic board, taped with silver masking strips into rectangular blocks, often askew from repairs with traces from pipe or roof leaks.

What's up there refers to fire, smoke, bad air, loud noise, theft, accidents, and the repairman: the ceiling as service center, a covering for wires, cables, tubes, ducts, immediately accessible for maintenance. Here is one more instance of interior, designed not for the nine-to-five inhabitants of that interior but for the maintenance crew, not for pleasure of use but for occasions of breakdown. It is like choosing your clothes in the morning to wear for an accident.

I want now to claim that the ceiling is the most neglected segment of our contemporary interior—interior in both architectural and psychological senses of the word. Whether oppressively close and ugly as just described, or removed altogether in vaulting A-frames or atriums to the roof, the ceiling is the unconsidered, the unconscious, presenting interiority without design, with no sense of inherent order.

What statements are these ceilings making? What are they saying about our *psychic* interiors? If looking up is that gesture of aspiration and orientation toward the higher order of the cosmos, an imagination opening toward the stars, our ceilings reflect an utterly secular vision—short-sighted, utilitarian, unaesthetic. Our heads reach up and open into a meaningless and chaotic white space. The world above has merely a maintenance function, God the repairman called on when things break down.

Curiously, however, the *perspective* from above still remains. Look at our usual blueprints, our usual models. They are drawn from above as floor plans; the view is down from the ceiling. The place from which the Gods have fled is now where the planner sits. We must remember here that renewal of spirit occurs within an enclosed space, under some sort of ceiling. Ancient kings, as far back as the pharoahs, placed themselves under a canopy, a tent, a dome—walls were incidental—and thereby the interior man, the soul, received renewed vitality. The ceiling did indeed refer to heaven, to *ciel*, as our popular and mistaken etymology of ceiling continues to insist.

## Etymology

For *ceiling* doesn't come from *ciel*, French for heaven, sky. Covering the room, enclosing it, that feeling of interior designed space—that there is design to the interior, and this design renews the human spirit—is the true root of the word. It derives from *celure*, via Middle English (*celynge, silynge, syling,* and *selure* [*celure*]) for tapestry, canopy, hangings, finally coming to *ceil*, meaning "to line with woodwork" (1400–1600).

Ceilings became white only during the Enlightenment, the eighteenth century, with the refinement of the plasterer's art. Previously all the detail was exposed: joists, beams, the reverse of the floor above. Then the detail was enhanced by carving the beams, painting, gilding, stucco, plaster, so that looking up fed the imagination. The eye traversed an intriguing pattern of rhythmical and inherent relationships—where function (joists, floorboards) and beauty were inseparable. Ceilings emphasized design—and I do not mean only the magnificent ones painted to represent the heavens and the Gods.

Inside the Latin root of the word itself (*celum, caelatura, caelo*) is the idea of design as burnishing, chiseling, engraving. The upper aspect of our interior space is an intricately fashioned and figured design. The ceiling is a place of images to which imagination turns its gaze to renew vitality. The true ceiling, then, as derived from the word is not a flat white rectangular space studded with incidental equipment, but a magnificent artifice of imagery. The ceiling up there corresponds with the richness of human imagination. It is this our heads can open into and find protection under.

## Ceiling Lights

Which brings us to the quality of light and ceiling fixtures. You all feel the difference when the overhead light is turned off and standing lamps, table lamps, go on. You know the kind of interior that emerges—like a Vuillard or a Bonnard room, an effect used in the movies to change the atmosphere toward intimacy and interiority. Single uniform brightness gives way to shadings of color, reflection, and the sense of nearness to the light within the reach of the hand—as to a candle or a fireplace.

Overhead lighting belongs originally to large state halls, banquet rooms, exhibitions, factories, and markets, where very high ceilings and expansive floorplans demanded flooding of light from above. A splendor both marvelous and functional; indoors, yet lit as the sun-filled world. The light fixtures themselves became objects of awe. They have of course given way, in most cases, to what the maintenance crew can get at and clean up, as low-cost as possible.

Now we apply the same overhead lighting in the smallest cubicles with the lowest ceilings. We sit bathed in a merciless, shadowless enlightenment, democratically falling on all alike,

straight down—a spotlight like that used to break criminals into confession, a brilliant clarity like for an anatomical dissection. The light does not group the furniture, encircle it. Instead, each thing is distinct, isolated from each other thing. Interiority is gone: the flickering feeling of the cave, lighting that makes this piece of room here different from that over there. The room receives the massive doses of illumination of summer outdoors: uniform, bright, cloudless. And timeless: it is always noon indoors. We cannot tell because of these ceiling lights what time of day it is, what the weather, what the season of the year.

Moreover, you do not want to raise your eyes, to look into fluorescent fixtures, at the bright bulb in the track can. You keep your head down—a depressive posture, outlook limited to the horizontal or the downward state. In such light what does the soul do with its shadows, where find interiority? Does the soul not shrink into even deeper personal interiors, into more darkness, so that we feel cut off, alienated, prey to the darkest of the dark: guilts, private sins, fears, and horror fantasies. I am suggesting some of our most oppressive psychological ills come out of the ceiling.

## Moldings

To conclude this psychoanalysis of the ceiling, a word on moldings. At the retreat of The Dallas Institute on Architecture and Poetry, Robert Sardello gave a remarkable, thought-provoking paper in which he examined the place of the right angle in the design of modern cities. He pointed out that the right angle is an abstract expression for the ancient archetypal directions of heaven and earth, Sky God and Earth Mother, the vertical and horizontal dimensions reduced to a simple pair of intersecting lines, much like the tool used by carpenters, the square, the Greek word for which is *norma* (from which we have norms, normal, normalcy). The simple right angle normalizes our entire world from the grid plan of city plats to the graph paper on which we calculate and display the living curves of economic activity.

Modern Bauhaus design exposes this conjunction of father sky and mother earth. The joint is laid bare. Moldings resolve the shock, the violence of their direct rectangular conjunction. Moldings provide a skirt, a curtain covering the exposed pornography, the crotch shot of ceiling joining wall in bare fluorescent light. Moldings are not merely a Victorian cover-up, a delicate discretion—they are an erotic moment in a room, a detail that softens the vertical, letting it come down gently through a series of ripples, heaven into earth, earth into heaven, the secular and the divine, not cut apart and placed at right conflicting purposes, a leap, a gap (as we often see a black line at the ceiling's edge where the two directions have receded from each other, the sheet rock not quite meeting, the taping and mud inadequate).

The problem of how to conclude a ceiling, its edge or end, was particularly a concern of Islamic builders, who had to set circular domes on square rooms. Squaring of the circle and circling of the square, the meeting of two worlds, gave rise to extraordinarily ornate corners rich with embellished moldings. Rich fantasies develop at the juncture where the ceiling descends into the living space of everyday.

Let's now come to a close. I deliberately chose a small subject because in this city we all think so big and bold. I chose ceilings for this exhibition of interior design because just these minor forgotten matters are the more psychological. But now let me be bold: it doesn't so much matter how tall and what color the next huge building downtown, what the library, the symphony hall, the museum look like from the outside. These considerations seduce us into staying outside, playing planner and developer ourselves. It's what's inside that counts, says the psychologist. And the very interest in the exterior of projects—the Arts District, the malls—reflects the exteriorization of our inner concerns. Human beings adapt to their surroundings, and we shall have human beings designed like our interiors, human beings of gold and silver and glass, with hollowed atriums, uniformly illumined by shadowless light, without upper orientation, and with only the crassest, simplest right-angled norms and straight rules for connecting the principles of the heavens with the ways of the earth. These shall be the inhabitants if these be our habitations.

I am suggesting, by means of ceilings, that our buildings are not truly inhabitable—that we must become a certain kind of person with strange habits of soul in order to stay in such rooms under such ceilings for the major part of our conscious life. I am suggesting that many of our social evils and psychological troubles—and even economic ills, such as low productivity, inefficiency, absenteeism, sexual harrassment, job turnover, quality decline, on the job addiction (whether valium, alcohol, coffee, or soda pop)—are psychological results of interior design. To believe still that our psychological problems have economic causes and economic solutions is not only crude materialism, it is crude to the soul, psychologically unsophisticated. I am saying that until we recognize the design of interiors on our interiority, we shall be living in a kind of Orwellian repression, that is, disguised and unnoticed, like living in his book *1984*.

For repression, as Freud discovered it—and he considered repression the greatest of his discoveries—is never where we believe it lies. That's its very meaning. We cannot be aware of it; it is unconscious. So, the repressed today is not where we think it is, in our sexual feeling, racial prejudices, family knots, and hidden motives. We are far more aware of these interior events than in Freud's day. Today the

repressed is less in our interior life, and to search still for it there only furthers the main repression: our unconsciousness regarding the interior psychic reality of the external world. Today the repressed is outside of us, and we are anaesthetized and tranquilized to the world we inhabit, what has been called "psychic numbing" which refers not only to possible nuclear catastrophe, but to every detail of soullessness from our coffee cups to the sounds and light and air, the taste of water, and low maintenance clothes we put on our skins, discomforting but so easy to maintain. By repressing our reactions to basic simple details, like ceilings, by denying our annoyance and outrage, we actually maintain an unconsciousness that estranges and disorients the interior soul.

I am not calling for more potted plants, for sweeter manners, for longer coffee breaks to humanize the interiors of the office. Nor am I beating the antique drum, going back to old ways: historic preservation, nostalgic inspiration from European palaces, ceilings like that in the Sistine Chapel, Disneyland imitations, Red-North-Valley-Center-Preston-Wood Mall. We don't need to build them like we used to—we can indeed build better, as the slogan goes. Restoring and preserving the old, worthwhile as it is, remains a lesser concern because it can become a literalization of what we truly are after: preservation and restoration of the human tradition, the tradition that shapes in replication of the cosmos, where the roof over our heads brings imagination into our minds.

The interior sense always seems a minor matter when compared with the public arena—whether to build aircraft carriers and what kind, whether the deficit should be $90 or $120 billion—these abstract issues that seem so mighty are really the advertising campaign of governments to keep us buying their product, that is, government, to keep us believing that it is dealing with the important issues of "reality." The reality of the soul, however, must be affirmed again and again in this city, for the city is an invisible, spiritual city, not of buildings only but of small sensitive things that give life to its soul as a city of soul and spirit, of sensitivity and inspiration.

So, my intention has not been to suggest how rooms should be built— even if I have drawn attention to moldings, lights, ceiling height, arrangement. My purpose with these physical details is to make a psychological point. I want to preserve and restore the simple gesture of looking upwards. If our society suffers from failures of imagination, of leadership, of cohesive far-sighted perspectives, then we must attend to the places and moments where these interior faculties of the human mind begin. Remember the psalm: "I shall lift up mine eyes—from whence cometh my help." That primordial gesture toward the upper dimension, that glance above ourselves, yet not lofty, spacey, and dizzy, may be where the first bits of

interior change take place. This change of soul can take place inside our ordinary rooms.

# Architecture as Ritual

## Vincent Scully

I don't know whether what I have to say today has much to do with Dallas, though I think that it has implications for this city and modern urban life. I was asked to talk about ritual and the city. It is probably better to draw a world-view of that question by focusing on an architecture that you literally can't see unless we understand the ritual which shapes it. In a certain sense that is true of all architecture which always shapes its own ritual. But for the modern pueblos, this is especially true. I want to talk about the pueblos and how we can see them, how we can understand them, how in fact, we can experience them as works of human art.

First, it is difficult. There is great poverty—the people are very poor. If we come and look at them without knowing what they are for, or how they are sited, all we see are a few rundown buildings, some abandoned automobiles, and we see the architecture of abject poverty.

At Taos we have first the mountain. And down below it we have the North House. Up in the mountain is the water—the sacred Blue Lake. Then, from the mountain some water

is squeezed, and it comes down in a never failing stream. It's the glory of Taos, and it runs all winter, and it runs also in the dry days of summer.

The great North House is where all the dances culminate. That's the heart and the climax of Taos. It doesn't stand alone. Not only the House is Taos. The mountain is Taos, too. As we approach the North House, we see the especially touching quality of pueblo architecture, that unlike the other architecture of Mesoamerica, is not symmetrical; it is not just a temple base but is a communal dwelling. At the same time, it is a pyramid, a concealed pyramid. As we look at it, it steps back, it goes forward, and it picks up the shape of mountain. . . . We find out that it not only reflects the mountain but it also clarifies and picks up the other great element in the landscape, the shapes of the clouds. . . .

I show you now a painting of a "dog dancer," painted in the nineteenth century. This is the kind of dance that calls to those nomads who are just on the other side of the mountain, and who were drawn on their horses—the Kiowa, the Comanche, the Apache—were drawn through the narrow pass, and they came to Taos because that is where the power is. That's where enough human beings are together in one place, in a city, to wrest some of nature's power to themselves. That dance is the war dance of the city. It is a city stating its power. . . .

The beat of the feet of the dog dance is like the beat of the building and the beat of the mountain. You feel the beat of the man-made, of the architecture, and nature, all together. . . .

In winter, especially, are the great animal dances. They shovel the snow away from the North House for the buffalo dance. At Taos, unlike other pueblos, they wear the whole buffalo head, as the Plains Indians did. Some-times it is a blind head; some-times there are no eyes in it. At Taos the buffalo dancers carry one arrow and they come in a herd, blindly shuffling. There is a real sense of the animal coming, moving, turning, dancing. . . .

Now that principle, of the work of men imitating nature, drawing power from that, is worldwide. It is broken, finally, by the Greeks. The Olympian gods are in the human image. And they have a house, and that house is a temple. It is a great exterior body; and it doesn't look like nature at all. Natural forms are also sacred—mountains and sky and earth. But the temple is a great worshipped mass, and it images new things for the Greeks—a kind of revolt of human beings against nature's laws. . . . That is what is finally embodied in the imperial Athe-

nian state, which breaks all the previous laws and enters into a great hubris which brought about her partial destruction, but out of which all Western civilization grew.

Now, it isn't a short road, but it's a fairly direct one from Athens to the modern city, where man controls, apparently, the whole. Here, it is the automobile which gives the human being a velocity, an apparent command over space, and a power that the individual never had before. And our buildings are successors of the Parthenon in that they rise up as images of purely human action, human pride, in the landscape. Now that's true of course of all great skyscraper centers in the United States, but it is especially true in the sunbelt. It's certainly true here in Dallas. . . . It is an architecture of exile from the earth, of humans who are in fact making their own world, with their own systems of power. That certainly will never change so long as the earth lets us get away with it. If it does change, and poverty ensues in that power, then maybe other problems might arise. . . .

The Pueblo Indians, as you know, learned the hard way. Their ancestors depopulated the buffalo; and then the earth out there began to dry up, thousands and thousands of years ago. They became poor. And only in their poverty did the great structure of their ritual become necessary to them. To the rich, only money is necessary, or so it seems. But to the poor, a more intense view of how one can get along in the world may be felt.

# Architecture and Poetry

## *Christian Norberg-Schulz*

The philosopher Martin Heidegger did not leave us any text on architecture. And still, it plays an important role in his philosophy. His concept of being-in-the-world implies a man-made environment, and when discussing the problems of "dwelling poetically," he explicitly refers to the art of building. An exposition of Heidegger's thinking on architecture therefore ought to be part of our interpretation of his philosophy. Such an exposition may also contribute to a better understanding of the complex environmental problems of our time. . . .

A building according to Heidegger is, or may be, a work of art. As a work of art the building "preserves truth.". . .

Heidegger wants to remind us of the fact that our everyday life world really consists of concrete "things," rather than the abstractions of science. In his later writings he moreover offers an interpretation of the totality of things as a "fourfold" of earth, sky, mortals, and divinities:

> Earth is the building bearer, nourishing with its fruits, tending water and rock, plant and animal.
>
> The sky is the sun's path, the course of the moon, the glitter of the stars, the year's seasons, the light and dusk of day, the gloom and glow of night, the clemency and inclemency of the weather, the drifting clouds and blue depth of the ether.
>
> The divinities are the beckoning messengers of the godhead. Out of the hidden sway of the divinities the god emerges as what he is, which removes him from any comparison with beings that are present. The mortals are human beings. They are called mortals because they can die. To die means to be capable of death as death.

Each of the four is what it is because it "mirrors" the others. They all belong together in a "mirror-play" which constitutes the world. The mirror-play may be understood as an open "between," wherein things appear as what they are. . . .

What a poem and a work of art have in common is the quality of image. A work is in addition a thing, whereas a thing proper does not possess the quality of image. As a gathering it mirrors the fourfold in its way. . . .

Although poetry is the original art, it does not exhaust the disclosure of truth. In poetic language truth is brought "to work." But it also has to be "set into words." Human life takes place between earth and sky in a concrete sense, and the things which constitute the place have to be disclosed in their immediate presence. . . . Thus Heidegger says that man dwells "between work and word." The word opens up the world, the work gives the world presence. In the work the world is set back on earth, that is, it becomes part of the immediate here and now, whereby the latter is disclosed in its being. . . .

Heidegger says: "The buildings bring the earth as the inhabited landscape close to man and at the same time place the nearness of neighborly dwelling under the expanse of the sky." This statement offers a clue to the problem of architectural gathering. What is gathered, Heidegger says, is the "inhabited landscape." An inhabited landscape obviously is a *known* landscape. An inhabited landscape is brought close to us by the buildings, or in other words, the landscape is revealed as what it is in truth.

What is, however, a landscape? A landscape is a space where human life takes place. It is therefore not a mathematical, isomorphic space, but a "lived space" between earth and sky. . . . It is impossible to consider the world separately from language, which is understood as the "House of Being." Language names things which "visit man with a world," and man's access to the world is through listening and responding to language. . . .

To give the world immediate pres-

ence, however, man also has to "set truth into work." The primary purpose of architecture is hence to make a world visible. It does this as a thing, and the world it brings into presence consists in what it gathers. . . .

The inhabited landscape therefore is a manifestation of the fourfold and comes into presence through the buildings which "bring it close to man." We could say that "inhabited landscape" dominates the spatiality of the fourfold. This spatiality becomes manifest as a particular "between" of earth and sky, that is, as a *place*.

When we say that "life takes place," we imply that man's being-in-the-world "mirrors" the between of earth and sky. Man "is" in this between, standing, resting, acting. The natural and man-made things which constitute the boundaries of the between also stand, rest, and tower. . . .

The words "extension," "delimitation," "standing," "resting," "towering" refer to modes of being-in-the-world in terms of spatiality. Although the possibilities are infinite, the modes always appear as variations on archetypes. We all know some of these, such as "column," "gable," "arch," "dome," "tower." The very fact that language names these things proves their importance as types of images which visualize the basic structure of spatiality. . . .

Today we are at a new beginning in architecture. This is apparent in architectural practice, where functionalism is being abandoned while a new architecture of images is emerging. Heidegger's thinking may help us to understand what this implies. In his essay *Building, Dwelling, Thinking*, Heidegger in fact concludes that "thinking itself belongs to dwelling in the same sense as building. . . . Building and thinking are, each in its own way, inescapable for dwelling." In other words, we have to give thought to the thingness of things in order to arrive at a total "vision" of our world.

# The Poetry of Water

## Dan Kiley

You cannot approach design by designing, but by living. Design is a matter of sensitivity. Things need to be apt for the place. . . . Landscape design is like a walk in nature; but it is not a copy of nature—the process of nature is completely different. It is copying an end result that comes from all kinds of factors. . . .

Nature resents generalizations, said Emerson, and insults philosophers every moment with fresh particulars. You cannot get away from copying things. Architecture has always come from need, and the forms come from that need. . . .

Dallas is empty at night—but there is nothing wrong with a dead city at night—the activity is going on some-where else. . . . Maybe the buildings need to rest at night. You cannot force things on people— they have to come the other way. We lack green space in the cities because of the auto-mobile—each takes up about 350 feet. . . . But there is a lot that can be done in Dallas, not all concerned with water. The main thing is the spatial idea of the city. It is necessary to get it into some kind of beautiful form, an experience that is continuous. An ex-ample of this is the city of Boston. You have to get green spaces in the city—and Town Lake would not help this much. . . . If you look at the city plan, I bet there is a way to get a new green system that penetrates the whole city, and every two, three, or four blocks there would be a place to sit down. I used to say that I had to go to Europe to get a place to sit down, but now America is doing better at this.

People are afraid, and that makes planting trees as they should be planted in the city difficult—they need to be dense, not one here, another forty feet away. The way we like to do it is the way nature does it—plant them very close. That gives texture. The city is hard. We are trying to soften the city by giving it texture, depth, shade, and shadow. You have to think of water as part of the space. Trees, space, water, and movement— that is all you have to have. It is a very simple thing, but it means giving up a little—maybe on the edges of sidewalks. I used to measure the value of a city by how wide its treestrip

was. When you have a wide treestrip
you get put back in dimension—the
cars are then out there, separate from
what is most human. . . .

Trees are as important as water—
possibly more so. They develop spatial
movement in the land. . . . People do
not like to move directly to something
—that misses the experience of the
space, the experience of coming and
arrival.

Right in the city you can have quiet
places, places of mystery and repose
even in the heart of the city. We
designed the gardens at the Oakland
museum with this in mind. . . .

Water has to be a system you are in
rather than something that you look
at. That is what I am seeking —that
kind of depth and continuity that can
be done with good patterning. . . .

# Chinese Water Gardens

## *Edwin T. Morris*

I want to look at water from a more poetic and aesthetic point of view, which for the Chinese is in the terrain of magic, the terrain of the garden. The Chinese garden was a boiling down and a concentration of the whole cosmos. The cosmos of China is a cosmos of two things: high, steep, rugged mountains and a filigree of water magic—waterfalls, lakes, which went into the three enormous river systems of China and then out to the sea.

Most of China's water magic and water imagery is always fresh water; the water in the garden is sweet water, the water of the hillside and the countryside, not marine water. So the Chinese garden was a distillation of the water that was encountered in the countryside. The ideology that made for the boiling down and the creation of the quintessence of nature within their own garden property was Taoism. Tao is the Chinese word which means 'the flow,' or 'the current,' or 'the flux.' One must feel this great flow of the Tao for it cannot be named. The force is often described under the analogy of water. Another

example of the force of Tao is the grain of wood, the pulsation of the bands of the wood. Another example are the strata in nature, the folding in rock. . . .

Now Chinese philosophy sees no breakage between man and nature. So one could not be true without remaining close to water, rock, plants, and animals. However, all of this closeness to nature is balanced by a tenderness for the body politic, or Confucianism. There is a feeling that "all the world are my brothers.". . . But how could one be close to others and at the same time be up in the mountains, close to nature? The dichotomy was solved by bringing all the terrain of nature into the city. This is the meaning of the Chinese garden. It was the terrain of the Taoist hermit in the woods. . . .

The Chinese garden served to refresh you when you became tired of the fatigues of political living or the fatigues of family living. It was meant to be a hatchery of dreams and reverie. One walked down winding paths that gave arresting vistas of this scene of water or that clump of rock or that orchard of fruit trees in full bloom. . . . The idea was that in all the ramblings one loses one's normal perspective and goes into a kind of fairyland. . . . The work of the garden designer was called "half of heaven, half of man." The half that man produced was pavilion architecture. The pavilion was meant to set off a beautiful hillside in your garden, and a vantage point for dreaming. The Chinese say: "In the large we have the small, but in the small we have the large." On a large hillside we have a small pavilion, but as you actually sit in the pavilion the eye rambles widely across the land.

As one walked from pavilion to pavilion, one was carried not only by paths that were treated very sensitively but also by covered arcades that allowed one to ramble across the terrain without getting wet in the rain or covered by snow in the winter. They made a great art of letting these covered arcades go where they will, so that you could enjoy a kind of poetic trance or poetic reverie. . . .

The Chinese temperament could not stop and enjoy the beauty of nature without feeling the stirrings of hunger. What could be more civilized than sitting in a beautiful chair in a comfortable pavilion and having tea brought to heighten the enjoyment of this beautiful terrain; and even more beautiful, to be joined by friends to enjoy the moment together. . . .

The Chinese loved accessories that were of the most perfect quality possible. So, the tables that were used in these pavilions were beautifully polished hardwoods so that one could admire the perfection of the grain. Chairs were brought from the inner apartment out into the garden so one was not sitting on roughhewn furniture; and one could sip tea from eggshell-clear porcelain.

The Chinese garden was never constructed by a designer; one let it come from one's own spontaneous creativity. In order also to let these feelings be more expansive and beautiful, they would wall away an objectionable view. Water was particularly important in this technique because water is a mirror, and the Chinese say one could borrow from below the heavens. Sun would not only be in the heavens but rippled on the surface of their water. . . .

No Chinese garden is without water. The Chinese say that a portrait without eyes is a garden without water; it has no smile, no glint, no sparkle, no animation.

# The Psychology of the Fountain

*William S. Burford*

For all its abundant display there is something secret about a fountain; though designed for the public's pleasure, it keeps a strange sort of privateness; despite its apparent vitality when we see it from a distance—at the end of a vista—it is a kind of phantom, a white plume, a ghost in the sunlight. Though happy, the fountain weeps.

These paradoxes make up its fascination and guide the art of the creators of fountains, who work in an uncertain element between the solid and the aerial states. The fountain promises never to fail, and yet hovering within it, or at the source from which it springs, is the specter of its sudden cessation. The fountaineer, as he is called, the man who creates fountains, is not unlike the mountaineer on the side of Everest. He works in the precarious....

In the past, the fluid element, welling up, gathered and dispensed by the public fountain, gave life to what otherwise would have been dead stones, dust. Water was thus sacred and the central element of religious rites. The fountain was not merely a decorative display, as it usually is today. It was not exclusively a feast for the eyes, an extravagant goblet. The fountain was the deep spring, the fons surging up, from which men directly drank and women dipped their jugs.

The removal of the source of water in modern times, from this direct path to man, from his immediate sense of touch—so that water reaches us only after passing through the complex machinery of filtration plants and reservoirs, so that fountains are only to be seen and not touched or drunk from—means a profound change in the sense of the city as a site chosen because of naturally flowing water. The modern fountain, designed as part of an architectural plan, shows the abiding human need for the presence of water, which the fountain celebrates. However, a feeling of unreality has crept over this modern fountain. . . . Instead of the restless, uncertain, unresolved secret life of water that man has always tried to catch and contain, we now have a controlled element, a dependable supply, on which the immense modern cities draw, without which they would quickly die. . . .

The fountain, in its essential mode,

has always been our assurance that the waters of our earth will not dry up, that there is an inexhaustible source. It is proof also of our belief that the human heart will not be cut off from hope—what else is meant by the fountain that opens in the side of the crucified Christ when the spear pierces him, the stream of blood and water caught in the cup that becomes the chalice of the mass from which men sip to renew their thirsty souls.

In this recalling of miraculous phenomena associated with the fountain, we must add, of course, the Fountain of Youth, and the spring opened on Mount Helicon sacred to the muses when Pegasus struck it with his hoof —the waters of these legendary fountains all acting to release men from the heaviness of gravity, letting it drop away from us, the gravity of aging, the gravity of being uninspired, of having no language, no singing and dancing, which the fountain restores to us. . . . I describe the past of fountains in order to reach now what seems to be the truly modern fountain, one that we happen to have in Dallas. . . .

The creators of the fountain at the Flora Street entrance to the Dallas Museum of Art may never have been tempted to echo in its design the mythology of the Roman goddess of flowers for whom the old and once obscure little street was named. The style of the building itself would have resisted, in any case, an eighteenth-century Roman fountain, in which none of the actual forces of the city

could have been recognized. So, we have a circle of granite curbing that evokes no fanciful legend about the waters leaping up within it. Instead, there are two upward pulsations, the second springing from the first just as the first begins to fall, so that the monotony of a single pulsation always rising to a fixed height and stopping there is avoided by this doubling of the impulse. The reserves, so to speak, of the fountain seem profound. We are not facing a shallow display. But what is this strongly endowed water doing at this place?

A museum is a collection and repository of forms. Where do forms emerge from? From the brains of artists, who have the form-making power out of which painting and sculpture comes into existence. . . . The contents of a museum catch some of this form-making; the whole of it is ungraspable; the enormous process can be suggested but never held. The fountain, when its makers have perceived their task clearly, can best reveal this continuous forming, this tossing up of structures that collapse back into the surging stream, only to be built up again in renewed forms. In the fountain's tossing one can see entire buildings raised in an instant and then dissolved, as if the fountain were the genie in the tale of Sinbad who could create a city in a night or snatch it away. The speed at which the material world can be shaped will vastly increase, if this fountain is to be believed.

However, the fountain is not an op-

timist; it does not offer a tribute to
the modern world, or to a society
avidly drawn to art. . . . The fountain
is beautifully indifferent like the smile
of Dionysos which his statue, carried
to the theater in Athens, maintained
throughout the performance of the
tragic play where life tore itself to
pieces on the way to forming a new
meaning. But the fountain is not as
philosophic as tragedy—nor as unruly
as the volcano. Its waters place us at a
place between natural chaos and
human artifice.

# Gather by the River

## *Roy P. Harrover*

From 30,000 to 25,000 years ago, the last great ice cap which covered North America melted northward, and as it did so, torrents of water carried rock and sand and silt into the Gulf, filling it almost to its present configuration. The final melting carved the lower Mississippi River valley.

All great rivers, in their length from headwater to mouth, go through stages which may be likened to the ages of man's life. At its beginning, the river is youthful, skipping and dancing as it falls from pool to pool over surface rocks. The young Mississippi begins at Lake Itasca in northern Minnesota and flows to the Falls of Saint Anthony in Minneapolis where it begins its vigorous, strong, and mature midlife, cutting through earth and rock down past Saint Louis, where the Muddy Missouri joins, to Cairo where its last major tributary, the Ohio, flows to meet it. Below the mouth of the Ohio, the river widens, slows, begins to drop silt and soil over a vast alluvial flood plain, enters the final phase of its life, and becomes Old Man River.

The Mississippi and its tributaries collect the waters of half this country —hopes, dreams, and memories were to flow with the sweat and blood of America in: the Allegheny and Monongahela, the Ohio, the Illinois, the Tennessee and Cumberland, the Missouri (also called Big Muddy and Old Yellow); the Black, the White, and the Red; the Buffalo—the Little Buffalo—the Wolf and Pigeon; the Platte, Big Horn, and Little Big Horn; the Sunflower; the Nonconnah, the Yalobusha, Tallahatchie, Yazoo, and Atchafalaya; and into the father of waters, Mark Twain's magnificent Mighty Mississippi, "rolling its mile-wide tide along, shining in the sun."

This river system was used by Indian nations to build a vast trade network in support of highly developed cultures which peaked about the time Hernando De Soto led his small army of Spaniards westward in search of seven mythical cities of gold and became the first white man to see the Mississippi, near Memphis, in 1541.

More than 100 years later, Marquette and Joliet, and then La Salle, came down the Mississippi from the north, claiming it and all the land it drains, for France. During the eighteenth century, Spain, France, England, and later the United States struggled for control of the lower river and its valley. Spain eventually ceded its claims to France, who sold them to the United States in 1803 with the Louisiana Purchase. England's claims finally died with the Highland regiments who fell piping in the mist at New Orleans before the long rifles of Jackson's small crew of Tennesseans, Kentuckians, effete New Orleanians and free blacks, and the cannon of Jean Lafitte's pirates.

Enter the land speculators. Like John Neely Bryan, they were lawyers from Nashville. In 1795 John Overton bought, for $500, the highest, largest flood-free bluff on the lower Mississippi. He went home and sold half interest in this future site of Memphis to his roommate, Andrew Jackson, for $100. To successfully promote the sale of land, they had to get rid of the Chickasaw Indians, who claimed it as hunting grounds. Jackson did this in 1818 when he negotiated a treaty for the United States government that removed the Indians to Oklahoma along the trail of tears. The city was laid out in 1819, chartered in 1821.

Through the nineteenth and early twentieth centuries, blessed by the Mississippi and its fertile delta, Memphis grew rapidly, surviving the Civil War and repeated epidemics of yellow fever, to become the cotton trading capital of the nation and a major distribution center. Through World War

II and the fifties, downtown Memphis was the regional shopping center for western Tennessee, Arkansas, and Mississippi and the playground for delta planters.

Dramatic changes were imminent for the city. In 1968, Martin Luther King came to Memphis to lead marchers in a peaceful sanitation workers' protest. Across from his motel a vague figure rested his rifle on a window sill and, as King stepped out for a breath of air, fired, mortally wounding him. Caught in an accident of time and place, such as Dallas has known, Memphis and its downtown would never again be the same.

Although no one was killed in the rioting that ensued, no one hurt, no buildings burned, within two years almost all the shops and stores and hotels in the downtown area had closed. Now to the lure of the suburbs was added the fear of racial violence and crime in the inner city. Real estate speculators were delighted as farmland became subdivisions and shopping centers. Thus, the city sprawled without commensurate population growth.

When a Latin people—the Spanish, French, Italians—found a city, they put people-places—plazas, courts, promenades—on the waterfront. When Anglo-Saxons found a city on the water, they consider the waterfront a place of rough commerce, build wharves and warehouses, and live as far away as possible. Memphians had not lived downtown on the river for over a century. No one lived downtown, not rich nor poor, white nor black. In the early '70s the city fathers decided that downtown must be saved. It had symbolic value, it had potential tourist value—and it had the Mississippi River, which had given birth to the city and which was magnetically appealing and magnificently beautiful.

It was wisely decided to encourage new residential development downtown by the adaptive reconstruction of vacant warehouses, office buildings, and hotels into apartments. The best way to bring vigorous new life to a downtown is to have people live there, and this worked! A whole new generation or two of suburbanites were harboring a secret desire to live downtown by the river. But they needed nearby a large recreational park, and there was no vacant land downtown for such a park. So the city decided to build this park on a fifty-acre portion of a sandbar offshore in the Mississippi that had always been known as Mud Island. My firm was chosen to design the entire park. We were told only to make it useful and beautiful.

I knew we would have to raise the fifty acres of island fifteen feet to get it above flood level. Although there existed a service road over to the island some two miles north of downtown, I knew we would have to have a pedestrian bridge directly over from the center of the downtown core to the park. And I knew we did not want automobiles in the park. I knew we

wanted open playing fields and wooded areas and picnic areas and a children's playground. But I struggled for two months trying to find that organizing principle which would give the park a special meaning, a special order. Without this, it would just be another park, albeit a good one, enhanced by the river.

Then the simplest and most obvious concept came to me. Why not have the park tell the story of the lower Mississippi River and its valley; its natural and cultural history; its people and their struggles, their folklore, food, and music; its wildlife and vegetation; the river itself—how it was formed, its meanderings, how man fought to tame and control it, to use it, to simply coexist with it. A fitting theme for the park—Faulkner's two ancient protagonists: man and river.

This concept gained immediate support from the mayor and the city council, the media, and the banks and business community. But all was not easy nor pleasant. Many suburban residents resented such a huge expenditure of city funds in a downtown area which they considered a slum that they would never visit. Suburban real estate interest encouraged this attitude. Many times the project slowed, but it never stopped. It cost $60 million and took eight years to complete. It opened in July 1982 and was an immediate success, drawing a million and a quarter visitors the first year.

# Economy

Economics, in its original sense, does not concern money, but the care of the household of the world. A money economy characterizes only the modern world, and the present time constitutes a peak as well as a point of transition, a period during which 'the bottom line' seems to be everything while at the same time we are awakening to understanding such a view as illusory. Instability is the law governing transition. For some, change brings fear of death; for others, it is a moment to capitalize on the confusion of others; and for still others it is a time for reconsideration of basic assumptions. All these responses to instability go on at the same time, producing the simultaneous operation of several economies. One economy, in effect, is the same as politics—the manipulation of oil prices, the 'de facto' default of the debt of many Third World countries, economic sanctions against countries as a retribution device, the shifting of interest rates. Another economy, recognizing money as a technological medium, does not concern itself with the 'reality' of money but with the control of information on the stock market, produces vast shifts of power daily. A transaction of millions of dollars from one part of the world to another takes no longer than eight seconds. Consequently, money no longer grows or circulates, it appears and disappears in accordance with the laws of dreams of power, not reality.

A third economy goes on underground. Part of it is underworld—drug related, illegal activities, crime, which according to some estimates approach in quantity the Gross National Product. The other part concerns cooperative, altruistic economies of barter, voluntary work, and subsistence by choice as alternatives to anonymous control. A fifth economy can be seen in attempts to recover the reality of money as care of the household by establishing "local" currencies backed by tangible resources.

Looking at this list alone—and surely there are more—the odds are against recovering a care of the household of the world. These odds just might be shifted through recognizing that the faltering of the economic system does not stem from lack of inventiveness, but from domination of a mode of thought, calculative reasoning. The essays in this chapter are of importance because they introduce a different level of reflection sorely needed by the 'science' of economics. Cultural reasoning operates on a higher plane, and thus demonstrates the presence of human freedom, a breath of spirit in an otherwise dismally deterministic discipline. The action of human freedom, to be effective, is not a matter of speculation, which always sets up its opposite, but a matter of using it so that it shows itself. As with any human organ, when not utilized, it atrophies. The problems of the economic system might well be due to the withering away of this most central component.

*Robert Sardello*

# The Qualities of Money

*Robert Sardello*

Taste concerns qualities—the tangible but immeasureable life of imagination within the heart of landscapes, trees, houses, animals, people, buildings, offices, schools— the very living body of the city. A city is tasteful when it is alive and fully itself. It lacks taste when it is an imitation, dummy thing, the outcome of clever ideas, or the importation of fanciful delusions.

How can money help Dallas in its awakening to its own imaginative life? Are there ways to consider money in the city that increase the probability of enhancing life, which, of course, is more than comfort or convenience or amenities. . . .

While taste can never be guaranteed, the likelihood of its occurrence increases if money transactions can be apprehended in their qualitative dimensions. So, I want to consider with you the qualitative actions of money. . . .

To begin with, money remembers. The energy, aspirations, and achievements of the ancestors of the land who stood for and brought values into the community are com-memorated on each denomination of currency passing through our fingertips, greening our hopes for the future. The five-dollar bill remembers Lincoln as a hero of the land. Through the currency bearing his image we hear again the resounding words of the Gettysburg Address, smell the gunsmoke and hear the cannon fire of the Civil War, feel the wounds of internal dissension, anticipate emancipation. . . . We so readily take for granted the magic ritual of the transformation of a bit of green paper into the actualization of a desire that the background making this possible goes unnoticed until it cries out that we have become inflated with our own sense of worth. The quality of money is governed by the liveliness of action, the formative visions of the body of ancestors still circulating in our midst—Abraham Lincoln, George Washington, Lady Liberty, Alexander Hamilton, Susan B. Anthony, and the rest. When money comes to be measured independently of memory, cycles of inflation and depression occur, which are states of the human soul before they are notations on an accountant's ledger. The rise and fall of money serves as an index of the acuity of communal memory. . . .

The qualitative economy of the city, too, needs public recognition of its obligations to its ancestors in order to release the forces of imagination into financial matters. Portraits of the heritage of civic leaders displayed in city hall, public statues, fountains, and festivals honoring our local heroes—from John Neely Bryan through Erik Jonsson—would serve as daily reminders protecting the memorial values of currency in the city. . . .

Our first step, then, regards money as value. Money values by connecting us with memory. Money is also wealth, and this term needs to be taken into an economics of imagination.

The word wealth means well-being; it refers not only to individuals but also to the community, the commonwealth. Well-being is also related to health, which means wholeness of being. The wealth of money is imagined as gold. In spite of the fact that paper money has not been backed by gold since 1934, there is something permanently golden about money. What is this gold quality of greenbacks?

Gold provides in tangible form a small glint, a touch of immortality within the world. What else could possibly account for the greed, the raw passions that money evokes than to have the golden touch of immortality—the final security each of us spends our life pursuing?

But the quality of gold that most relates to taste resides in the fact that far more gold is fashioned into art, jewelry, and crafted objects than is preserved as bullion. Gold, then, takes us into the quality of money as art. Money is an art when its golden qualities craft the things of the city. As long as money carries golden fantasies, the circulation of currency keeps the element of craft close in touch with the things of the city. Then things, each in their own proportion, have golden qualities—attributes of permanence, beauty, solidity, fineness, the touch of the human hand. The art of money in Dallas can too readily be converted into Dallas art. When this occurs, the rare and valuable experiences of everyday life get removed from the street and placed into the specialized world of taste. Taste is vaulted behind monumental museum walls, concert halls, and expensive districts. Slowly, the crafting of the city drains away, the golden opportunities for the common sense of taste, lost. . . .

In 1908, before the gold standard was abandoned, Freud had already discovered that the standard of wealth had shifted from the touch of immortal splendor in the world to the lowliest place imaginable, for he declared that money was equivalent to human excrement. Few paid attention to such an absurd-sounding statement, but Freud was getting at some very important qualities of money with this metaphor. We speak of dirty money, filthy lucre, the smell of cash, holding companies, putting someone on a retainer, tight money, loose money, cash flow. Money matters have a dirty side; they take us right into the messes of the city, and I for one admire those who are not afraid to get their hands dirty. . . . The only difficulties inherent in this image of money come from holding on too tightly, from thinking that the whole point of money is to accumulate it. . . . The real contribution of Freud's insight is his reconnection of money matters with the vital processes of the body, the sense that the health of the communal body depends on the choreographed movement of money. The circulation of money gets stopped up when the point of it is simply to make more money. I think that the point of money is to make the living body of the city. . . .

Reimbursing money with the value of memory and the wealth of craft leads us to a third and final consideration; money as a medium of exchange. Imagine giving twenty-five cents for an apple. . . . I reach into my wallet, purse, or pocket and give the clerk a quarter and receive a particular apple, the one that has caught my fancy. The apple draws the quarter from my pocket as the quarter gives tangible substance and particularity to my imagination. . . . To think of this moment as spending is to operate out of an image of money as the action of retaining and letting loose. The quantitative approach isolates the exchange and forgets the relationships to the store in which I stand, the clerk whom I face, the employer who paid my salary, the family budget which portioned the earnings, the desire which brought me to the store, the company which owns this store and the employees which it retains, the produce merchant who brought the apples in, the farmer who grew the apple, the tree from which it came, the earth from which it sprouted, the rain which moistened it, the clouds which shaded it, and the sun which reddened it. . . . We are what we purchase; that can be as narrow as greedy functionaries or as broad as guardians of the earth. It all depends on the extent of our emotional relationship with money. . . .

Money is a kind of magic talisman through which transformations of the city take place. The medium is the message. When we think of this medium of a quantity, we are in an economics of fear and power. Those with the greatest quantities protect their interests; the city develops in lopsided ways, like a body with a tumor.

qualitative actions, we are in an economics of delight. . . . Herein lies Dallas's greatest hope for taste. Commerce is the very myth of this city—it has been since its beginning. Dallas carries, then, the potentiality of discovering its true identity as the city of relationships. That, I think, is its secret life, yet unfulfilled, and what will make Dallas one with itself. Our wealth is to be found in an exchange of care for each other.

# Economics of Taste

## *Donald Cowan*

Taste is a dangerous thing to talk about. Nothing so raises an audience's indignation as for someone to presume to specify taste. The part of caution demands that it be left wholly relative —one person's taste is as good as another's. But caution lies next to cowardice, and I shall enter no such caveat today. . . . my aim is to attempt to see the social structure in its relation to taste, since I am convinced that taste is not a mere decoration upon society but one of its sources of energy.

Taste, then, I define as an inner response of recognition that some action or object in society is genuine in itself and fitting for the situation in which it participates. Fitness implies a standard of taste that serves as a shared norm for society. Taste is a social phenomenon. . . .

Artists and taste are not bedfellows, not at least in a generative sense. Taste cohabits with the audience, not with the artist. An artist is impregnated with something much more profound than taste, something more archetypal, more robust, more brutal, and if what is produced by that union is a true art

piece, then taste, though jarred and insulted, redefines itself to encompass this new revelation of being. . . .

Taste, then, as I am defining it, is not the inner vision of the artist, nor is it that strange and wonderful faculty that recognizes the essence of an art piece in any medium—poetry, drama, music, painting, sculpture, out of an era, wherever it occurs—what I can only call its *truth*, quite independent of any consideration other than the piece itself. . . .

Nor do I go with Immanual Kant in letting taste be the ability to recognize *beauty* and to render an *a priori* judgment that something is indeed beautiful. Taste *is* aesthetic but does not require beauty as its object. . . .

Our topic for this conference, "The Economics of Taste," couples together three different realms of society. Let me borrow for a moment Daniel Bell's three components of contemporary society that he sets forth in his book, *The Cultural Contradictions of Capitalism*. First, he speaks of the techno-economic, then the polity, and third, the culture. Taste, I say, governs the third of Bell's categories—culture, the realm of the symbolic . . . those forms which seek to explore and express the meanings of human existence in some imaginative form. Those meanings, Bell notes, stem from the existential agonies which confront human beings through all the times—how one meets death, the nature of tragedy and the character of heroism, the definition of loyalty and obligation, the redemption of the soul, the meaning of love and sacrifice; the understanding of compassion, the tension between an animal and a human nature, the claims of instinct and restraint. I would apply this to not only the arts but folkways and events. And I would append to his litany of agonies a brighter listing of those instances of interaction that yield pleasure—breaking bread together, celebrating, playing, communing. . . .

The techno-economic sphere is in radical disjunction from the culture. What Bell calls its axial principle is *functional rationality* whose regulating mode is *economizing*, that is, efficiency, least cost, greatest return, maximization, optimization, productivity. The structure is bureaucratic and hierarchical. Authority rests in position, not in persons. Taste, seemingly, would enter this realm only insofar as it affects the market for goods and services produced.

The other component, the polity, is the arena of social justice and power, exercised in conformity with a society's tradition or its constitution. The axial principle in a democratic

society is governance by the consent of the governed. . . . Taste has no standing under law, but because the polity operates by tradition, the persistent residue of culture, it is not in so marked disjunction as is the economic segment.

. . . When industrialists try to correct the problems of the cultural segment by technocratic means or when representatives of the polity seek to alter it by political procedures, they are naive and misguided, however high-minded they may be. In this third segment, culture, different purposes prevail and different ends are sought; and therefore governance—by boards and even by administration—is largely fictional. These institutions belong to their purposes and are directed by them. Seemingly they submit to no adequate measure of success or failure. . . . An adequate study of management for these nonprofit institutions would involve a rethinking of the economics in terms appropriate to the ends sought. . . .

How does taste grow and spread? First of all by the presence of good design. Taste reinvests in itself, so to say. Design generates the *concept* of design in its observers. And, unlike the products of the money economy, for taste it is plentitude that increases value, not scarcity. The more taste there is, the better the market for it. . . .

Second, taste grows by the action of critics—those who write for newspapers and journals—who perform part of adult education. Those who have accepted a professional responsibility for judging artifacts are generally worth listening to. Their function is not so much to pronounce as it is to make one reconsider, to awaken an inner action of taste. . . . But more than design or criticism, education is the chief disseminator of aesthetic sensibility.

Society has turned over to schools the development of taste in children, just as it has the development of virtues. The fun and then the joy of music establishes a foundation in the early grades; and at the secondary level, a group experience in chorus or orchestra, under a demanding director whose taste is impeccable, invests the student with an intuitive nonverbal critical judgment that serves as paradigm for all later expressive experience. Beyond the high-school years, the importance of music as a formative experience diminishes, while the visual arts and poetry do not flower until later because their aesthetic has philosophic dimensions. . . .

Education is an activity of culture and has as its chief—though often forgotten—end the perpetuation and enhancement of culture. The services it renders to the political and economic realms are by-products. . . . What a curriculum must do is awaken desire and guiding taste for symbolic experience—such as reading and calculating. All of us, educators included, are so conditioned by functional rationalism to the techo-

economic mode of thinking that when we are put in any post of authority, such as board member, administrator, or curriculum director, our references are immediately efficiency, completeness, productivity borrowed from the techno-economic realm. We forget that our task is to engender pleasure as an inner instructor, the young person's self-instructor for life. . . .

I want to grant the importance of the concept of productivity, which, remember, is the number of units of goods produced per man-hour of labor. In the industrial world, the gain in productivity is the chief thing that allows an increase in individual income without inflation. Our state of affluence is a reflection of productivity. Our ability to compete in the world market depends on a high productivity. It is an important index to our economic health. Yet it is somewhat ambiguous and difficult to assess even in the industrial world. . . . I suspect you can readily see the complexity of any such measure of productivity in the realm of the polity. It can hardly be the number of laws passed per legislator or regulations issued per bureaucrat. Some social scale of value is needed.

Gains in productivity are brought about by better production tools, by greater investment per person in equipment. . . . An industrialist looking at an enterprise so labor intensive as education—something like eighty percent of expenditures goes for salaries and wages—immediately thinks in terms of equipment, of capital goods replacing labor. Hence the enthusiasm a few years back for teaching machines and computer-assisted instruction. The supposition was that through such means costs could be cut drastically. Indeed, they could not. . . .

Let me back away, however, from outlawing the application of productivity to health, education, and welfare, the symphonies, museums, performing arts generally, and all the symbolic expressions in their creation and display. The situation is that we—each of us—are inhabitants of all three realms of society. . . .

Putting it positively, each of the realms is in the service of the others. The affluence of the economy in monetary terms elevates the other two to greater output—what might be called affluence—in their terms. Similarly for cultural and civic endeavors. When one segment of society seeks to divest itself of the other, it harms the whole body. . . .

The danger, then, lies not so much in the techno-economic realm taking over the other two realms as in a failure of the other two realms to make equivalent gains in their own terms. . . . The cultural realm, in the end, is the crucial element. To what purpose is the success in the economy and of government if not for the satisfaction of the higher desires that life presents—not an inordinate indulgence in amusement and divertissement but a participation in the symbolic expressiveness that the human

kind discovers in communion with others—largely, I would say, in a committed work, gaining a livelihood in an enterprise that accomplishes this end.

It is taste that guides one, taste—that faculty of choosing what is most fit and pleasing to the community—that must spread and elevate. It is no new Eden that I project, no paradise on earth. Those old existential agonies are ever with us. We shall know pain and anguish, witness death and come to it ourselves. But these, too, in that strange way that issues in art, take on a pervading symbolism that lets us know we have tangled with reality and found it deeply pleasing.

# The City as a Bioregional Economy

## Robert Swann

I am particularly interested in the small scale—in how we can encourage, nurture, and interest the small scale developments in our cities and in our lives in general. It is because of this interest that I began to study why we do not have more opportunities for the small shopkeeper, the small business, the small industry. . . . One of the key problems that we are faced with today is that our present financial institutions are not inclined to encourage the small scale. It is much easier, much more profitable for banks to make large-scale loans. When it comes to the actual paper work, making a large loan is as easy as making a small loan. So the key question, if you are going to encourage small businesses, is how you are going to create small loans. . . .

When I moved to Great Barrington, Massachusetts, we started a small cooperative to purchase food. But the question kept coming up—where is this food coming from? Why can't we get more of this food locally? We discovered that we were buying carrots and onions from Idaho. You can grow carrots and onions in Great Bar-

rington. We talked with some farmers and asked them if they would be interested in growing these crops locally. They said yes, but there was no market for them. We told them that we would buy from them—a few tons at least, to distribute among the members of the cooperative, and that we would pay them in advance. Farmers aren't used to the notion that somebody should pay them. They assume that they should take all the risk. They grew the crops and it is all working out very well. . . .

We have now set up a structure where farmers will grow a few acres of diversified food, and we will pay them in advance. The advantage will be that we will get some good quality food, locally grown. . . .

The same principle can be applied to the cities. We have started a small loan program. We call it Self-Help Association for a Regional Economy—SHARE. The unique idea about it was that we would deposit our funds in our local bank, which would be a joint account with the SHARE program. The loans would be made by the bank. We, the depositors, would guarantee the loans with our deposits, which would be used as collateral. . . .

The first loan we made was to a woman who raises goats. . . . She wanted to make goat cheese, from a recipe from a French source. She said that she would need about $3000 for the equipment, but that she always paid for things in cash and thus did not have a credit record and could not get a regular loan from the bank. We made her the loan. She now makes the cheese and sells it in our town, and the members of the SHARE program—about sixty people—are the people who promote the cheese. . . .

Then, we decided that what we needed is a local currency, something that will just work here in the community. . . . We wrote the Treasury Department and asked if there was any reason we couldn't do this. They said that as long as we paid taxes we could do what we wanted. So we are now in the process of beginning to develop a local currency. . . .

The first question that came up is how we could guarantee that the currency is real. It needed to be backed by something. . . . We thought, what are we producing here in our local area, the most common denominator that would make sense? We have a lot of trees. They grow easily. . . . What we get from them is wood for burning. We've learned how to burn the wood and take care of our heating needs. Everybody here knows that wood has value because you can burn it and heat with it, which is important

when oil and fuel costs are going up almost daily. Over fifty percent of the people in Vermont are actually heating with wood. In our area, about forty percent do. So we thought that cord wood ought to back our currency. . . . We began to compare the price of cord wood with the consumer price index to see if it made any sense. We knew that if we were going to have a currency that was going to be attractive to people, a currency that was feasible, it had to do something that federal dollars didn't do. One thing that federal dollars do is lose value, so if we could get a currency that didn't lose value we would have something people would want. So we traced the value of cord wood compared with the consumer price index and discovered that the value indeed does continue to increase. The price of cord wood goes up at about the same rate as the consumer price index. We began to index cord wood with the dollar. An average price of cord wood in our area is about $90 per cord. Soon $100 will equal one cord of wood— very convenient.

We began talking with some of the merchants in the area, and they got the idea. Local currency cannot get out of the area. . . . One of the merchants then suggested that in the beginning we index cord wood at a one-to-one ratio—$100 per cord. Since the current value of a cord is $90, we would be encouraging the currency— the BERKSHARES, as we call the currency. . . .

The bank was a little skeptical. We simply asked to be able to exchange BERKSHARES for Federal Reserve notes. We said we would sell BERK-SHARES for dollars, have the bank hold the dollars, and let merchants exchange BERKSHARES for dollars if they wish. . . . We are now in the process of negotiating this with the Banking Commissioner and the State of Massachusetts.

If you take this one step further, the fact is that cities are being stifled by national currency. National currency works to depress cities because cities belong to natural bioregional complexes which have their own life, their own development, their own directions. It does not go up and down with the national economy. . . . A national currency, completely issued from one source, can only deal with the economy in a general way. It can't deal with it specifically through the region. It increases or decreases interest rates according to the data that comes in at the national level. But that might be very bad for Dallas and it might be very good for Detroit, or vice versa at any given moment. What has to be done, what is essential for the further development of cities, is that cities must have their own currency so that they can develop in their own ways. . . .

# Six Agricultural Fallacies

*Wendell Berry*

1. *That agriculture may be understood and dealt with as an industry.*

This is false, first of all, because agriculture deals with living things and biological processes, whereas the materials of industry are not alive and the processes are mechanical. That agriculture can produce only out of the lives of living creatures means that it cannot for very long escape the qualitative standard. That is, in addition to productivity, efficiency, decent earnings, et cetera, it must have health. And so the farmer differs from the industrialist in that the farmer is necessarily a nurturer, a preserver of the health of creatures.

Second, whereas a factory has a limited life expectancy, the life of a healthy farm is unlimited. Buildings and tools wear out, but the topsoil, if properly used and maintained, will not wear out. Some agricultural soils have remained in continuous use for four or five thousand years or more.

Third, the motives of agriculture are fundamentally different from the motives of industry. This is partly accounted for by the differences between farming and industry that I have already discussed. Another reason is in the fact that, in our country and many others, the best farms have always been homes as well as work places. Unlike factory hands and company executives, farmers do not *go* to work. A good farmer is *at* work even when at rest. Over and over again, experience has shown that the motives of the wage earner are inadequate to farming. American experience has shown this, but it is perhaps nowhere so dramatically demonstrated as in Soviet Russia, where small privately farmed plots greatly outproduce the communal fields.

And, finally, the economy of industry is inimical to the economy of agriculture. The economy of industry is, typically, an extractive economy. It takes, makes, uses, and discards. It progresses, that is, from exhaustion to pollution.

Agriculture, on the other hand, rightly belongs to a replenishing economy, which takes, makes, uses, *and returns*. It involves the return to the source, not just of fertility, of so-called "wastes," but of care and affection. Otherwise, the topsoil is used exactly as a mineable fuel, and is destroyed in use. Thus, in agriculture, the methods of the factory give us the life expectancy of the factory—long enough for us, perhaps, but not long enough for our children and grand-children.

2. *That a sound agricultural economy can be based on an export market.*

We should begin, I think, by assuming that a sound economy cannot be based on *any* market that it does not control.

And we should assume, further, that any foreign market for goods *ought to be* temporary, and therefore, by defini-tion, not dependable. The best thing for any nation or people, obviously, is to grow its own food, and therefore charity alone would forbid us to de-pend on or to wish for a permanent market for our agricultural products in any foreign country. And we must ask too whether or not charity can ever regard hungry people as "a market."

But the commercial principle itself is unsafe in agriculture if it is not made subject to other principles. One of the principles that should everywhere con-dition the commercial principle in agri-culture is that of subsistence. Commer-cial farming, that is, must never be separated from subsistence farming. The farm family should live from the farm. Just as the farm should be, so far as possible, the source of its own fertility and operating energy, so it should be, so far as possible, the source of food, shelter, fuel, building materials, etc., for the farm family.

Thus the basis of the livelihood of the farming population is assured. In times such as these, when costs of purchased supplies are high and earnings from farm produce low, the value of what-ever the farm family produces for itself is high, and involves substantial saving. What is exported from the farm, in whatever quantity, is properly re-garded as surplus—not needed for sub-sistence.

But at every level of the agricultural system the subsistence principle should operate. The local consumer popula-tion in towns and cities should subsist, so far as possible, from the produce of the locality or region. The primary reason for this, in the region as on the farm, is that it is safe, but there are many other benefits. It would tend to diversify local farming. It would sup-port the local farm economy. It would greatly reduce transportation and other costs. It would put fresher food on the table. It would increase local employ-ment. And what would be exported from the region would, again, be regarded as surplus.

The same principle should then apply to the nation as a whole. We should subsist from our own land, and the surplus would be available for ex-port markets, or for charity in emergencies.

The surplus should not be regarded as merely incidental to subsistence, but as equally necessary for safety: a sort of "floating" supply useable to com-pensate for both differences and vagaries of climate. Because of droughts, floods, and storms, no farm or region or even nation can be forever assured of a subsistence, and it is only because of this that an exportable surplus has a legitimate place in agricultural planning.

3. *That the "free market" can preserve agriculture.*

The "free market"—the unbridled play of economic forces—is bad for agriculture because it is unable to assign a value to things that are necessary to agriculture. It gives a value to agricultural products, but it cannot give a value to the sources of those products in the topsoil or the ecosystem or the farm or the farm family or the farm community. Indeed, people who look at farming from the standpoint of the "free market" do not understand the relation of product to source. They believe that the relation is merely mechanical, because they believe that agriculture is or can be an industry. And the "free market" is helpless to suggest otherwise.

The "free market" values production *at the cost* of all else. And this exclusive emphasis on production, in agriculture, inevitably causes overproduction. In agriculture, both high prices and low prices cause overproduction. But overproduction leads only to low prices, never to high prices. It could perhaps be said, then, that on the "free market" agricultural productivity has no direct or stable relation to value.

When this is so, agriculture overproduces, and the surplus is used as a

weapon against the producer to beat down prices, either in the service of a "cheap food policy" for domestic consumers, or to make our agricultural produce competitive in world trade.

In a time when urban investment in agriculture ("agribusiness") stimulates a higher productivity than the urban economy can provide a market for, then the rural economy can be protected only by controlling production. Supplies should be adjusted to anticipate needs, and those needs should always include surpluses to be used in case of crop failure. Such an adjustment can be only approximate, of course, but since we are dealing with an annual productivity, yearly corrections can be made. Thus the sources of production can be preserved by preventing runaway surpluses and the consequent low markets that destroy both people and land.

The "free market" is economic Darwinism, with one critical qualification. Whereas the Darwinian biologists have always acknowledged the violence of the competitive principle, the political Darwinians have been unable to resist the temptation to suggest that on the "free market" *both* predator and prey are beneficiaries. When economic ruin occurs, according to this view, it occurs only as a result of economic justice. Thus Mr. David Stockman could suggest that the present dispossession of thousands of farm families is merely the result of the working of "a dynamic economy," which compensates their losses by "massive explosions of new jobs and investments . . . occurring elsewhere, in Silicon Valley.'' That these failures and successes are not happening to the same people, or even to the same groups of people, is an insight beyond the reach of Mr. Stockman's equipment. By his reasoning it may readily be seen that the poverty of the poor is justified by the richness of the rich.

The "free market" idea is the result of a lazy (when not felonious) wish to found the human economy on natural law. The trouble with this is that humans are not *of* nature in the same way that foxes and rabbits are. Humans live artificially, by artifice and by art, by human making, and economics will finally have to be answerable to this. Unbridled economic forces damage *both* nature and human culture.

There are, I suggest, two *human* laws of economics, very different from the laws, in fact both unnatural and inhuman, that govern the "free market":

a. Money must not lie about value. It must not, by inflation or usury, misrepresent the value of necessary work or necessary goods. Those values must not, by any devices of markets or banks, be made subject to monetary manipulation.

b. There must be a decent balance between what people earn and what they pay, and this can be made possible only by control of production. When farmers have to sell on a depressed market and buy on an inflated

one, that is death to farmers, death to farming, death to rural communities, death to the soil, and (to put it in urban terms) death to food.

4. *That productivity is a sufficient standard of production.*

By and large, the most popular way of dealing with American agricultural problems has been to praise American agriculture. For decades we have been wandering in a blizzard of production statistics pouring out of the government, the universities, and the "agribusiness" corporations. No politician's brag would be complete without a tribute to "the American farmer" who is said to be single-handedly feeding fifty-seven or seventy-five or God knows how many people. American agriculture is fantastically productive, and by now we all ought to know it.

That American agriculture is also fantastically expensive is less known, but it is equally undeniable, even though the costs have not yet entered into the official accounting. The costs are in loss of soil, in loss of farms and farmers, in soil and water pollution, in food pollution, in the decay of country towns and communities, and in the increasing vulnerability of the food supply system. The statistics of productivity alone cannot show these costs. We are nevertheless approaching a "bottom line" that is not on our books.

From an agricultural point of view, a better word than *productivity* is *thrift*. It is a better word because it implies a fuller accounting. A thrifty person is undoubtedly a productive one, but thriftiness also implies a proper consideration for the means of production. To be thrifty is to take care of things. It is to thrive—that is, to be healthy by being a part of health. One cannot be thrifty alone. One can only be thrifty insofar as one's land, crops, animals, place, and community are thriving.

The great fault of the selective bookkeeping we call "the economy" is that it does not lead to thrift. Day by day, we are acting out the plot of a murderous paradox: an "economy" that leads to extravagance. Our great fault as a people living in this economy is that we do not take care of things. Our economy is such that we say we "cannot afford" to take care of things. Labor is expensive, time is expensive, money is expensive, but materials—the stuff of creation—are so cheap that we cannot afford to take care of them. The wrecking ball is characteristic of our way with materials. We "cannot afford" to log a forest selectively, or to mine without destroying topography, or to farm without catastrophic soil erosion.

A production-oriented economy can indeed live in this way—but only so long as production lasts.

Suppose that, foreseeing the inevitable failure of this sort of production, we see that we must assign a value to continuity. If that happens, then our standard of production will have to change, indeed will already have changed, for the standard of pro-

ductivity alone cannot assign a value to continuity. It cannot permit us to see that continuity *has* a value. The value of continuity is visible only to thrift.

5. *That there are too many farmers.*

This has been accepted doctrine in the *offices* of agriculture—in governments, universities, and corporations—ever since World War II. Its history is a remarkable proof of the influence of an idea. In the last forty years this idea has supported, if indeed it has not caused, one of the most consequential migrations of history: millions of rural people moving from country to city in a stream that has not slackened from the war's end until now. And the motivating force behind this migration, then as now, has been economic ruin on the farm. Today, with hundreds of farm families losing their farms every week, the economists are still saying, as they have said all along, that these people deserve to fail, that they have failed because they are the "least efficient producers," and that America is better off for their failure.

It is apparently easy to say that there are too many farmers, if one is not a farmer. This is not a pronouncement often heard in farm communities. Nor have farmers yet been informed of a dangerous surplus of population in the "agribusiness" professions, or among the middlemen of the food system. No agricultural economist has yet perceived that there are too many agricultural economists.

The farm-to-city migration has obviously produced advantages to the corporate economy. The absent farmers have had to be replaced by machinery, petroleum, chemicals, credit and other expensive goods and services from the "agribusiness" economy, which ought not to be confused with the economy of what used to be called farming.

But these short-term advantages all imply long-term disadvantages to both country and city. The departure of so many people has seriously weakened rural communities and economies all over the country. And that our farmland no longer has enough caretakers is implied by the fact that, as the farming people have departed from the land, the land itself has departed. Our soil erosion rates are now higher than they were in the time of the Dust Bowl.

At the same time, the cities have had to receive a great influx of people unprepared for urban life and unable to cope with it. A friend of mine, a psychologist who has frequently worked with the juvenile courts in a large midwestern city, has told me that a major occupation of the police force there is to keep the "permanently unemployable" confined in their own part of town. Such a circumstance cannot be good for the future of democracy and freedom. One wonders what the authors of our Constitution would have thought of that category, "permanently unemployable."

Equally important is the question of the sustainability of the urban food supply. The supermarkets are, at present, crammed with food, and the productivity of American agriculture is, at present, enormous. But this is a productivity based, at present, on the ruin both of the producers and of the source of production. City people are unworried about this, apparently, only because they do not know anything about farming. People who know about farming, who know what the farmland requires to remain productive, *are* worried. When topsoil losses exceed the weight of grain harvested by five times (in Iowa) or by twenty times (in the wheatlands of eastern Washington) there is something to worry about.

When the "too many" of the country arrive in the city, they are not called "too many." In the city they are called "unemployed" or "permanently unemployable."

What will happen if the economists ever perceive that there are too many people in the cities? There appear to be only two possibilities: either they will have to recognize that their earlier diagnosis was a tragic error, or they will conclude that there are too many people in country and city both—and what further inhumanities will be justified by *that* diagnosis?

Both parties to our political dialogue seem to have concluded long ago that the dispossession and disemployment of people by industrial growth are normal and acceptable. The liberals have wished to support these people with welfare giveaways. The conservatives have instructed them to become ambitious and get jobs. Both are ways of telling the unprivileged to go to hell —the only difference being in the speed with which they are advised to go.

6. *That hand labor is bad.*

This too is accepted doctrine, and it will be found to be one of the chief supports of the doctrine that there are too many farmers. The forced migration of farmers from the farm will be easier on the general conscience if it can be supposed that bankruptcy and dispossession are ways of *saving* farmers from work that is beneath their dignity.

We can only assume that we are faced with an unquestioned social dogma when so astute a writer as Jane Jacobs can say without blinking that "cotton picking by hand is miserable labor; driving a cotton picker is not." But a great many questions would have to be asked and answered before this assertion could be allowed to stand. Wes Jackson is certainly right in his insistence that the pleasantness or unpleasantness of farm work depends upon scale—upon the size of the field and the size of the crop. But we obviously need to know also who owns the field. We would need to know the experience and the expectations of the workers. We would need to know about the skill of the workers and the quality of the work. After consideration of such matters, we can say that probably *any* farm work is miserable, whether done by hand or by machine, if it is economically desperate—if it

does not secure the worker in some stable, decent, rewarding connection to the land worked. We can say that hand work in a small field owned by the worker, with the expectation of a decent economic return is probably less miserable than mechanized work in somebody else's large field. We can suppose with some confidence, moreover, that handwork in the company of family and neighbors might be less miserable than work done alone in the unrelieved noise of a machine.

The fact remains, of course, that millions of hand workers have been and are being replaced by machines, and that the farmers now losing their farms are to some extent being so replaced. Many people apparently assume that this process of "labor saving," the substitution of machines for people, can continue indefinitely, and to the unending betterment of the human lot. Even so, we must continue to ask about the possible necessity, the possible goodness, and the possible inescapability of hand work.

My own suspicion is that, especially for the private owners of small properties such as farms, hand work may become more necessary as petroleum and other "industrial inputs" become more expensive. Increasingly too, I think, farmers will find it necessary to substitute their own hand labor, in such work as carpentry and machinery repair, for more expensive city labor.

But I suspect also that a considerable amount of hand work may remain necessary for reasons other than economics. It will continue to be necessary in the best farming, because the best farming will continue to rely on the attentiveness and particularity that go with the use of hands. Animal husbandry will continue and require the use of the hands. So, I think, will much of the work of land restoration, and we are going to have a lot of that to do.

Judging from our epidemic of obesity and other diseases of sedentary life, and from the popularity of the various strenuous employments of the "physical fitness movement," the greatest untapped source of useable energy may now be in human bodies. It may become the task of a future economy to give worthy employment to this energy and reward its use.

# Money and Nature

*Randolph W. Severson*

In the New World nature, earthy, loamy, *natural* has disappeared. Since the Industrial Revolution, and perhaps before, our lives have grown more and more technologically texturized with the latent, arcane rhythms of the body absorbed into an artificial cycle. The invention of the photograph climaxed this evolution because the camera ejects not a replica of nature, but a double, a quasi-presence, a secret sharer that disputes the autonomy of the original. As primitives often divined, the camera steals away the soul of things and submerges it in an alien order, the order of technology. In the Age of the Photograph a thing retains its independence only by belonging to a network of relations extending beyond the camera's range.

But what if the whole earth could be photographed? What if the totality of these relations could be captured? This would entail the end of nature and the final triumph of technology. And it has happened: Hitler's smile launched a thousand rockets, and though many toppled over on the launch pad, fiery phoenixes that never rose, one of these rockets, ours, finally reached the empyrean where, bathed in intersellar light, it relayed back a photograph, an image of the whole earth, round and glowing. On this epochal day technology, ontologically, superseded nature.

In today's world money has become the new nature; it has gathered to itself all the qualities traditionally ascribed to nature so that if the distinction between them once mattered, it no longer does. A direct phenomenology foregrounds the identity, supporting this claim.

Money, like nature, is a feminine reality, evolving out of a whole cluster of feminine words and meanings that reach back to the Latin *Moneta*, a feminine noun and epithet for the Queen of Heaven.

Only money governs our lives as both money and nature once did. Nature—storms and draughts, immeasurable spaces, the rhythms of the body—has ceased to rebuff ambition or to thwart even the wildest arc of desire. Do you want to freeze in summer and sizzle in the cold—the thermostat will enforce your desire. Or do you want to jog in Central Park at dawn and dawdle in a Parisian café at dusk—a super-sonic jet awaits you. Or do you want to conceive a child without ever being touched—that too is possible, all assuming of course that you have the money and that you pay your bills. Weather, space, the human body: the will transcends them; only money moors us to the earth.

We now cultivate money the way humankind once farmed the earth. Two primary actions define this relation: taming and tending. The desire to tame stems from the fear of money, fear of a reality that violently erupts—who fears nature anymore, really? We respond to this threat with rituals of taming—steady jobs, on-time payments, budgets—all of which we hope will appease that power, deferring any doomsday until tomorrow. And neither the rich nor the government can dodge that threat; they too can be pauperized overnight; they too develop taming rituals.

The desire to tend comes from our confidence in money's bounty, its ability to produce what we want. As nearly everyone in America, except the poor, once tended their garden, raising vegetables to supplement their fare, so each of us today tends our tiny basket of cash, our plot of greenbacks, and tries to harvest from it the means to buy some little extra luxury, a present, or a pleasure. And the rich with their stocks and CDs and money market funds, excel at this, their fields of cash repaying cultivation with a bountiful yield.

nearly everyone in America, except the poor, once tended their garden, raising vegetables to supplement their fare, so each of us today tends our tiny basket of cash, our plot of greenbacks, and tries to harvest from it the means to buy some little extra luxury, a present, or a pleasure. And the rich with their stocks and CDs and money market funds, excel at this, their fields of cash repaying cultivation with a bountiful yield.

Despite our best efforts, money, as did nature once, retains an irreducible core of mystery, transforming even the brightest scheme into an ultimately futile, though sometimes lucky, wager. In fact, so rich is money's mystery that it more resembles "real" nature than anything since Newton or Descartes. It teems with quirks and sprites, energies and power, recalling the pre-Newtonian nature. And we, like our medieval forbears, cannot shake the superstition that these powers obey some occult law, so we importune squads of wizards, economists and accountants, the new glamour guys of business, and bid them yoke the demons, but their spells —theorems, equations, formulas, and laws—shatter on a stony silence that yields no final mystery and answers to no charm.

And though nature atrophies, poisoned and abused, money breeds and branches, parthogenetically divides, a rush of liquid, a wild exfoliation, a wad of green.

Money appeals to the senses as a

lovely, heavy jangle of coins in a pocket. Taste and texture, as well, are absorbed into this new nature, emerging as a silver tongue and a golden touch.

Finally, the four ancient elements compose money. Earth appears in the filthy rich and dirty deal; air courts recognition as inflations, depressions, soaring interest rates; fire roars up in hot deals, hot checks, money to burn, a live savings going up in smoke; water surfaces in staying afloat, floating a loan or a deal, going to the well one time. True, these are metaphors, but who is to say that they do not correspond to some perception, some carnal wisdom of the body?

Yes, money, alive, abounding in forms and fables, is the new nature, the only alternative to technology, the last stand of the soul. With that odd cunning that borders on Providence, history foreshadows this exchange. In 1935 the old nature flourished in a few isolated spots, but only in Tibet did it form the basis of a culture; a pattern of human life. In 1935 the last Dalai Lama was born; after him there would be no more, as there would be no more Tibet, and perhaps no more nature, not in the way we once knew it. Also in that same year the dollar bill was reissued, unscrolling on its crisp green face a tableau of symbols identifying it as the new wilderness. The celestial eagle, usurped symbol of native America, adorns the bill, and the number thirteen, the number not only of the original colonies but also a number sacred in Mexican mythology, the number of Quetzalcoatl, supplies the basis for an occult mathematics, permuting endlessly: thirteen stars, thirteen stripes, thirteen olives, thirteen arrows, thirteen layers of stone on the pyramid on top of which reposes the sacred eye. Beneath the pyramid appears a banner with the inscription *Novos Ordo Secolorum*, the new order of the ages.

Today this new nature, this new wilderness, stretches out before us, arousing a crowd of conflicting emotions: greed and generosity, fear and hope, ambition and desire. Whether these emotions will convert into a new policy of exploitation, the creed of the quick fix and the quick buck that pays no heed to the wisdom of the past nor the needs of the future, or whether it will inaugurate a new ecology, a numismatic one, sensitive to the intrinsic rhythms of money and to its place in the general economy of culture, *this* remains to be seen.

# Women Mean Business

## *Gail Thomas*

I want to talk about how women bring to business a new kind of economy.

Many voices are now having the courage to say that our present economy is dying. We have only recently heard this cry in Texas, perhaps because we have been one of the last frontiers. Reasons for decline are found, in many cases, outside the economic structure—the way we use resources and raw materials and the energy-intensive type of technology we have developed. When we hear these predictions, it is important to ask, "Which part is dying?" I think we can see that the part which is declining is a particular type of industrial society based on excessive resource consumption and on non-renewable resources. What is growing is the *renewable resource economy*. Another way to say this is, the economy which is dying is the one which believes we can continue to use up resources without replenishing them; the one which is growing and coming into its own is the one which believes the First Law of Ecology—that everything is connected to everything else, and that the ecology that must be restored and re-

balanced is our human ecology of values.

Women understand renewable resource economy because they are the originators of it! Women, and the category which we represent—the feminine—are the renewable resources of the universe. Forgive me for making it so pointed, but women, like the earth itself—Mother Goddess Gaia—can and do continue to renew the resources of our world. The masculine side of things simply cannot. It continues to use them up.

In considering the connection between women and business, we can ask, "Why is it that the present economic structure has such difficulty in allowing women position and power?" The answer, I believe, goes back a very long time and cuts deeply into the historical, psychological and religious roots of our culture.

Most of us have learned but may not remember that the world "economy" comes from the Greek word *oikonomia* which means "house-hold management." The root word is *oikos* which in Greek means "house." The word "ecology" also comes from the root word "house" but ecology is the *logos* of the house—the divine law governing the house, or one could say it is the house itself speaking—the *oikos* or logos. The word "ecology," then, is saying that there is a wisdom or word or law of the house—like our notion of a balanced ecological system —and that the "economy" is saying there is a management—a *nomos*—of the house.

To remember that economics comes from household management is important from several standpoints. For one thing, it allows us to get an image of economics and we are part of that image. If economics is merely a word, a concept, it anesthetizes us to the complex world of exchange and relationships in which we are all involved. It also makes us feel not connected. So much of our lives is determined by economic trends and policies of which we do not feel a part. The image of economics as "the house," now, that's helpful! We can imagine that the first economic structure evolved from the attempt to satisfy the needs of the various members of the household. All members are considered, regardless of age or sex, as are their needs for food, clothing, shelter, work, play, and love. Secondly, the notion of economics as household management is important because it helps us remember the "unofficial economy," the one not considered for the GNP—Gross National Product. We as women know this "unofficial" economy as the traditional heritage we share of cooperation, gift-giving, volunteering, homemaking, child-bearing and rearing. It

also includes home fix-ups and mechanical repairs, home workshops, and craft production, furniture refinishing, gardening, food production and preparation, caring for the sick and the aged—all those activities which center around the home. It begins to be easy to see why an economic system which will not admit "home-centered" activities as official contributors to the Gross National Product also will not admit women into its Inner Circle of official decision making processes. . . .

There is a growing rejection of competition as the basic way of fueling our kind of economy. As far back as 1937, in her book *The Neurotic Personality of Our Time*, the psychologist Karen Horney describes what she calls the particular American neurosis brought about by excessive competition. She says there are three characteristics of the American neurosis: "first, that of aggressiveness so stimulated that it begins to conflict with the tenets of Christian brotherhood [Sisterhood]; second the desire for material goods so vigorously stimulated that it can never be satisfied, leading to widespread dissatisfaction; and third, with expectations for untrammeled freedom soaring so high, people can not square them with the societal limitations that eventually surround us all."

We need a value-based economy, an economy based on need and use rather than on "what we can get in the market-place," an economy which remembers the First Law of Ecology —that everything is connected to everything else and depends upon a balanced system of values; an economy which remembers its origin is the house, and that the first house is the womb, the house of the child, and that even before that, the house is the earth itself, the Great Mother Gaia.

An economy is needed which, when considering what is valuable, recognizes the irreplaceable value of feminine gender-related activities. This economy would allow women to assume their goddess-given roles of authority, power, and position without aggressive competition, each one helping, encouraging, the other, making a place for the next one to come along.

I would like to call for a new GNP, a new way to measure the economic level of our nation. It would be the "Gross National Psyche." It seems to me that "psyche"—the Greek word for "soul"—would more completely encompass and reflect a balanced, value related economy than does the word "product."

This is the way I see women doing business in the future—women as creating, initiating, begetting, nurturing, helping, bringing along. Women as product-makers, as gift-givers, as law-makers, as healers. Women as teachers, women as learners. Women as heads of state and heads of households, fully as women, women in all of their awesome power, dignity and stature.

# Psychological Benefits
# of Capitalism

*Robert J. Sardello*

I speak as a psychotherapist, as one engaged, with care, in the disease of economics; as one who adheres to the therapy of the word, taking things as they are, working to sense more fully the value that lies within symptoms. My technical knowledge of economics may be off. My nose for the inner workings of the disease is not.

Methodical, systematic, continuous pursuit of gain with avoidance of all pleasure characterizes the original spirit of capitalism, born of the Protestant Reformation. The relation between capitalism and psychology, as far as I know, has never been explored, an apparent oversight, since the two begin at the very same moment. The great Phillip Melanchthon, friend of Martin Luther, fellow theologian, supported and gave clear formulation to the respectability of restrained accumulation of capital. He also introduced the word 'psychology' into the modern vocabulary. I hope to show that because of Melanchthon, modern economics consists of a single, simple psychology of individual subjectivity projected onto society, and that the final benefit of such economics lies in the breakdown of human subjectivity, leading to the discovery of reality. . . .

Psychological sensibility has been around in the Western World since Heraclitus, 500 B.C. Psyche, or soul, permeated everything and was not limited to human beings. The world was ensouled, and economics simply meant the care of the household of the world. Heraclitus put it this way: "You could not discover the limits of the psyche, even if you traveled every road to do so; such is the depth of its meaning." The care of the household was not simple, nor automatically given as some primordial contact with the beauty of nature. It took place through ritual oriented toward conforming human life to the life within the cosmos; it took place through disciplines such as astrology recognizing human reality as a microcosm of the macrocosm; it took place through including care of all objects of the household as part of the familia, the family, and thus all objects as alive.

Melanchthon, by naming a field psychology, by limiting psyche to what goes on in individuals, stopped soul from appearing in any place but individual subjectivity; and economics changes from care of the household of the world to the pursuit of personal gain. . . .

Capitalism has come a long way—from the pursuit of limited gain with the avoidance of pleasure to the pursuit of unlimited gain in order to produce pleasure. Melanchthon's psychology lies behind it all. The first part of his *Loci Communes Theological* presents a simple model of individual psychology. He says:

> We divide man into only two parts. For there is in him a cognitive faculty, and there is also a faculty by which he either follows or flees the things he has come to know. The cognitive faculty is that by which we discern through the senses, understand, think, compare, and deduce. The faculty from which the affections arise is that by which we either turn away from or pursue the things known, and this faculty is sometimes called 'will', sometimes 'affection', and sometimes 'appetite'.

This definition of what constitutes the human soul founds the capitalistic spirit. Knowledge of what is to be done comes from cognition. Will, which contains the appetites, cannot be trusted and is therefore turned over to the guidance of God. People may know what to do to acquire gain. That greed may enter, cannot be controlled, but they may proceed as long as they have turned their will over to God, pursuing gain without seeking their own pleasure.

Adam Smith's classical economics

wrote the divine out of individual psychology and thus out of economics altogether, replacing the element with propositions concerning human nature, claiming acquisition as an innate human trait. He says: "The desire of bettering our condition comes with us from the womb and never leaves us until we go to the grave." This version of Melanchthon's psychology serves as base for his primary economic proposition: "Every individual is continuously exerting himself to find out the most advantageous employment for whatever capital he can command."

Unlimited acquisition becomes respectable and acceptable by interpreting it as rooted in human nature. Such an interpretation represents the elevation of a culture-bound historical orientation to a universal principal.

The psychology of self-interest puts a severe strain on restraint, a central element of capitalism. The utilitarian psychology of Jeramy Bentham and John Stuart Mill heightens self-interest even more, for they say the basic individual propensity is to seek pleasure and avoid pain, though pleasure is defined as long-run pleasure, not immediate satisfaction. The direction of economics, in keeping with this view of human subjectivity, turns from valuing labor to valuing the production of goods, the crack in the door that will change the word 'goods' into the word 'commodities'.

Neoclassical economics, whose founder was the British economist Alfred Marshall, the originator of micro-economics, introduced efficiency as the center of a psychology needed to accomodate pleasure. Once pleasure is introduced as the purpose of economics, the danger arises that behavior incompatible with economy will surface—the disinclination to work, art, the senses, meaningful work—for these are all pleasures. The new variation of Melanchthon's psychology says that it is natural for human beings to maximize monetary or consumptive gains. Opposing forces, values, and interests are balanced in such a fashion that they maximize advantages—this is the definition of efficiency. Marshall states:

> And in a money economy, good management is shown by so adjusting the margins of suspense on each line of expenditure that the marginal utility of a shilling's worth of goods on each line shall be the same. And this result each one will attain by constantly watching to see whether there is anything on it which he is spending so much that he would gain by taking a little away from that line of expenditure and putting it on some other line.

This is of course the budget, and the budget is a way to manage satisfaction of pleasure efficiently. Economics becomes the management of pleasure. The new psychology states it is natural to seek more and more satisfaction by consciously, deliberately maximizing all gains at a given moment.

This new psychology shifts the whole sense of economics. The classical economic individual was supposed to maximize something concrete: income, wealth, savings, investments, capital, durable goods, durable posses-

sions. Efficiency is based on manipulative maximizing of pleasure, of inner psychologcal states, the efficient management of desire. It is entirely relative what one chooses to maximize. It could the pleasure of cocaine or the pleasure of giving to the poor; it makes no difference. . . .

This position, where we are now, opens the way for consumer economics, the manipulation of goods and services through attaching them to pleasurable states which have nothing to do with said goods and services, through advertising. Economics turns into public relations and promoting the satisfaction of subjective states.

I read the history of economics since the sixteenth century as the history of human subjectivity separated from the world we inhabit; economics is the psychology of an uninhabited world. The new emerging economics, so aptly under creation by Hazel Henderson, an economics of the household of the planet, is the first sign that we just might be able to forego the glorification of subjectivity. But, one more hidden element of Melanchthon's psychology must be exposed. All economic theories begin with the proposition that it is natural for man to be greedy, and that the best way to make society consists in harnessing greed. It is impossible, however, to base economics in a psychology of greed without greed becoming the single creative factor in the world. Restraint only proves the necessity of the proposition. Greed produces restrained greed which accumulates in the world. A second factor also enters. Since all economic theories are based in speculation about individual psychology, we must also say that subjective psychology is the same thing as the psychology of greed. Basing psychology on the nature of persons rather than on the nature of the psyche, which includes far more than greed, makes greed into the primary virtue; since greed, according to economic psychology, is the basis of human nature, greed must express itself for us to be true to our nature. Economy, from this point of view, is nothing more than human nature, greed, expressing itself in the world, creating a world, without the burden of guilt. If greed could be felt with its attendant affliction of guilt, there would be spontaneous movement out of subjectivity into care for the world. The third factor in all economic psychology which makes this movement impossible is that all such psychologies include rationality as basic to human nature, along with greed. But since, like greed, rationality is defined in such a manner as to be contentless, without a world, the content of rationality has to be greed as the content of greed is that greed becomes harnessed to rationality. That is all there is to work with in economic psychology— greed and rationality playing off each other. The primary way greed plays off rationality is by rationalizing greed so that guilt does not accompany the affliction of greed. The result when all this is leashed onto the world over a period of two hundred years is one gigantic psychopathic world; we do not

live in a world of anxiety or hysteria, or depression, or a schizophrenic world, but a psychopathic world— very successful, very adapted, very clever, but there is no feeling of affliction. That is the psychological benefit of capitalism. All possible fantasies can be enacted in the world without inhibition because nothing hurts, nothing feels wrong, nothing feels off the mark. It can all be rationally justified as being good if individual gain is involved.

Now, to the real psychological benefit of capitalism. Economic psychology, bringing about individual gain, has made the world sick. Well, now there is something real to care for. And since psychology made her sick, psychology must be central to her healing. But the whole paradigm must be shifted. It is we who are dead and the world is alive and in pain. We can no longer trust our humanity, no matter how much we sugar-coat it with the psychology of peak experiences, the return to feelings, and more body; it's all psychopathic. All you have to do is spend one evening watching television to see that every human emotion possible is now under the domain of manipulation for gain. But the world does not lie about its afflictions, and it does not cover them, for it has no ego to protect. The terrible misery of the world has nothing to hide behind. And I mean the world in a concrete, particular sense. The room with its false, water-stained ceilings, hollow doors, skyscrapers forced to act like neon signs, the most atrocious, nasty images polluting the room, emanating from the television eight hours a night, fabricated foods, cancerous plastics, ugly computers. These things I trust. A new economics must be based in a psychotherapy of the things of the world, a care for the psyche within things, a care for their afflictions. Now that may be the psychological benefit of capitalism—there is so much sickness to care for—it forces us to forget ourselves and return to the world to recover its soul, its mana. We cannot help ourselves anymore or rely on ourselves to make a decent world. We are failed, and now we must care. We are totally anesthetized to human suffering. But the afflictions of the things of the world still have power to move us.

The approach to caring for the world I have in mind can best be carried forth in daily life in the city. Think of it as saving $80 an hour for visiting a psychologist in an office who treats your illness and sends you back out into a sick world. First, there must be the felt recognition that the city, in spite of its glitter and flash and self-promotion, is dying. Once we get through the process of denial, a response of rage follows. We all feel it at moments. It is an important feeling; it scares us because it is not subjective. It is a feeling that breaks through the numbness of anesthesia. If it is acted out, however, rage would meet with powerlessness, and isolated subjectivity would return. Rage, felt, held, not shut off nor denied, leads then to compassion. It is the point it dawns

on us that the loss of sensibility we suffer is also suffered by the things, the material things of the city.

Compassion is the capacity to be with the suffering of another; but this capacity is not limited to human relationships. It can be developed to the point of suffering with things. Let me assure you, this is not foolish, merely an unusual way of understanding. Thinking that the world is dead is a relatively recent historical development —since the sixteenth century, the time modern economics took hold. It is a development that has allowed us to gain power over the material world by declaring it dead; and it is the stance that makes us live with the fear of holocaust, the final result of taking the world as dead. So, imagine caring for the things of the world, giving them time and attention, sensing what they need, as an act of anti-nuclearism, as psychological activism against the literal bomb. As the viewpoint of subjectivity breaks down, as it is now doing in this great age of transition, we are provided with an opportunity to enter a new age, a new economy of care for the world. I think it can be the age of life—not utopian and spectacular, but simple attention to reality, a simple recognition that human beings are nothing more than emanations of the world; her first, us second. If Dallas is really the city of the future, then it ought not to rely on a dead world view. This new age can be ushered in right here in Dallas. All that is needed is a recession; a recession of human subjectivity.

# The City

The ingredients of the city—the architecture, roadways, rituals and ceremonies, mores, businesses, arts—are like threads of a woven fabric within which we wrap ourselves so that our city becomes like an outer skin. We live in utmost intimacy with the city and are divorced from it only through abandonment.

Plato says the city is the soul of the individual and if we consider it, it seems to be true. If the city is my soul—that which is in me as I am within it, which animates and which I animate, which deepens me and within which I deepen, which is the source of meaning and to which I give meaning—then I care for it, pay attention to it, lovingly embrace it, am critical of it, scold it, repair it, listen to it, am guided by it, and am formed and shaped by it. Because we live so intimately with the city it becomes difficult to gain the objectivity necessary to fully comprehend our life within it. A mysterious "coniunctio" unfolds continually, revealing the city as the collective psyche of the people and, at the same time, unveiling the city's own particular genius, present from its founding.

Cities were first formed as a holy rite—a demonstration of devotion to the gods—and were the outward construction of humankind's greatest dream; cities offered the opportunity to experience one's own creative expression and, simultaneously, to live in service to the divine authority. The founders of cities were told by augurs where to place the boundary markers. The gods had chosen the site; death would come to those who questioned. And death came! Some have pointed out that the founding of a great city is always an act of patricide, fratricide, or genocide. In this way, the city is an *opus contra naturam*, the making of a city goes against natural laws; it obeys a calling from another realm; the city is "divined" to be what it is.

Each city has its own mark, a genius which has accompanied it since its birth, and continues through ages of growth and change to fulfill the destiny implicit within it from its own beginnings. Christian Norberg-Schulz calls it the "genius loci." It is present in the lay of the land, in the way the wind blows, in the plants and wild life which come naturally to the place. It is there in the founding acts of the city—the circumstances which determine its boundaries. It is in the spirit of the people who are drawn there and in the psyche of the people born there.

The essays in this chapter invite a different perspective on the city—sensitivity to its function, attention to its physical ingredients, appreciation for its essence, and a determination to care for its soul. Those who have contributed these thoughts ask us to live in the city with an awakened heart, a posture we achieve when we acknowledge that the city has a life of its own with which we are able to participate. With such a perspective, we do not plan the city, nor do we build it; we join with it in its making; we celebrate the city.

*Gail Thomas*

# Planning the City

## *James Rouse*

In the summer of 1963 I received an invitation to give a speech at Berkeley on "Metropolitan Growth." We had already begun planning the city of Columbia, Maryland, but now I really had the opportunity to think about it. What is the purpose of a city? Since we are going to build one, what is it? What is its highest goal? What is the best that a city could be? What is the North Star you guide by? And in that talk at Berkeley I said that I had reached the conclusion that the most legitimate goal was a biblical injunction to "Love the Lord thy God with all thy heart and all thy mind and all thy soul; and love thy neighbor as thyself." It doesn't matter that this is remote. It doesn't matter that this is unattainable. But to have that as the direction—what a difference planning would be. How this would affect the whole process of planning! What kind of city might emerge? A city that respected the individual and the family, that encouraged tolerance instead of bigotry, that encouraged the emancipation of people to follow their gifts and their taste. The whole notion of a city built this way was a very stimulating and releasing thing. . . .

This way of thinking has several parts. It is fundamentally focused on people as the purpose of all planning and development. It seeks to identify the circumstances under which men, women, and family can grow in their individual personality, their character and spirit, and then tries to find a way to shape institutions, land uses, buildings, and services to create communities and projects so as to provide maximum support for the people who live, work or shop there. It believes that people can have a good life and can live together and grow together. It looks upon everything short of that as a malfunction to be corrected, not as a condition to be worked around. It proceeds always with the purpose and belief that the good life, the good community, the good project is available if we will but build it; and that our job is to plan and produce it. It believes that these purposes are among the most important in our civilization and that those engaging in them are at work in the most important task that can possibly consume their lives.

It is a way of thinking that is geared to victory and not just to fighting better battles. It understands that important values are created by the most effective interrelationship of all of the pieces of the city and all the processes and institutions supporting life in a community. The beginning point of planning is to discover the best that ought to be and then reconcile the individual pieces into the most feasible solution toward those ultimate goals.

This approach to planning asserts that the processes of development and change, while focused on human values, must be undertaken within rigorous disciplines of sound economics and the best available knowledge of development techniques. It knows that the creation of the economic values generates the earnings to attract the private investment that invigorates the entire process. . . .

The real way of thinking in its summary is: if faced with a problem, don't beat at it, leap over it. Find the solution before you deal with the problem. Find what something would be like if it worked. How do you get there? And often you don't have to face the problem. You don't have to deal with the adversary. They disappear in the bright light of the rational answer. . . .

People are thrashing about the cities today. They want the city to work and they don't know what it means. They want a vital, lively center. . . .

The city is not the meeting place it is meant to be: the heart of the town. People come to the center of the city for a slice of life. They come to an office building to work, to a hotel to stay, to a library to get a book, to a museum to see a picture, to a restaurant to eat. But there is no place where people just come to downtown to "be there." And that's what the city needs. The center of the city needs to be the center place of the metropolis, where all kinds of people feel the presence of one another. It is the place that provides an alternative to the isolated, segregated, rigidily divided suburban developments. The regional mall is a very good place to shop. And we built a lot of them. We own a lot of them—55, as a matter of fact. But that is a very special purpose. It doesn't create community among people, in the sense that the center of the city can. . . .

When we went into Boston and opened Faneuil Marketplace in 1976, Boston was a very forlorn city downtown. Boston had no belief whatsoever that Faneuil Hall Marketplace would work: not the bankers, not the merchants; it was looked upon as "What in the world do they think they are doing?" . . . A hundred thousand people came the first day it opened. Ten million people came the first year to Faneuil Hall Marketplace. *Overwhelming* response. The yearning was there. . . . And then we went to our hometown of Baltimore. . . . We built Harborplace on the waterfront in Baltimore, and eighteen million people came the first year. And then, recently, The Rouse Company opened the project in downtown Milwaukee, which is something you may have seen. If you haven't, you should.

There is a whole new life in the center of Milwaukee. . . .

When I retired from The Rouse Company I created the Enterprise Foundation, which is at work on housing for the poor; raising money to build, staff and provide the financial and staff support to small nonprofit neighborhood groups in cities around the country that are working with the poorest of the poor. Not with middle-income housing, but with the *very* poor—to make their housing fit and livable and through their housing to work with health care, jobs, to help lift poor people out of the cycle of poverty and into the mainstream of life. The Foundation is now in Oakland, Denver, Chicago, Cleveland, Pittsburgh, Baltimore, Washington, Lynchburg, soon in Philadelphia. We will be in twelve cities by the end of this year, and we propose to be in fifty cities in five years, building a national network working from the bottom up with little groups. . . .

It is the responsibility of the city government to provide for the future of the city. It is not the responsibility of business; it is not the responsibility of a citizens' group. It is the responsibility of city government to provide for the future of a city. . . . Twenty years from now what Dallas is will depend upon the strength, the power, the leadership, the imagination, the effectiveness, the caring of the government of this city and the people who hold office in it.

That is the city's job—everywhere. That is why we have city government.

And there is nothing that anybody has to fear in that. Their business is not going to be worse in a well-organized city. A developer is not going to be worse in a well-organized, well-planned city. A developer is not going to make less money because things are organized in rational relationships with one another. People are not going to be abused or oppressed because the gross is stripped out and the good is supported in advance. Everybody does that—developers do better, the whole life of the city is better. The job the city faces is to look at what it ought to be. It is to look beyond the problems, to fashion what Dallas best ought to be ten years from now, twenty years from now, and then determine how to get there. To schedule it, cost it, make it real—not a watercolor of what the city ought to be, but a hard-headed, carefully developed projection of what the city ought to be. What a city this would be! How much more vibrant, alive; how proud the people would be of that kind of a city. And we have the capacity to do it. There is a throbbing spirit here. Coincidence of events has brought me here four times in the last six months. In every situation it has been fascinating, inspiring to see the spirit that there is here. The desire to do something. The real, legitimate concern on the part of people. It is a great, good spirit. There is deep caring, and there is deep concern, and it has not functionally expressed itself yet to the extent that people hold it and want to express it.

# Poetic Form and Place

## *Louise Cowan*

Poems are made of words crafted to create a texture of sound that reveals and sustains meaning. Behind poems lies poetry, the mysterious movement of the soul that stems from the interaction between the self and things, which is, as Jacques Maritain has said, a kind of divination. *Poems*, in a sense, are only one of the manifestations of this movement. *Poetry*, if I may continue with Maritain, is the "secret life of all the arts"—literature, drama, architecture, music, the dance. Beginning with a moment of creative intuition and incarnating that "flash of reality" in a medium, it works through the imagination to give form to a particular work, be it lyric, drama, novel, or building.

It is in this sense of poetry as the secret life of all the arts that one can conjoin architecture and poetry. There are verses that are not poems—that lack that inner animating principle. So, too, do many buildings lack it, and I think one could say that those that do not possess it are not genuine works of architecture. Wherever the embodied work is an art form, therein poetry has its secret dwelling. . . .

In her essay "Place and Fiction," Eudora Welty speaks of place as one of the "lesser angels that watch over the racing hand of fiction" and indicates that this guardian spirit has been neglected of late and perhaps could do with a little petitioning. . . . "It is only too easy," she continues,

> to conceive that a bomb that could destroy all traces of places as we know them, in life and through books, could also destroy all feelings as we know them. . . . From the dawn of man's imagination, place has enshrined the spirit; as soon as man has stopped wandering and stood still and looked about him, he found a god in that place, and from then on, that was where the god abided and spoke, if he ever spoke.

. . . This is the overt mark of what we might call the sacred—the conviction that some places are intimately bound up with divine presences, that gods abide in places of their own choosing—in shrines—and that human beings should rightly build their cities around those shrines and hold them sacred. . . . The shrines of the Olympian gods in the Greek cities—in Troy, Thebes, Argos, Delphi, Athens, and others—gave all the activities within the cities order and stability, a rich pluralism, a drama and a destiny.

. . . But the Biblical tradition presents another set of images and another attitude toward place. For the ancient Hebrew in particular, rootedness to place was relatively insignificant. Henri Frankfort has pointed out that "the desert as a metaphysical experience loomed very large for the Hebrews and colored all their valuations." . . .

Yahweh, unlike the native gods of the pantheons, is fittingly found in the wilderness, as opposed to the cities, marketplaces, or grainfields. The unearthly landscape of the desert is not God's "home," but a scene appropriate to him, for he too is unearthly. Matthew Arnold's insight in his essay "Hebraism and Hellenism" grows constantly more applicable in our time; in Europe and America we stand before two conflicting visions of the world, the Hellenic and the Hebraic—one, we could say, concerned with space, the other with time; one a world of beautiful forms, the other an absence, a vastness; one exhibiting concern for the sacred, the other for the numinous, the holy. Zeus appears to human beings as a swan, a bull, a sheath of lightning; Yahweh uses the burning bush as a sign; He is not in it: He has touched it. The shrine of Apollo is sacred; the ark of the covenant is holy.

Our attitude toward place is at the very heart of our dilemma today; too much emphasis on it seems idolatry; too little, impiety. And yet, as we know, human building stands under the curse placed upon the Tower of Babel and

further indicated by the invisible God of the ark of the covenant, when He would not allow a temple to be built for Him in David's newly won city. How do we resolve this conflict in our soul and in our cities? . . .

Martin Buber, the twentieth-century Jewish theologian, has written: "We expect a theophany of which we know nothing but the *place*, and the place is called community."

Place is indeed, then, sacred to us; but our real place is community. Place is not nature, or man-made objects, but community—a group or groups of people united by a common endeavor and by love and trust. Wherever community appears, spirit descends. But, since man is in motion, community may have to take on new forms. Family may never again in our time be a real source of community; only with vast trouble and some sentimentalizing do we renew neighborhoods in a modern city such that they become true communities; institutions may not now as they did in the past provide the vitality of community that we not only desire but desperately need. Buildings that we love may have to be removed to make room for new growth. We may have to make our own communities, wherever we can find them; we cannot always choose our place. But we can from time to time return to our roots, the sacred things in our lives—and "know the place for the first time."

Memory, imagination, and spirit must redeem the "exasperated soul," caught in a desire for order and stability.

We must learn to live in cities that are constantly being built and constantly passing away. The city the poet builds, according to Allen Tate, is Memoria. And when memory catches up the past, imagination gives it a new form, and spirit illumines it, what is achieved is community, that one perpetual truth which, as Tate has said, must be constantly rediscovered. Jerusalem—people —and not Babylon—buildings—must be the image we hold of our city.

# The City and Blake's Poetry

## *Kathleen Raine*

Those who know me know that my only title to speak at a conference on the theme of the city in architecture and poetry is as William Blake's secretary. And because Blake is of all English poets the supreme poet of the city, what he wrote on his own city, London, must surely have some significance here in Dallas; for what he had —has—to say about London has little to do with such matters as a town planner, or a writer on buildings of architectural interest might have to tell us about London. For Blake a city is a living organism, "a human awful wonder of God," as he wrote; it is the inner lives of its inhabitants as these act and interact upon one another. . . .

The city, then, is for Blake a living spiritual entity. He called this interior city "Golgonooza," from the root *golgas*, a skull, because the city's existence is not outside us, but within us, in the human brain: "Golgonooza, the spiritual four-fold London eternal, / In immense labours and sorrows, ever building, ever falling.". . .

The city of Golgonooza is fourfold because we are ourselves fourfold, a realization far older than C. G. Jung, who has in our own century made clear the fourfold nature of the human psyche in the four regions of reason and sensation, feeling and intuition. As the human psyche, so the human city. Golgonooza is the labor of men and women in this world to realize in time an image of eternity; to build the outer city in the image of the inner city, or to use the phrase of George Russell, the Irish mystic, to make the "politics of time" conform to the "politics of eternity." This has been the theme of Plato, of Aristotle, of Saint Augustine, and of Blake's own teacher, Swedenborg. . . .

The poets, painters, musicians, and architects—remember eternity, or as we might say, perceive more clearly the inner pattern of the archetypal world of the Imagination. It is these who are able to build Golgonooza according to that pattern "laid up in heaven" as Plato says, heaven being, as the Gospel also teaches, within. Works of art serve to awaken and remind those who cannot themselves perceive the originals. . . .

We must not consider the cities

humanity builds when the agent is not the Imagination and the human spirit but the empirical ego of natural uninspired man, who Blake calls, in distinction from the "Divine Humanity," the Imagination, "Satan the Selfhood!"

The Satanic city, built by the natural man, "the worm of sixty winters" and "seventy inches long," without imagination, without the vision of the archetype of the human spirit, recalls Dante's City of Dis, built in the darkness of hell.

No phrase of Blake's is better known than "those dark Satanic mills"; which of us has not felt those words to be an apt description of the landscape of England's Industrial Revolution? What is less well known is that those words do not in fact describe the mills and factories of an industrial landscape, but the philosophy—the ideology—which gave rise to these: that of mechanistic materialism, which Blake identified by those names he associated with this deadly ideology, Bacon, Newton, and Locke. . . .

There would be little point in my presence here as Blake's spokesman if it were merely a matter of the "history of ideas," safely isolated from the present as something over and done with, belonging to the ignorant past. But on the contrary, whereas scientists themselves have meanwhile advanced into a universe very different from that mechanistic hell, our society is still in the power of our machines, our computers and mechanical brains and all the rest, with our humanity

enslaved to these idols we have ourselves created. . . .

When I was young and, together with my Cambridge contemporaries, more or less influenced by Marxist idealism, we were supposed to admire the newly built Battersea Power Station. It was the work of one of our best architects, Giles Gilbert Scott, and conceived as an example of architecture embodying the socialist ideal of a worker state; a totally work-oriented state of collective effort toward a materialist Utopia, I suppose. There was much talk of building beautiful factories for the workers in those days and adorning them with the best modern art. And yet, the utile, however worthy the purpose or technically impressive the construction, has never yet succeeded in creating an architecture that speaks to the imagination in its own language. Blake would have seen, in merely decorating factories or machines in themselves expressing false values, a false view of men and of work, only an evasion of the fundamental issue. Technology does not address the soul. We may—indeed we must—admire the functional utility of Battersea Power Station, but we cannot love; our imagination cannot live in it. . . . It surely remains true that whereas the materialist ideology, against which Blake so set his face, can produce machines of a precision to make us marvel, that in its cities we fell perpetual exiles from something that is not here, but whose absence is ever-present to us. . . .

It was Blake who said to the

Worm, "thou art my mother and my sister." We can love the humblest of living things, but not the machine; whatever has not life does not reflect and express the human, remains forever outside "the divine body of the Saviour . . . the Human Imagination" which Blake calls "Eden, the land of life."

# Conditions of Culture

## *Jacques Barzun*

Nearly every city that has left a trace in history has done so by virtue of its culture; that is, its characteristic forms of art and of life, from manners and customs to architecture. You might think that great battles have given cities fame. But great battles are not fought in cities. They are fought on a flat place *near* a city.

In modern times, the city state has enlarged into the nation or the continent. But—this is my thesis—culture continues to arise in the city. It is local in origin and it gets merged only later into the mingled stream we call national or international—American or European, British, Western—whatever.

The first reason for this local origin is that the culture-makers are, of necessity, individuals. The city fosters individuality; it takes the person out of the kinship pattern into a larger, freer one. No family or clan has ever taken seriously an artist who is one of their own. But of course boys and girls may be born anywhere for whom the only important thing, the only thing they want to do, is sing or tell stories or paint or build buildings or write poet-

ry or go on the stage. In the city or from the city they learn about practical possibilities; they are taught by the example of those who have gone before. But when we speak of some young person's native gift, innate talent, we recognize something that is not the result of teaching. That is why, if every scrap of music were destroyed tomorrow, together with every instrument and recording and memory of the past, you may be sure that music would be re-invented in some form or other by somebody musically impelled, who would soon get together with others of his kind.

That coming together of human beings who share a talent is the great fact that makes cities essential to culture. The talented youth who must live an isolated family life on a farm is not likely to burst out in great song or epic poetry. Culture, in the honorific sense of the arts, needs fostering through several favorable conditions. One of the first is: an audience. The artistic impulse is communicative, and the audience provides the stimulus of eager receptivity. The primitive poet, who probably sings what he has to say, wants willing listeners, and they listen because they want entertainment, a pastime dosed with novelty. That is the reason why the early bards, like the later troubadours and our modern country singers, go from place to place. One can't imagine Homer reciting the entire *Iliad* to the same people every Tuesday night. But we can readily see why the Athenians went outdoors to hear Herodotus deliver another installment of his travels, day after day, till he was finished.

In mentioning Herodotus and his listeners, one is speaking of a highly developed city culture. The people of Athens were known for their insatiable curiosity, which may be why the young man from the small town of Halicarnassus in Asia Minor undertook his travels, hoping that he would have something new and important to contribute to the center of civilization. The products of culture must be made and felt as a revelation.

This example, which I picked almost at random, shows us the pattern of culture-making. The impulse arises in the individual, in the country, the provincial town, or the metropolis. But it generally leads him to the last, because for his full flight there must be a willing audience; and what he offers must attract and entertain, by its skill and freshness or novelty, people who know and who care.

These are the conditions for the birth of culture; there are others for its growth. Consider the advantages of a city. In a city the audience is large and self-renewing. Not everybody turns out at one time, so there are several audiences for each event, the first viewers or listeners promoting by word of mouth the appearance of the later comers. And all these can pay for the artist's support. As Ogden Nash put it in his excellent poem, "The City,"

> Artists speak of everything urban
> As the W.C.T.U. speaks of rye
>     & bourbon
> And they say cities are only
>     commercial marts.
> They fail to realize: No marts, no arts.

Gradually, the city organizes the various kinds of cultural activity into institutions: There is a theatre, a concert hall, a speakers' forum, ultimately a museum and a library.

Equally important is that the city exerts a gravitational pull on talents of a like sort. The first ballad singer wants, as I said, an audience who are eager strangers, not his unappreciative family. But curiously, he also wants to be with fellow performers. He wants to compare notes, discuss his craft, and perhaps feel that he belongs to a group apart, more "spiritual," less worldly, than the paying public. The contact with others of his trade spurs invention. It also permits borrowing, copying, stealing ideas; or again, it intensifies originality by showing what has not yet been done. Call it competition or emulation, the effect is to make culture *hot*, lively, self-multiplying. The city—and in modern times a certain district of the city—becomes truly the hotbed of one or more of the arts. It is the Left Bank, Greenwich Village, or Chelsea, where artists feel at home because they are together and can work and live as they please—a life of endless argument—and irregular hours. This is just as natural as the concentration of stockbrokers at the Stock Exchange.

What I have described has been the rule, with local variations, from time immemorial. But recently—during the last half century or so—a new variation has been introduced which is worth a little thought. I mean the new self-consciousness about art. Through the ages, the motives for cherishing the native artistic impulse have been much the same. Art was used for entertainment, as an accompaniment to religious ritual, or for the greater glory of the city, the king, the pope, or the patron. In our day we have added to these motives a kind of sociological, hygienic notion of art's purpose. We think that just as we must have a balanced diet, with plenty of vitamins, and keep down the level of cholesterol, so in a proper society we must have plenty of art—every kind of art—and keep down the level of philistinism.

This Medicare role is expressed in the deliberate things we "do for the arts"—from grants and fellowships, public and private, to the innumerable programs, schools, societies, groups, foundations, and other devices for getting as many people, young and old, somehow involved in the arts. Art has

become a cult. It is in fact *the* cult of western civilization in the 20th century, the chief substitute for religion. To put it in most general terms, artistic culture is now thought normal and necessary for everbody. It is a democratic right, and it is the only democratic right which is also a duty. That being so, all of us as citizens face questions—not to say problems—about the best way to cultivate culture.

Indeed, with our nefarious modern habit of engineering everything, of turning activity into projects, of giving specifications and asking for evaluations and interim reports, we the audience run the risk of steadily manufacturing mediocrity and discarding talent. Just think: why is government support of the arts so unsatisfactory? It is because of unavoidable system and method. Recall what John Sloan said on the subject. "I'm in favor of government getting into the arts; then we'll know who our enemy is."

Does this mean that the public should make no demands whatever and take from the talents what they choose to give? Up to a point, yes; but only up to a point. Once an artist has brought forth the considered product of his spontaneous desire (which can perfectly well mean a work that has been commissioned), he must stand up to be criticized like everybody else. The audience is entitled to *some* satisfaction; it mustn't take art as a punishment good for the soul. The state of culture is no better when the public meekly accepts the work of charlatans than when it rejects the work of geniuses.

The prosperity of a local culture, then, comes down to critical judgment on both sides. The artist should know his audience and please it without pandering; the audience, on its side, must show its approval and disapproval without destroying the supplier of its pleasures. A local tradition, a special genre or mood, a particular art cultivated in one spot over a period, will often help to achieve this ideal give-and-take.

But nothing is perfect and there are bound to be grievous errors and misunderstandings. The strong and sympathetic Irish plays of John Synge were met by angry denunciation in the Irish national theatre. Often a local tradition will get too firmly set and will shut out the artist who would have given it new life. And there are talents that refuse to converse with their contemporaries, local or global. They must be content to wait in the grave for rediscovery. There are also a few creators who prefer the anonymity of a village or a megalopolis to the warmth of regional appreciation.

All a city can reasonably expect is that through sincerity and enthusiasm, coupled with a simple, modest attitude toward culture, the local talent will thrive and produce. The resulting culture will be a good in itself year in and year out; it will steadily educate the feelings of all who approach it; and it may at some point burst into brilliant flower. How this comes to pass no one knows. Why in earlier centuries it was Venice, Florence, or Rome, Amsterdam or Paris, remains a mystery. In this country, the glow of Boston at one time, then of San Francisco, Chicago, or the South at other times, cannot be explained.

But that is only another reason for nurturing wisely at *all* times the local culture which is the source of all culture. Keep working and hoping: nothing in the melodious syllables "Dallas, Texas" prevents them from being added some day to the list of the world's high-water marks of culture.

# The Economy of Cities
## Jane Jacobs

**Note:** The following is a portion of a video-taped interview between Dr. Gail Thomas and Jane Jacobs made in the home of Jane Jacobs in Toronto on April 6, 1986. The interview was shown as part of the What Makes a City Conference.

**G.T.:** Would you relate to us what constitutes the ingredients of a great city?

**J.J.:** It has to have a good economy because that supports everything else. A good economy to me means diversity. It has to be a very diverse economy; it cannot depend on one thing or a very few things. And over the course of time it ought to grow continually more diverse. It also has to be a continually rejuvenating economy. It has to have new activities and new enterprises or it just gets old and grown, idler, obsolescent, lackadaisical.

The more diverse the city's economy, the better the chances for new enterprises and new activities because they don't have to depend so much on themselves. There is a symbiotic nest of other producers who can help get other things started. . . .

Then, of course, the city is not entirely economic. It has to have citizens who care about the city, who care about cultural things and educational things . . . all things that go into making a great city. But underlying it, I want to emphasize, is this support by the economy.

**G.T.:** You speak of a healthy city as one which continually renews and regenerates its own resources. You call this process "import replacing." Would you tell us more about this process—is it more than a city just growing older?

**J.J.:** Oh, yes. You could also make an analogy with the natural world, in the way forests regenerate and watersheds, farms, and the soil. There are regenerative forces working if given a chance and time. Now, to get to a city specifically. It sounds very vague that you figure out what's needed here, what should we be replacing. I think it has to be a little more concrete. Cities used to replace imports very vigorously and spontaneously. But they are not doing that any more. In Eugene, Oregon, a young woman named Elena Probst has started a most remarkable program. What she and her staff do is go to businesses and ask them what they are planning to import during the current year. Then they circulate that information to other companies in Eugene and find who can produce these things or would like to, solicit bids from them and get the bids to the company that plans to do the buying. In the very first year, contracts amounting to one and three fourths million dollars were given local companies. . . . This is the kind of thing I think cities have to do. They have to give an intelligent shove to the process. . . . The initial thing is not to think too big and ambitiously. . . .

**G.T.:** How does a city like Dallas, which is a trade city, become import replacing?

**J.J.:** There is no such thing as just a trade city. If it were just trade, it would be a market town. It would be a little town. I think if you look at Dallas, you will be surprised how many things are produced there. A trading city doesn't really become a city unless there are goods and services not directly exported or imported.

**G.T.:** Would you define Dallas as a 'city region' the way you speak of such regions in your book?

**J.J.:** I don't think Dallas is notable as a city region. It has a hinterland from

which it draws things. But a city region would be a case where the city overflows with a lot of its things. And the region, in quite a large sense, becomes a very mixed agricultural and industrial and commercial area. A city the size of Dallas is bound to have some of that beyond its suburbs. But I don't have the impression that it is a big city region; or a very intense one. . . . For example, in the United States, New York created a great city region. It's decaying to quite an extent now. And Boston has a very large city region, and it is very alive now. It is moving outward into southern Maine and southern New Hampshire.

**G.T.:** What would it require for Dallas to become a city region?

**J.J.:** I think good, big episodes of import replacing are the thing that creates a city region. Import replacing adds jobs very fast. It adds new or expanded work very fast. It generates capital very fast. . . . And city region activity is often the saving of small towns, which, without this activity would just dwindle. . . . We are so fixated on national economics and national problems that we tend to think of imports as meaning foreign imports. It is obvious that American cities are not replacing foreign imports plentifully any more. . . . The point I want to make, though, is that American cities are not good anymore at replacing domestic imports. A city that is not any good at replac-

ing domestic imports is not going to
be good at replacing foreign ones. . . .
Import replacement is the very opposite of being parasitic. . . . Self-
reliance is an important concept in
this; not isolation. A city that replaces
imports doesn't stop importing because of that. It just switches to other
imports, and it doesn't hurt the world
outside because of that process. It's
no economic gain for the world outside, but it's no economic loss either.
. . . And in the city itself that is import replacing and in its region, if it's
spilling over, there is actual expansion. So, it's economically expanding.
. . .

# Culture and Agriculture

## *Wendell Berry*

I am here, by a kind of affirmative action, to be the country person among the speakers. I can't help but feel that it is an interesting time for a country person to be asked to respond to Dallas. These great buildings of Dallas are property that results from a lot of money. My life, for a long time, has been devoted to the possibility of a livelihood—a decent, small livelihood—as a result of a little property. The country and people I belong to are a colony of the economy that is building Dallas. Dallas is growing. My country and people are dwindling; they are representative of the whole rural countryside of the United States.

I don't see how one could fail to be impressed by the view through the windows of City Hall in Dallas. There is a monumentality to the view. I looked and looked, and finally I realized that the people out there look awfully small. They look to be scaled about like the people in the mountain paintings of the Chinese. Then I realized something else. Those buildings are symbols. They stand for *some* people. They literally stand *for* some people, who are not little. The message of those buildings is: this way

of things will last forever. Great concentrations of wealth and power have occurred before. They built great buildings before with the same message. And they have always, to date, been wrong about economics, nature, and human nature.

The buildings of Dallas, like all those buildings before, are living on the exhaustion of their sources. And like those others before, they are going to create, in opposition to themselves, minds that are not abused by that occupation. And eventually, we will again make the noise of subversion, and that noise sounds like this: "We hold these truths to be self-evident, that all men are created equal, that they are endowed by their Creator with certain inalienable rights, that among these are life, liberty, and the pursuit of happiness." Then, we are back in our dear America.

I made, in preparation for today, a series of proposals:

1) We live in a wilderness in which we and our intentions occupy a tiny space and play a tiny part. We exist under its dispensation and by its power.

2) This wilderness, the universe, is

somewhat hospitable to us, but it is also absolutely dangerous to us. And we are absolutely dependent upon it.

3) That we depend upon what we are endangered by is a problem not solvable by "problem solving." The human condition does not have what the industrial economy would regard as an answer.

4) There does exist a possibility that we can live, more or less, in harmony with our native world. This possibility of harmony comprehends all the possibilities of good and of goodness in our life here. The role of human intention in human good, though critically important, is small.

5) It is not possible for very long for humans to intend their own good specifically or exclusively. In the long run, we cannot intend our own good without intending the good of our place as a whole, which is to say, the good of the world as a whole. But there is no *practical* way we can intend the good of the world as a whole. Practice can only be local.

6) The role of human intention in the making of harmony between human life and nature is therefore smaller than humans are accustomed to think. And often, intention must be manifested in negative ways. We must not intend too much. We must not intend the wrong thing.

7) We are dependent upon some things that come to us from the wilderness directly and are directly useable by us. We must not obscure the sunlight or pollute the rain or the air. Typical behavior of the industrial

economy is to take something that is free and depreciate it, to the point that it has to be replaced by something expensive.

8) Once the limits of intention are understood and the need for restraint accepted, then we may consider the role of positive intention: work, or the use of nature. The human use of nature either must fail or submit to the rule of two necessities. First, to preserve the natural sources by care, thrift, and replenishment. And second, to preserve the human users and the tradition of good use. Whereas the industrial economy always proceeds from exhaustion to pollution, the good economy would proceed from taking from nature, through use, to return.

9) Humans are not a "resource." To the extent that they come from nature, they are products. But to the extent that humanity is a product of human culture, human beings are sources.

10) It is possible, by the too strong enforcement of human intention, to diminish our access to our sources in nature and to diminish those sources themselves.

11) It is equally possible for intention to diminish the sources of humanity in the lives of human beings. It is evidently a fact that humanity as we have always known it is well advanced into obsolescence. More and more human abilities as well as more and more humans have been depreciated and replaced by industrial devices that "work" and "think." This human obsolescence, as well as an obsolescence

of nature, appears to be institutionalized in planned communities in which
everything is designed. In such places,
geography and human usage, time and
history, nature and worth, have become forceless. Intention has become
the exclusive forming principal. The
overwhelming feeling in such a place is
that something is missing. What is
missing is virtually everything that
makes life desirable.

12) An authentic human dwelling
place, on the other hand, is the result
of a long conversation between local
humanity and local nature. It is partly
its own memory of itself as a human
dwelling place. It is partly its own continuous work in its own making. It is
partly its sense of the possibility of its
continuance. If it is to continue, it
must preserve its sources; it must be
properly thankful and responsible for
all goods that originate beyond its intention; and it must not yearn for
what it cannot be.

# Adventures in the Undergrowth

## *Denise Scott Brown*

It seems to me that cities have to do with the massification of society, with the growing size of groups, and with the forming of connections between groups. . . . And as the society becomes a mass society, you can make the case, and I have heard it made, that industrialized agriculture belongs in the definition of the city, whereas downtown, where we have, in the North and now in the South, recent migrants, may be all rural. So the definition of a city is very much up in the air right now when one is talking about the structure of a society. . . .

Now, as for the economic definition of a city, as a student I was fascinated by the concept of "Regional Science," a discipline which deals with the space economy, and is based in essence on the statement that "here is nearer than there." The cost of carrying goods affects where you put cities. And if a product becomes lighter through the manufacturing process, it makes sense to locate it in one place, whereas if it becomes heavier in the process, it may make sense to locate it in another place. These kinds of analyses lead to interesting patterns which ought to be fascinating to urban designers. As ought the notion of "linkages." The best definition I have of linkage comes from experience. Our office is on Main Street, and opposite us is a small store that has a wonderful variety of items. The owner said to me the other day that it was a shame that all the people who come into our office didn't come also into their store. And the truth is there is no reason for people visiting us, short of wanting to buy a bar of candy, to go into their store. And that's the trouble with Main Street. It doesn't have good linkages. People go for one thing and then they go away.

Now, more and more, cities are beginning to realize that if you can have a city where you do several things at once, all sorts of opportunities are open to you. The Dallas Arts District is obviously based on this notion of good linkage. The daytime uses of the parking structures are for one thing, the nighttime uses for another, weekend uses for another. The art museum can rub off on the commercial district. All this is based on the economic notion of linkage.

Patterns such as these change with changing technology. And we have had several changes coming and going. The economists like to talk about the fact that the only people who really need to be downtown anymore are those who need to listen to each other. This means architects, because I really must talk with my client across the table. Talking on the telephone is a substitute, but only after you have had a whole lot of things worked out. . . .

Now, a series of definitions within the city. For example, "civic" obviously means city—it has the same root—and "civic" might be contrasted with "public." A beach, where you might sun yourself, but while there you try very hard to ignore the other people. If you observe people on the beach, they space themselves as far as they can from each other. . . . They are all enjoying the same opportunity, trying very hard not to notice that other people are there. That's a public place. In a civic place you want to wear a suit, walk nicely, and think of yourself as a citizen. That cities combine public, private, civic, is a fascinating notion. . . .

There are certain necessary polarities in the city. I like to talk about "grit" and "glitter," "utopia" and "reality." When I came into urban planning, people were quick to talk about "the perfect vision—the year 2020." The city may look like this now, but in the year 2020 it will be perfect. For me, particularly downtown, there should be a little of everything. I would like to see downtown become an upward mobility machine, a place where low-income people whose neighborhoods ring all our downtowns, can learn to become middle-income people. . . . I think we should think of downtown as a place where low-income people can learn to use skills, but we should also try to get the upper-income families too, and we should try for artists, and we should try for yuppies. We should have a little of everything and something for everyone downtown.

# The Morality of Water

## Geoffrey Stanford

Let me begin with some facts about water. You and I are about 60 percent water; and if, on the average, you and I weigh about 130 pounds, then, although I imagine I am talking to about 200 people, I am also talking to 2000 gallons of water.

Water is strange, unusual, mysterious. It has a dreamlike character, even in terms of chemistry and physics. For its own molecular weight, which is low, it has an unusually high melting point and boiling point. One of its strange characteristics is that as it cools it gets more dense, it contracts until it gets to 4°C, and then it starts to expand again. So, hot water is lighter than cold, hot water rises to the top, cold water sinks to the bottom, and that is how the hot water system works in the home. Now, imagine a world in which the cold water went on getting heavier, and all the ice sank and stayed down at the bottom of the sea and lakes and never melted; the world would get colder and colder.

Water expands when it turns from water to ice; it occupies more volume than the water did. That is why it is important to have trees, so that land and rock will not be eaten away too

rapidly. But this expansion also fluffs up the surface soil for the farmer, so that when he makes a seedbed in the fall, all the soil is fluffed up by being expanded, and then is powdery so that the small, delicate young roots coming out of the seeds can quickly get down out of the range of the hot sun and live. . . .

Water has a high dielectric constant, and many things dissolve in it. It is a good insulator when it is pure. But when salts dissolve in it, it becomes a good conductor. . . . It has an extraordinarily high heat capacity; you can store heat in it very well. . . . Clouds in particular conduct heat. The climate, to a large extent, is controlled by water as a vapor. . . .

Now, let us look at the city's water supply, its water cycle. We build dams to make reservoirs that are going to get silted up in twenty to fifty years. We build pump stations to pump up underground water, which we know will diminish; we are using 30 million-year-old water which we know will not come back. . . . This water is pumped to some central point where chemicals are poured into it, and then we try to get them out the

best we can—the process of purification. Then it is piped to the homes
where about twenty to forty percent
leaks out on the way. Here in Dallas,
we use about half of that water for irrigating our lawns and cleaning our
cars. The other half we use for
flushing our toilets and bathing. About
one half of one percent is used for
drinking and cooking; that is all we
need that is of drinking quality. All
the rest is cleaned for no good purpose. . . . This is exceedingly expensive; it would be much cheaper for the
city to supply people with half purified
and unpurified water and a bottle of
distilled water in every home on demand.

The toilet water that is flushed
down into our sewers has a fiftieth of
one percent of factory-made chemicals
in it and something like a fiftieth of
one percent of human organic fer-
tilizers in it. This is pumped back
through another set of pipes to
another central point, a sewage treatment plant; there it is cleaned by settling it, blowing air through it, settling
again, and then putting chemicals in it.
Then it is piped into the river—water
that has been collected at enormous
expense, barely used, purified at great
expense, and then dumped. Then it
flows downstream to the next reservoir for the same treatment all over
again. . . . This is done fifteen times
along the Mississippi River. This is the
first time in history that a city has
ever let any water out of its confines.
Cities could not afford to waste water
in the past, any more than they can

afford to waste it now. It is exceedingly expensive in energy to do these
things to water. . . . . And the Environmental Protection Agency tells us
that around seventy percent of the
sewage treatment plants in this country do not meet the regulated requirements imposed on them—they
do not work adequately. . . .

Rural waste-water treatment plants
are so small that they are often ignored by agencies, and we do not
know whether they are working at all.
Some facilities have not been visited in
years by inspectors. Consulting engineers often recommend expensive,
complicated processes which cannot be
properly supported. . . . In a south
Texas community, such engineers
recommended a $500,000 treatment
plant which would serve about 200
people. . . .

In one large city that we investi-
gated we found that the director of
water utilities would not even consider
water conservation as his policy; if
water consumption were to drop, his
revenues would also fall, and the city
would be unable to pay the existing
debt service and maintenance costs.
This man is put in a morally horrible
position of having to recommend
squandering a precious commodity. . . .

We were told that the consulting
engineers of a large city said that it
would be uneconomic to send waste
water twenty-four miles upstream for
farmers to use, but that it would be
economic to collect water from a
reservoir eighty miles upstream. . . .

A major city has to install twelve-inch diameter water mains to supply its fleet of fire trucks wherever they might go to put out a fire. But they can control a fire only up to seventy-five-feet high; after that, the builder has to put in automatic sprinklers. Those sprinklers could all work in any building from a four-inch main. So why don't we save our money in twelve-inch mains and put fire sprinklers in every home?

Having offered some strange facts in several different ways, I am going to suggest some sensible solutions. First, we should adopt water conserving principles. Don't build any more dams; then we would have to use less water or conserve water—at the same time preserving farmlands. . . . Second, put many more trees on the hillsides to store water from the rainfall. . . . Third, pump used water back onto farmland and parkland for irrigation or fertilization. The water thrown back into the river after treatment by Dallas and Fort Worth is presently worth somewhere between $3 and $11 million a year. . . . Fourth, use weeds and rushes to clean water—it is very effective. . . . Fifth, you can divide your genuine sewage from wash water and drinking water . . . which cuts the water consumption in half. Sixth, sewage could be irradiated with cesium. . . . It will kill the bacteria, and it is a safe procedure. . . .

There are obstructions to these suggestions. First, there is a firmly entrenched federal obstruction. The EPA has the responsibility for treating sewage water. It may not allow itself to recommend that sewage water be used for irrigating farmland. . . . And the Department of Agriculture cannot recommend putting sewage on farmland because that is the prerogative of the EPA.

There is also a strongly entrenched economic motive of the fertilizer industry and also of the water boards which do not want city water to go out cheap. There is in addition a professional block; engineers who design treatment plants are paid a percentage of the total cost of the plant. . . . No engineer can afford to recommend anything that will cut into his income. We need to devise a system whereby a reasonable fee is assessed for designing the installation and then giving a bonus for designing it cheaper. . . .

The next thing is public anxiety—brought about through the press and media . . . that the people who are benefiting from the present system can afford to advertise in. . . . And lastly, we are not allowed by Texas law to do water planning on a regional basis.

New and better systems are available. Science and technology have solved the technical problems; good methods are available for saving water, for cleaning waste water, and for re-using water cheaply, safely, and wisely. . . . What is needed now is for moralists, economists, politicians, biologists, and the public to encourage our engineers to use these new systems.

# H₂O and the Waters of Forgetfulness

## *Ivan Illich*

*Peace of Mind*
*If the pool were still*
*The reflected world*
*Of tottering houses,*
*The falling cities,*
*The quaking mountains*
*Would cohere on the surface*

*And stars invisible*
*To the troubled mind*
*Be seen in water*
*Drawn from the soul's*
*Bottomless well.*

Kathleen Raine

I am told that for the last seventy years there have been citizens in Dallas who have urged the construction of a midcity lake. The community expects this lake to water finance and fantasy, commerce and health. . . . Dreams have always shaped cities, and cities have always inspired dreams, and traditionally water has quickened them both. I have serious doubts that the water is left that can connect the two. Industrial society has turned $H_2O$ into a substance with which the archetypal element of water cannot mix. . . .

Dreams perform catharsis, which means: they clean, and dream waters can clean in several ways. The sprinkling quenches curses, dispels the pollution that lingers at certain places, can be poured on the hands, the head or the feet to wash off impurity, blood, or guilt. But there is another catharsis which only the dark, mythical waters of Lethe perform: in myth, Lethe's water detached those who crossed them from memories and allowed the blessing of forgetfulness. . . . This makes my question about the proposed city lake very narrow: Can the soul's river of forgetfulness which flows into the social pool of remembrance reflect itself in the purified disinfectant that is metered, sewered and piped, and then poured in an open air reservoir downtown? Can the city child's dreams about "letting go and forgetting" be watered by the liquid that comes from taps, showers, and toilets? Can purified washwater "circulate" in fountains or lakes that mirror dreams? . . .

Bruce Lincoln has shown that, at the bottom, Greek, Indic, Nordic, and Celtic pilgrims on their way to the beyond cross through the same funeral

landscape designed according to the same mythical hydrology. The slow flowing waters the traveler crosses are those of the river of forgetfulness. This river has the power to strip those who cross it of their memories. . . .
However, what the river has washed from those on their way to the beyond is not destroyed. The traveler is only divested of the deeds by which he will be remembered. The river carries them to a spring where they bubble up like the same at the bottom of a cosmic well to serve as drink for the elect: the singer, the dreamer, the seer, the wise. Memories return as poetry, music, prophesy, wisdom—as the oral tradition of storytelling. . . .

However, this archaic well of oral tradition has no place in the classical cities. The classical cities of Greece and, above all, Rome are built around aqueducts piping water to fountains. . . . Remembrance as the throbbing source beyond the river of forgetfulness is replaced by a new kind of memory—writing replaces oral culture, and legal order replaces old customary order. . . .

The complaint that cities are dirty places goes back to antiquity. Even Rome with its 900 fountains was a dangerous place to walk. A special kind of petty magistrate sat under umbrellas on one corner of the Forum; they heard and adjudicated complaints from people hurt by excrements thrown from windows. Medieval cities were cleaned by pigs. . . . However, the perception of the city as a place that must be constantly deodorized by washing has a clearly defined origin in history; it appears at the time of the early Enlightenment. The new concern with scrubbing and cleaning is primarily concerned with the removal of features which are not so much visually ugly as objectionable in an olfactory sense. The whole city is now for the first time perceived as an evil-smelling place. . . .

Only during the last year of the reign of Louis XV was an ordinance passed making the removal of fecal matter from the corridors of the palace of Versailles into a weekly procedure. Below the windows of the minister of finance for decades pigs were slaughtered and the walls of the palace were impregnated with layers of blood. People relieved themselves as a matter of course against the wall of any dwelling or church. The odor of shallow graves was part of the dead's presence within the walls. . . . This olfactory nonchalance came to an end when a small number of citizens lost their tolerance toward the stench from burial places with churches. . . . The new olfactory sensitivity to the presence of corpses was due to a new kind of fear of death. . . .

Intolerance against the smell of feces took much longer to develop. Attention was drawn to the issue at first only by public-spirited scientists, who studied "the airs"—today we would say gases. . . . The treatises on odor deal with the seven smelly points of the human body that lie between the top of the head and the interstices between the toes; they classify the seven odors of decomposition that can be observed in succession in a rotting animal body; they distinguish disagreeable odors into those which are healthy like dung and those which are putrid and damaging; they teach how to bottle smells for later composition and the study of their evolution; they estimate the weight of per capita exudations of city dwellers and the effect of their deposit-by-air in the city's vicinity. . . .

During the first half of the nineteenth century the English have already set out to wash their cities and to pollute the Thames. In France, and in general on the continent, public opinion is not yet ready for such profligacy. L'Institute, in a report of 1835, rejects the proposal to channel the excrements of Paris into the Seine. It is not concern for the river, nor mere anti-English prejudice, which motivated this decision, but the calculation of the enormous economic value that would thus be lost. . . .

To deodorize the city the English architects proposed to use water. As early as 1596 Sir John Harrington, the godson of Queen Elizabeth I, had invented the water closet. . . . Then in 1851 George Jennings installed public WCs in the Crystal Palace for the Great Exhibition, and 827,280 persons, 14 percent of the visitors, tried them and paid for their use. The "convenience suited to the advanced age of civilization" was perfected by a

Mr. Crapper, a foundary owner. The "anus mirabilis" water flush reserve valve was patented in England, and the English word "WC" became an integral part of every civilized language. According to a United States government report, Baltimore was the last eastern city to produce its fertilizer in a natural way before it switched to mandatory flush in 1912.

Until the beginning of the nineteenth century, all American cities had obtained their water from local sources, from wells, cisterns, and springs. Water was mainly used for drinking and washing: one to three gallons per person and day. At the beginning of the nineteenth century, the large fires in wood-built cities led to the demand for water to be used in firefighting. By 1860, 136 waterworks had been constructed in American cities that brought water from across the city line. When tap water was introduced directly into the household, water consumption increased by a factor of 20 to 60: 30 to 100 gallons per capita became typical figures. During the next twenty years, for the first time in history anywhere on a large scale, households became dependent on water for the transport of their waste. . . . For the first half of this century the accent was placed on the sterilization of the water supply. . . . Then, toward midcentury . . . public emphasis could shift toward the "purification" of sewage and the salvaging of lakes. The cost of sewage treatment and collection by 1980 has become the greatest expense of local government. . . . We have now followed the water of history from archaic Greece to the ecological tap. . . . We have understood that city water, in western culture, has a beginning and therefore might have an end. It was born when the artist domesticated each of the waters of Rome at an appropriate fountain where it was used to tell its own unique story to the citizens' dreams, and it is threatened when the suction rotors of waterworks make it into a cleaner and coolant. We have come to wonder about the coexistence between wealth and dreams. . . .

Looking back on the course of historical water through the cities of the west, we can now recognize certain points:

1. Dreams need to be reflected in the cosmological water corresponding to their age if they are to water the city.
2. The cosmological water in which dreams are reflected determine the range in which dreams can speak.
3. . . . The aliveness of a city depends on the bond between its waters and its flow of dreams.
4. As far as we could see, it is a unique feature of the modern city to degrade the ecological element metaphorically, turn it into $H_2O$, and thus extinguish its ability to reflect the water of dreams.

This road following water has not been a pleasant one, but along it lies the only hope to find a trickle of water for our thirsty dreams. If you want to create inspiring beauty with water in Dallas, you cannot but start with the question: Is there any water left? It might be more healing for the dreams of your children to mourn rather than to exalt the loss of water to $H_2O$.

# Man and Beast in the City

*Bill Porterfield*

It is spitting in the wind to think that Dallas will preserve the buildings of its past. We never have, and it's hardly likely that we will start as long as the city continues to grow and attract new blood. The idea of preservation is anathema to our expansive character. It is like asking a strapping fellow in his boisterous prime to lie down and soak in a coffin of formaldehyde. In fact, it is damned near un-American. . . . . "The American journey has not ended," the poet Archibald MacLeish wrote, "America is never accomplished, America is always still to be built—West is a country in mind, and so eternal."

. . . We have always left things behind, traveled light, carrying only those things which were disposable. If something doesn't suit us—a territory, a job, a house, a horse, a wagon, or a woman—we leave it and skedaddle in search of something new. Walls could not contain us, just as the past would not constrain us. Even if we threw up walls, we raised them tentatively, flimsily, like tent cities which were made to be broken down and packed away as soon as it was time to move on. Home may have been where you hung your hat, but it was mobile. The covered wagon became the trailer house, the chuck wagon the fast food joint.

Not even the communities we paused to create were meant to last. The ghost towns were an American phenomenon. "It was enough to make them move if they saw they were not likely to prosper," historian Daniel Boorstin wrote of our great-grandfathers. "They had come quickly and recently, and they could leave in just as short order."

. . . Thus everything had a thinner life, even property. Land and buildings were not to be held for perpetuity, for future generations, but they became a commodity to be bought and sold at will. Deeds changed hands as fast as coin. Property was like the land and the people and the idiom of our tongues. Possessions, like the language itself, were mediums of exchange, not treasures to be kept. Nothing was solid, nothing sacred save for our faith in greener pastures. Everything was soluble and for sale. We became a throwaway, moveaway people, nomads more restless than bedouins, harboring little unique except our incredible craving and capacity for change.

. . . Biologically, like all forms of life, it is quite natural for us to discard that which does not suit us. The snake sheds its skin, chickens molt. . . . The fall of an old building, however grand, may not be the result of war among us, but evidence of the ongoingness of life, the tossing off of a magnificent but expendable old turtle shell.

If the building is dear to us, and some of us fight for its survival, it is because it has become part of the culture, which is supposed to be antithetical to nature. Jung said that culture lies outside the purpose of nature. But it seems to me that culture without the vitality of nature is a dead end. . . . Is to embrace civilization and art to deny life?

. . . Some may think that man long ago began separating himself from the natural world, that he lifted himself by means of his soul and his mind, his art, and now, for better or worse, his science. But I wonder. I especially wonder when I look at our cities, these places supposedly synonymous with civilization. They bear no resemblance to anything civil and humane, and neither do they look like any imitation of the natural habitat.

. . . It seems to me that our greatest art, and our highest soul-searching, brings us back to earth again, not only to face the beauty and terror of life, but to endure its incredible indif-ference to the values we so heroically, and pathetically, in our brief flurry wave.

# Dallas

One of the first books published by The Dallas Institute was *Imagining Dallas*, a collection of short essays written by Fellows of the Institute about the city which has captured the fantasy of people all over the world. The beginning essay of that book, Donald Cowan's "The Myth of Dallas," is included in this volume because the section on "Dallas" seems incomplete without an understanding of the founding myth of the city.

"Imagining" seems necessary when it comes to Dallas. IMAGINE! . . . DALLAS! Dallas changes daily; buildings go down and others appear within weeks in their place; favorite bars and eating spots—"watering-holes"—disappear within the time frame of a weekly rendezvous; corporate leadership shifts and moves more quickly than computerized mailing lists can correct. Change, like trade and barter, is part of the imagination of the place. Movement, soaring, taking flight, is in the air all Dallasites breathe, possibly originating from the image of Pegasus who has flown over Dallas for half a century. Imagining Dallas is an essential activity in the city's making, possibly one reason people continue to say, "anything is possible here."

Visitors to Dallas comment on the energy of the city, the quick pace. When Christian Norberg-Shulz first came, he could not get over "The enormous sky, like a dome . . . and the great wind. . . ." The land and sky here give one the notion that there is room for a lot to happen.

When asked what it is about Dallas that draws energy to it, people usually reply, "It's Dallas' spirit. Dallas has a great spirit." Certainly, Dallas loves winners and it loves success. It is not sure what to do with sitting, standing still, and shadow. Shadow is important; it allows you to know where you are standing. It also brings depth and dimension. Dallas' shadow is that it has attempted to ignore its shadow—the shadow of spirit. If Dallas' founding myth is the myth of development, we need to acknowledge that Dallas' development has, for the most part, been up and out. It is time to develop down, grow a deep taproot to provide an anchor for its spirit.

One way of achieving depth and acknowledging shadow within a city is memory. Memory is essential for the making of a true city; it is the soil in which grows a culture. Why is it that the Caddo Indian massacre led by General Tarrant on the banks of the Trinity in 1841 is not remembered in the founding of Dallas? The circumstances of Dallas' beginnings mark it as having the destiny of a great city. Most important cities were founded by acts of homicide—Cain slew Abel before founding the city; Romulus killed his brother Remus as the boundary of the city of Rome was being marked off. The Caddo Village massacre freed up the land to be bought and sold. Its inhabitants gone, Bryan was free to stake his claim to the land.

The writer William Faulkner says the white man had no right to buy and sell the land—that it was not his to trade. Faulkner says the land itself is memory, that it belongs to all who inhabit it, not only humankind, but animal and plant life as well. Certainly the Indians never claimed ownership to the land. They considered themselves guardians of it.

Perhaps cities with such shadowy beginnings become great because the inhabitants carry the memory of their auspicious start as a constant reminder of the frailty and preciousness of life, and of the responsibility toward guardianship for it.

Dallas as a modern city has another death as part of the myth of its founding—the assassination of John F. Kennedy. It was after the tremors of this horrible act had reverberated throughout the world that Dallas leadership moved into action to build the city we know today. Erik Jonsson was determined to obliterate this ugly scar. He established Goals for Dallas which prompted the construction of the D/FW Airport, Dallas City Hall, the new Public Library, as well as the ''can do'' attitude which keeps the dirt flying in Dallas. Dallas' own dirt is retained in memory. In 1983, Dallas observed the 20th anniversary of the assassination of President Kennedy. In many ways, the Dallas we know today is only twenty years old. It is difficult to recall a freeway or building that existed before. Central Expressway and Neiman Marcus may be the only two. Like the Caddo Indian massacre, the assassination is part of the shadow of Dallas which seeds it for greatness.

The following essays offer unusual reflections on Dallas. The myth goes on.

*Gail Thomas*

# The Myth of Dallas

## *Donald Cowan*

John Neely Bryan seems not too unlikely a character to be the founder of
the Dallas myth. He was well edu-
cated, read for the law at Nashville,
but, being slow to recover from an illness, went off to live with the Cherokees in Arkansas to regain his health.
He learned the languages of several
Cherokee tribes and learned as well
the ways of the woods. His intention
was to become a trader with the Indians and, in time, he set off with an
Indian companion, a small stock of
goods, a pony, and a dog for the land
where the three rivers met—the Trinity. In November 1841, he set up
shop in his lean-to on a site near
where the old red courthouse now
stands. But just a few months before,
a raiding party led by General E. H.
Tarrant of the Republic of Texas fell
on the principal village of the peaceful
Caddo Indians at Village Creek, a few
miles from here, destroying homes and
crops. The heroes of that encounter
are memorialized in the names of our
two adjacent counties—Tarrant and
Denton—Captain Denton being the
only white man to fall in that
slaughter. A second party came upon

the village two days later and finished
its destruction. The Indians were dead
or dispersed and soon were banished
to the Brazos. The sad tale of the
Caddoes will someday have to be acknowledged. They are very much part
of the prehistory of Dallas, and surely
their spirit haunts the ground. But for
now our tale has to do with the white
man, John Neely Bryan, who came to
trade with the Indians but found his
market considerably diminished. Turning to entrepreneurship, he built a
ferry to serve the semblance of a road
that ran from Austin to Preston Bend
on the Red River—our present
Preston Road is part of it. He also
turned to real estate, marking off the
land he claimed in streets and city-
sized lots. Dallas, you see, was conceived as a city before it was born. (It
was Ebby Halliday country without
yet knowing it.) Bryan was a good
salesman who promoted his development with vigor to travellers and to
those he visited in other cities. As it
happened, a land company based in
Louisville had a grant for the entire
region and was busy promoting its col-
onization throughout the East, freely

using the name Dallas, so that its reputation as a city was widespread
before half a dozen buildings had been
constructed.

I submit to you that all this development—real estate and advertising—had
an imprint on the nascent myth of
Dallas. But there were other elements.
Bryan was a leader but by no means a
dictator. The leadership of the town
spread out among many. Civic awareness grew with every new settler. In
many ways Dallas was a Western
town; it had its outlaws, its saloons
and bordellos. But it passed through
these phases rapidly on the way to its
destiny of becoming a cosmopolitan
city.

The second major leader and the
city's first capitalist was Alexander
Cockrell, who staked out a ranch on
Mountain Creek about where the lake
is now. Cockrell bought out Bryan's
Ferry in 1853 and replaced it with a
toll bridge. He also bought what
Bryan had left of the town, constructed a sawmill, and built the finest
hotel in Texas. Bryan by this time was
drinking heavily, shot a man and
thought he had killed him, ran off to
California and returned some years
later, a more or less broken man.
Cockrell, his good friend who had also
spent some years with the Cherokees,
died in a duel with the town marshal.
All of this sounds quite lurid, like
something in a TV soap opera called
"Dallas," but actually the young city
was orderly and its progress uninter-
rupted by changes of leadership. And

thus the myth increasingly took shape.

One other aspect, more symbolic
than actual in its effect perhaps, is
worth a comment. In France, the fol-
lowers of the philosopher Fourier
formed a society to set up several ideal
communities—utopias of sorts. The
only one that actually came about was
at Dallas: Reunion it was called and
was located on Chalk Hill. (The present Reunion arena and tower take the
name but not the location—and actually, the name I suspect is more a play
on the old Union Station.) But the
serious intention of Reunion Arena
was to memorialize the French project,
in which some 200 French natives, ar-
tisans, and shopkeepers came trooping
over, full of high hopes and grand
ideals. The enterprise failed of course,
as all such settlements did, but many
of the French stayed in Dallas, giving
the city a cosmopolitan air and an infusion of the lofty hopes of Utopian-
ism. The myth, you see, has many
tributaries.

Dallas is no new Troy, no shrine for
local gods nor haven for ones from
afar, not a fortress to repel invaders or
protect against aborigines, not a capital
city, not a social center for landed
gentry, not a university town. It is a
commercial city—is now, was at its
beginning. Its Romulus and Remus
were trader and capitalist, their drifting
on the Tiber was a toll-charging ferry
for the intermittent floods of the
Trinity, their nurturing wolf-mother
the Cherokees with whom both lived
for a time. Almost every aspect of

Dallas has been commercial. Its invaluable Jewish community that so greatly elevated its tone arrived en masse as merchants when the first train pulled in on fresh-laid tracks. Finance was quickly at the heart of the Dallas myth, and a daring, bold financing it turned out to be. Moving along in time, Nathans Adams was first in the century to finance a venture on the security of oil still in the ground; Bob Thornton was first to finance automobile loans on the security of the car itself. Both of these moves were groundbreakers on the American scene—ways of multiplying the money supply. Perhaps it was innocent of them, but the belief was quite general among early Dallas citizens that making money is a good in itself—that everyone benefits from any one person's good fortune or astuteness. This same innocence assumes that people are supposed to be winners and that there isn't much point in backing someone for the sport of it. Dallas backs the best or those that expect to be so very soon. Consequently, everyone with any degree of standing is expected to take a role in civic affairs, and, as I suggested, gains stature in the process. But Dallas is not bourgeois in attitude; it has a strange sort of aristocratic spirit—much like that of the epic hero, noble and magnanimous, even though the epic venture is not battle, or dangerous journey, or clearing the wilderness, but increasing the world's wealth.

The myth of Dallas is a myth of leaders. I should like to take a moment to project for you a theory concerning the way in which leadership works, a theory that takes on the nature of allegory, a story of succession and decay.

Founders, builders, and managers represent three successive stages of leadership in a city. This progression is present in all institutions but is most apparent to us in large corporations. Perhaps I could use industry, then, as my illustration of how leadership works—even though my ultimate concern is the leadership of the city.

Founders are persons of vision and daring whose feet tread the edge of an abyss because there the view is better. What is to be seen from this perilous perspective is not a never-never land, a private mirage of something unattainable. But neither is it merely the next stop on an already existing path. It is as if the journey thus far has led to an apparent limit, a gap in the continuous progression of unfolding potentialities that history presents. A founder leaps that gap, spans it with his imagination so that a bridge is built for others to cross to a new found land. Now of course a founding rarely seems as dramatic as I have described it; it is tentative and probing and the vision is engendered by the doing, not by hanging over the void in dizzying contemplation of its depths. But in retrospect, with time foreshortened, we can see the epic dimension and the heroic action.

Builders, following the founders, catch the vision, solidify it, give it scope, and display its grandeur. Their work has the excitement of risk because once across the bridge they must fling their enterprise into the future with bravado and abandonment. Quite properly they estimate all foreseeable difficulties and prepare fallback positions, but any builder who supposes he is risk-free—that he has it all figured out—is committing the old sin of hubris, of pride, and he rides to a fall. I am sure we have all seen this spectacle at times of sudden interest increases or unexpected antitrust action. The mighty fall, and so do the lesser ones. But we would not have it otherwise. The drama of life is in the building, in the debt builders incur in the present so that the future will be greater.

Fortunate the enterprise where builder succeeds builder. But comes a time when recurring risk wears thin the nerve sheath, and safer ground is sought. The managers take over. System with them replaces genius. They improve, streamline, optimize. They observe the best of conventions. They take no risk. But in the flowers of security grow the seeds of decline. The graph line of growth, which under the builder climbed exponentially as one idea stimulated others, under the manager bends over, asymptotically approaching a limit because each successive improvement is less valuable than the more obvious preceding one. And ever the competition creeps closer, trimming profits, cutting off markets.

Good management, of course, is important, essential. Its danger lies in being on top, as frequently happens in the process of succession. Some wise and wide-seeing governor is needed to oversee a manager, to nudge him at times free of the system that is his self-made cage.

Let me clarify what I mean by this matter of genius, for its recognition is of some practical importance to one in charge of an enterprise. Genius does not belong necessarily to a person of exceptional brilliance or learning— quick, clever, or otherwise impressive. It implies a natural capacity for original or creative thought in a given field—in certain contexts an exceptional capacity—but, in my scheme of things anyone could have this ability if he would free himself from inhibitions and preconceptions. Few people are willing to do so, I admit; but originality is not inherently so rare a quality. The genius, as I use the term, is reflective and therefore likely to appear a little slow or reticent. He has an ability to take a new problem into his imagination and let it stay there, revealing itself at its own pace, not harried by an impatient inventiveness. He knows his chosen field from within, has an authority to speak for it based on fundamental understanding, not mere fact. This ability to be original can break through the asymptotic curve of growth and jump an enterprise into a new state of vigor. The quality of genius, therefore, deserves careful appraisal and reasonable protection by management.

A city has many entities, many kinds of institutions, each with its own leadership at different stages of development. Not only the economic institutions—industry and finance—but the political, educational, social, and art organizations run the same gamut. These leaders taken all together along with a selection from the professions make up the leadership of a city. It has been the genius of Dallas that this leadership has operated corporately, seriously concerned with the welfare of the entire city. In my terms, I would say that the early leaders were primarily builders, people who invested freely in the future.

Subsequently, the political and economic environment changed and a more cautious note developed. The city, I believe, entered the stage of management—not, of course, univocally, but in its general mode. When such a stage persists for a time, that old asymptotic curve comes into play. Then the city needs a new founding, a new vision of its purposes. I should say we got that new founding when Bob Cullum and John Stemmons went to Erik Jonsson and convinced him to take the mayorship.

Mayor Jonsson was not Old Dallas, had no ties to John Neely Bryan or any of his cohorts. His was a broad scope of imagination that envisioned an international role for Dallas and, internally, saw the city in terms of the

new social conditions in this country. His Goals for Dallas program was a movement to broaden the base of leadership in the city—to open it to much greater citizen participation. I cannot say whether the democratic question "Can things be equal and excellent too?" has been answered (we stand too close to the clock to tell the time), but Erik Jonsson's regime earnestly confronted the question. Things have changed, have moved. The leadership is broader if less corporate, and though we may look with nostalgia at the old fast-acting oligarchy, we are successfully into a new age.

Physically, at least, the builders are at work. Everywhere new structures challenge the sky. Downtown is largely rebuilt. But actually the pattern here is not greatly different from that of many other cities, seeming to be more a product of affluence than a new vision. No, I should say in the metaphoric but more basic sense, the builders have not yet arrived. Indeed, the founding itself is not far along.

Where are the new institutions, those that incorporate a wide participation and a dispersed leadership? It would seem that the new architectural constructions symbolize concentration rather than dispersal, that the mergers and expansions of big corporations represent triumphs of centrism, that deregulation opens the door to a final onslaught of industrial imperialism. But, as Marshall McLuhan pointed out back in the seventies, when a movement reaches a point in its exponential development where its increase is excessive, it flips to its opposite. Deregulation, in releasing constraints, subjects an enterprise to the rigors of the free marketplace that, by its very nature, minimizes profits, as we have been witnessing for airlines. Not losses, but marginal profits will become a way of life, as it has for the Japanese. Equity financing then becomes less appealing, and the door is opened for smaller entrepreneurs, a movement of dispersal. Another target of deregulation, banking, is in the process of dispersal, and though Merrill Lynch may indeed become a superbank, it is nonetheless blazing the way for smaller firms of different financial functions to federate and become competitive. These changes are national, not unique to Dallas, but they do represent penetrations of the material limits—new foundings, as it were; and surely there will rise up in our midst—in Dallas— new geniuses who will thrust their enterprises into the new age.

It is worth noting that the two branches of Mayor Jonsson's refounding are quite in agreement with the myth of Dallas. The wide participation in leadership he promulgated is an extension of the original spirit that drew men into the public arena. The other branch, the international role, is an extension of the very core of the myth— commerce, trade. And that branch has flourished. Dallas *is* an international city. Its ships go to the farthest ports, a Venice of the air. The trade marts,

the actual products we use, the investments from abroad made here, our local industries' outreaches—these all give testimony. Mayor Jonsson's airport is a manifest symbol of the reality of which it partakes.

And I for one do not demean the role of commerce. It is the drama of people interacting to mutual advantage. Trade is the weaponry of peace. Trade disappears when fighting begins. The two actions are immitigable opposites.

The way of commerce, just as the way of war, admits of posturing, pretense, trickery, knavery—like war, a game of sorts, a child's idea of conflict —bartering, swapping, trading. Yet at the core, both war and trade are serious, deadly serious for one, lively serious for the other. The motivation of trade is the increase of value, not its destruction; the *establishment* of ties, not their severance. And the commodity that is traded, therefore, is necessarily a good. Merchants of goodness—what is here for the good that is there.

Behind the mask of self-interest lurks the face of magnanimity, in the clatter of barter the rumor of nobility. Trust, probity, integrity are the conditions of exchange beyond any precautions of legalism that can fall through the interstices of international jurisdictions. The virtues are indeed powers.

Finally, then, I must say the myth of magnificence governs Dallas, its pace, its architecture, its festivals. Its way toward the realization of that myth is commerce—on a large scale. This unconscious commitment rules out the quaint, the nostalgic, the sentimental; and one must understand this renunciation if one is to understand Dallas. "It is a good way," as Sir Henry Harcourt-Reilly says in *The Cocktail Party*. Dallas's way is clean, frank, open to all, welcoming the stranger, celebrating the present.

There are two ways to deal with a new land: John Neely Bryan came to trade with the Indians; General Tarrant came to shoot them. Dallas is child of the trader. Consequently, its citizens must elevate that instinct for peace, that love of munificence into something increasingly imaginative and spiritual and make Dallas *in its own way* an instance of that one city people in all ages and climes have been laboring to build.

# Pegasus

## Gail Thomas

For those of us who have lived for awhile in Dallas, Pegasus is more than the myth of the winged horse; Pegasus is Dallas' image, its own symbol, a sign of Dallas' spirit. Growing up in McKinney, I remember coming into the city eager for the first glimpse of the flying red horse, brazen red in the sun or illumined in the sky at night! Seeing it, I became a part of the city; my imagination was taken in by it, soared with it.

It has not been surprising for me to find that the story of the flying red horse yields much in the search for the myth of Dallas. The legend of Pegasus—its ignominious birth, its heroic fantasies, its vaulting ambition—echoes the complexity and contradiction which marks this city.

The myth of Pegasus is a venture into the fabulous—fabulous animals, heroic deeds, winged flights, miraculous joint ventures. So compelling is the image of the winged horse that it seems to embody imagination itself. Pegasus has been there since man first carved in stone or painted on clay. His image has traveled on coins, on wine flasks and water jars. The myth in all its phases is reproduced on marble, bronze, and precious stones and is found on monumental works of art and in all the minor arts—in temple sculpture, wall-paintings, vases, cosmetics, textiles, on armor and weapons, on plates and drinking cups as part of the communal life of a people.*

It is little wonder that the image of Pegasus suggests imagination itself—the image in action. Pegasus is the offspring of Poseidon and Medusa. Poseidon is the earthshaker, looser of the passions of the soul, the god of the deep. He espoused the sea and became its ruler. In his aspect as "father," he is darker than his heavenly brother Zeus but not as dark as Hades, ruler of the underworld. He is identified with animal shapes and made the horse his sacred animal. It is said that Poseidon turned himself into a stallion to mate with Demeter after she had attempted to evade his advances by turning herself into a mare.

Medusa, whose name means "Ruleress," was known as "ruler of the sea" and as "the cunning one." Her parentage comes from the sea and from the

*For a complete history of the art which has accompanied Pegasus through the ages see *Pegasus: The Art of the Legend* by Nikolas Yalouris, Director of the Archeological Museum of Athens, published by Westerham Press Ltd., England.

region of the night. Her father is said to be Phorkys, the Old Man of the Sea, who marries Keto, whose name means "the sea monster." The three "Fair-cheeked" Gorgons were born to this union. Of the three, Medusa was the only mortal. Medusa mates with Poseidon to give birth to Pegasus. Pegasus, therefore, is both mortal and divine.

According to Hesiod, the Gorgons lived in the direction of Night, beyond Okeanos, "the origin of the gods" and "the origin of everything." Medusa lived beyond this boundary in the realm of Night, in a dark cave where only the moon's rays cast reflection. It was in this dark place, this primordial region, that Pegasus was born, bursting forth from his mother's neck when the hero Perseus severed the Medusa's head from her body. The landscape of the birthplace of Pegasus offers the setting for his story—a place beyond the boundary of the "origin of all things" in the realm of Dark Night who begets the world.

Sired by the Ruler of the Sea and birthed by the Cunning One, she who herself has golden wings, Pegasus springs to life. From his first appearance, Pegasus is the image of action. All accounts of his birth attest to this spirited entrance into the world: he springs forth, he bursts out, he soars.

Pegasus resembles his father, Poseidon, in his horse-like nature, and in his relationship to water. The name, Pegasus, means "geyser." Hesiod explains the name's etymology as deriving from the springs (in Greek, *pegae*) of the

ocean: ". . . the horse Pegasus, who is so called because he was born near the springs of Ocean." (Theog. 282) His name, then, carries his image: he springs, he is the springs himself. Little wonder, then, that when his hoof strikes the earth, a well springs forth! And even less a marvel that the muses gather about this well, relying as they do on the source of all things, the liquid element, the preserver of life. Pegasus *is* that source, and produces the spring called Hippocrene, on Mt. Helicon, "the fountain of the horse."

We know this fountain as the fountain of the muses. It is the place the muses gather to sing and dance. In one account of the many stories concerning the muses, the muses sang with such rapture that at the sound of their singing everything stood still—sky, stars, sea and rivers. As the story goes, Mt. Helicon itself began, in its rapture to grow up to heaven, until the winged horse, Pegasus, on Poseidon's command, struck the mountain with his hooves, whereupon arose the fountain, "Hippocrene."

This account of the origination of the "fountain of the horse" would suggest a danger in the voices of the muses. "The muses divert the mind," Hesiod said. It is danger of rapture, of being transported by lofty emotion, a danger of losing ground. Imagination checks the danger of rapture by bringing Poseidon's own deep running water, the waters flowing underground from subterranean reserves.

Pegasus strikes the ground bringing

forth the well, acting on the command of Poseidon, looser of the passions. The appearance of Pegasus at the moment of rapture, breaking the spell, setting forth the life-giving stream, is an echo of an earlier action—Pegasus springing from the Medusa. Like the turbulent waters which father this image, Pegasus surges in, breaks apart, dispells. In the place of rapture, Pegasus provides a well-spring which is, for the muses, a place for dancing, music, and song, a playful activity which replenishes, regenerates, and restores.

(A playful interlude. One of the few buildings in downtown Dallas to have its own water well is the Magnolia Building, the structure which supports the Flying Red Horse. The well goes 1600 feet deep into the ground and provided water for the building for decades. It has been for many years one of the few sources of water in the city during a drought. During the severe drought of 1956, after Dallas had become a metropolitan city, people came from all over the area to draw from this pure spring.)

It is the hero Bellerophon who charms the wild Pegasus, lying in wait at Peirene, the fountain of Corinth, with the golden bridle, given to him by Athene. Bellerophon, after having longed for Pegasus and having tried in vain to tame the horse, seeks the advice of the seer of Corinth, Polyidus, who instructs him to sleep on the altar of Athene. Athene appears to Bellerophon and, giving him the golden bridle, instructs him to sacrifice a white bull to Poseidon before attempting to

subdue the flying horse. The taming of Pegasus is brought about through the workings of Athene, she who above all others is concerned with the city and the makings of culture. It was Athene who turned Medusa into the intolerable image after discovering the gorgon and Poseidon in the act of copulation in her temple, a sacrilege the goddess would not allow. Throughout the Pegasus myth, animal passions are transformed by Athene.

The hero is a difficult problem which becomes more and more complex in contemporary culture as we lose any memory we may have had of a divine order. The hero is an instrument of the gods. It is for this reason the hero comes so close to divinity; he/she reflects the order of the gods and does its bidding. The danger for the hero is identification with the heroic action. If the hero identifies with the heroic action, forgetting that he is a mere vehicle of the gods setting into motion the right order, he attempts to soar to the Heavens, thinking himself fit company for the gods. This was Bellerophon's fate. With the aid of Pegasus, he kills the Chimaera, dissipates the Amazons and destroys the Solymi. Drunk with success, Bellerophon loses all sense of proportion and attempts to fly with Pegasus to Heaven. Pegasus turns into an instrument of divine justice when he throws Bellerophon and continues his flight alone to Olympus. Bellerophon falls to earth and ends his days in misery.

Perhaps it is understandable why the

hero is suspect in contemporary times; it is expected that he will become victim to hubris and fall. The hero lives close to Death, is fated to fall. However, if we shy away from the hero, we run the risk of losing the play that exists between the hero and the beast.

In this myth, the hero Bellerophon acts through the divine counsel of Athene. Together Bellerophon and Pegasus overcome the Chimaera, a monster (cousin by birth to Pegasus) with the head and body of a lion, a snake's head emerging at its tail, and a goat's head growing from its back, who threatens to consume everything on Lycian soil. Pegasus, tamed by Athene's golden bridle, overcomes the fearful forces which resemble his own wild nature. It is this sublimated imagination which fights the Chimaera.

The language of myth echoes in our ears as we consider this city, Dallas. Itself founded in a region beyond the ocean—flat and dry—with no particular reason for its coming into being: water as a precious source, the value of a spring; a huge sky, room for soaring, the brandishing of gold, opportunity everywhere; heroic deeds, divinely inspired— a body of leaders building a city without regard for personal gain. Can we also see the danger ahead for a city which has enjoyed the free soaring of the high flying horse? Development runs rampant without regard for neighborhood; leadership giving way to management through system; cleanliness, order and security killing off natural, instinctual life; high rise cutting off street life. A

tension is required, the tension between the constant interplay between the heroic guided by imaginative action and the natural forces of the Chimaera. Pegasus, tamed by Athene's golden bridle, mediates between both—the hero and the ever present Chimaera.

# Quality of Life in Dallas

## *Gail Thomas*

To speak of the quality of life of a city is like speaking of the personality of an individual—the way body, heart, mind, soul, and spirit conjoin within an integrated pattern to reveal the essence of a particular person.

The history of this city's personality is the history of individuals—people who have lived and dreamed here and who have given in to the spirit which moves this place. Dallas manifests a spirit of drive, daring, and generosity.

Take the founding of SMU. Dr. Robert S. Hyer, who was to be SMU's first president, wanted the new Methodist University to be in Dallas. Hiram A. Boaz, who was president of Polytechnic College in Fort Worth wanted it there—to merge and give prestige to his fledgling school. Dallas citizens went to work, knowing what an important institution of higher learning would mean for the city. Will Caruth and others gave 662 acres of prime North Dallas land, and it was settled. Fort Worth had not acted quickly enough and could not make as generous an offer. SMU would be in Dallas!

When the State Fair of Texas was opened in 1886, Mrs. Sidney Smith, wife of the director of the Fair, was in charge of the "ladies department" and insisted that "art" should be displayed. The Dallas Art Association was an outgrowth of this first exhibit. It was ultimately the vision of Mrs. George K. Meyer, who for many years was the inspiration and working force of the Dallas Art Museum. She selected the paintings herself, hung them, and cajoled people into coming to look at them.

What about the city library? At the turn of the century, Mrs. Henry Exall formed the Dallas Federation of Women's Clubs in order to have a group to solicit Andrew Carnegie for funds for a library. Carnegie gave $50,000; the people of Dallas matched it with $50,000—and the Dallas Public Library was begun, opened in 1901.

Intellectual life has had a difficult time in Dallas where entrepreneurism and speculation have, since its founding, seemed more alluring than a quieter, more reflective life; but it was helped in the twenties by Elmer Scott, who formed the Civic Federation as a catalyst for community action. He brought in speakers from all over the world and established an open forum. The Civic Federation met in the upstairs auditorium of City Hall every Sunday afternoon and was open to the public.

Dallas Little Theater was formed after World War I during the heyday of small repertory theaters. It won the Belasco Cup several times. The Margo Jones Theater appeared in the forties and the Dallas Theater Center in the fifties brought the dramatic arts fully into the life of the community.

But quality of life is more than art and education; it is the physical configuration, the habits and mores, the rituals and ceremonies of the city. All of these bits and pieces form the personality of the city.

I am going to use this way of imagining the city as a means of addressing the quality of life within it; so, I will briefly consider the body, mind, soul, and spirit of Dallas.

First, body. Let us look at our city's body. How are we contained? How are we housed? How is our city adorned? These questions move us to consider Dallas' geographic configuration, our neighborhoods, downtown core, freeways, airport, public buildings, historic buildings.

Dallas was built on the Trinity River. It will never be navigable, it will never serve as a port, but it could be utilized to serve a more basic need. The need for water is archetypal—universally true for humankind throughout the ages. We have a need to be near water, to look at it, to put our hands and feet in it. Its presence calms the soul, stimulates dreams, and assures a sense of permanence and abundance. Every truly great city has had access to a body of water.

Other geographic considerations ask us to look at how our city is growing. We continue to develop industry in North Dallas. Is this perhaps shortsighted when we consider the quality of life of the entire city? Quality of life for whom? The citizens in the south and west sectors, seeking work, must rely on insufficient transportation to carry them to jobs. And those in North Dallas complain because of the traffic and congestion that prevent them from freedom of movement. We need to recognize what may be an unconscious reluctance to cross the Trinity River. Perhaps if the Trinity were a lake, inviting commercial, residential, and leisure development, this bias would disappear naturally. It seems to me that industry must be encouraged in South and West Dallas.

We are all now dedicated to a vital downtown core. We have seen what has happened to American cities which sprawl out toward one another in formless, cluttered growth. The term "urban sprawl" has, since the sixties, come to be synonymous with American cities. Suburban developments, mindless of the needs of neighborhood communities, continue to spread outward from the city, each demanding another concrete shopping mall, more churches, more schools, more city services, and more police protection against crime, which arises when people exist together without roots, memory, faith, and commitment. The downtown core is the heart of the city —its center—the vital, throbbing organ which nourishes life throughout its complex body. We are beginning to see that we must have urban housing to have a vital downtown. If we want restaurants, theaters, museums, art galleries, small shops, small parks, and most of all *people* downtown—all those ingredients which define vitality or life—then we must have people *living* in the heart of the city.

What about historic buildings? Our historic buildings are going down at breakneck speed. There are only forty historic buildings left in the downtown sector. Since the Baker Hotel fell, we have lost eleven—eleven in a year and a half! Why are they important to our quality of life? A building is the visible statement of our civilization—the reflection of our culture. Each age is preserved in stone, brick, or glass as a gathered construction of who we are as a people—of that of which our values consist. We know the technology, the theology, and the mythology of the Egyptians by their pyramids; we know medieval culture through Romanesque cathedrals, the Renaissance through Gothic. Dallas doesn't have these ancient architectural splendors, but it does have Victorian and Prairie style houses that reflect the style and condition of the soul of the people

who founded our city. It has a few grand brownstones, built with the dignity, security, and will of those first leaders of industry here and adorned with ornamentation which houses imagination and invites memory of our past. People cannot survive without memory. Without memory, we cannot leave our homes in the morning because we would not be able to return in the evening. Memory *allows* us to move, to grow, to develop because it is there reminding us constantly of who we are and of where we have been. What is it in us that suffers when the Trinity Methodist Church burns, when the Kress Building is defaced in the middle of the night, or when the Festival Theater receives the wrecking ball while we are at church on Sunday morning? Our soul suffers —the soul of the city suffers—because we have lost our memory.

Historic buildings should be regarded as civic treasures, our crown jewels—the way we revere the memory of the great leaders of this city whose spirit and drive provided the opportunities we now enjoy.

Speaking of this city's great leaders, there is a story about Erik Jonsson which we must all remember when we consider the body of this city. The story is that when Mr. Jonsson was mayor, he visited several of the magnificent cities of Europe to determine the essential ingredients required to prepare Dallas for its role as a great city. He realized that a prerequisite for excellence demands a public agora housing the public buildings of the city and a great park. He came back to Dallas and initiated plans for a new monumental City Hall with a public square, facing a grand city library; in another vision, lacking a seaport, he insisted on the construction of DFW Airport. Today, when guests come to our city, land at DFW, we take them with great pride to visit the city hall, Erik Jonsson's vision, I. M. Pei's art; the people of Dallas' conviction in its future.

Now, let's move from the body of the city to the mind of the city. If quality of life encompasses the total configuration of a body, mind, soul, and spirit, we must address the instructed principle of the personality— the mind. Quality of mind depends upon inherited capabilities and upon education. We can love this city passionately and remain blind to its deficiencies in education, but we cannot be responsible for it and do the same. Many of the future generations of Dallas are graduating from high school unable to read and write, unable to speak in sentences, unable to compute, and unwilling to be responsible citizens. The leadership of the city has responded to the needs of education, the corporate sector has pumped resources and expertise in the system through the "Adopt a School" program, but the fact still remains that Dallas has a long way to go to claim excellence in its public schools. The Dallas Institute brought Mortimer Adler to Dallas for a seminar, "Recess

is Over: The Crisis in Public Education," and, as a result of that seminar, brought him back again to work with DISD—actually teaching students in the classroom. Dr. Adler has dedicated the rest of his life to re-visioning public education and has been going about the country, working with students, and with teachers, inspiring students to learn and encouraging teachers to teach. Mortimer Adler reported to me his experiences in other cities. To my dismay, he said the Dallas experience was the worst; the students were unable to reason clearly and speak coherently. "It's not the students' fault," he said. "They have been badly schooled." If we are concerned with the quality of life in the city, we must pay attention to *what* our students are being taught and under what conditions they are expected to learn. We have been wrong to adhere to the utopian notion that teaching and learning can be made easy and rapid. Teaching is not a science—it is an art, and teachers must be encouraged to practice their art. It isn't possible in a given day when a student's time is filled with bus rides, recess, announcements, sports, and vocational training. And when a teacher's time is demanded for reports, psychological studies, evaluations, conferences, and meetings. Dallas has the needed prerequisites for an excellent educational system—a dedicated, knowledgeable, hard-working superintendent and a capable staff; excellent buildings and equipment; tax dollars to support it. We must encourage the art of teaching and *support* our Dallas teachers instead of allowing them to be wooed into industry for higher salaries. Finally, we must pay attention. *Care* is expressed by attention. The leaders of this city—the citizens who are responsible for its well being —must pay attention.

What about the soul of the city? Soul, of course, seeks depth and meaning and brings value, dimension, and differentiation. Soul can be found in the everyday things of the city—in fact, it is precisely the difference in the quality of a city. Soul is the very thing that is quality. When we say quality of life, do we not mean depth, value, meaningfulness, richness, diversity, choice—knowing what one desires and being able to pursue it? Soul allows for all of this. We call it "being true to one's inner self—being real." This same quality can be present in cities. Buildings have this quality. We know it when we look at a building or when we are in it. Intimate spaces, parks, public buildings, offices, or churches have this quality. It does not always come with being secure—perhaps the opposite. Like being lost in the labyrinthian maze at The Quadrangle. The diversity, the mystery in a place which gathers the Texas landscape has true quality and feels right when we are in it.

The soul of the city is reflected also in its tolerance for and support of the arts. The arts carry a transforming power, reminding us of another order which exists within us—an order having to do with form and beauty. It is an order which cannot be measured or evaluated for productivity or efficiency, but must be supported for its own sake.

Dallas, with its pioneer spirit, does not come easily to support of the arts or to an intellectual life, but a transformation is beginning. The symbolic gesture of building the Dallas Art Museum in the center of the city is evidence to it, as is the concentration now on the assurance of an Arts District, which should become what Philip Montgomery calls "a great river of life" for our downtown. Add to that river of life our new symphony hall, art galleries, small shops for crafts, places which would house poets and artists, and we do have the possibility for a renaissance of a cultural life downtown.

Dallas is changing more rapidly than we can absorb. With what seems to be all of the world moving into Dallas, it is essential that the leaders of this city prepare now for the amenities which lead to a fruitful and satisfying life for its citizens.

This brings us to the spirit of the city. It seems to me that the spirit of this city is in its leadership. More than any other city I know, Dallas has been blessed with powerful leaders who have taken the good of the city to heart and whose spirit has seen ideas into action. I have been greatly influenced by a newspaper interview several years ago with Erik Jonsson.

He stated in that article that what
Dallas needs is leaders who lead from
the heart. In my way of seeing things,
there is a great difference between a
leader and a manager, and I feel the
difference lies in the region of the
heart. A leader stands for what he or
she believes, stands under it, which is
what is meant to "understand." A
person who understands his or her
own convictions—stands under them,
upholds them—is willing to act in
their behalf, willing to take the consequences for those actions. A person
can be a good manager, can work
toward a more efficient system, but
not necessarily be guided by the heart.
In the final analysis, it is what is in the
heart of the leaders of this city that
will be built into the architecture of its
buildings, that will appear in its Arts
District, in its solution to transportation problems. It is what is in the
heart of the leaders of this city that
becomes the energy by which Dallas is
fueled. What do we hold most dear?
What forms of life do we cherish?
What basic values and traditions do
we feel we must preserve? The quality
of life in Dallas which we now enjoy
reflects what has been in the hearts of
our past leaders. The quality of life of
the Dallas of Tomorrow depends upon
the heart of Dallas' leaders today.

# What Makes Dallas
# a Different City

*A. C. Greene*

Most city definitions we hear are European; certainly our desiderata are European. Notice how often the description of the "good" city is European.

Or, just as often, a comparison involves New York . . . what was done in New York, what succeeded in New York or didn't succeed in New York, what New York planned or executed.

New York is *not* an American city. New York is a *European* city. Its public is a European public, not by birth but by influence. . . .

Dallas, on the other hand, is the quintessential American city. Not just in its cultural outlook, but in its problems and its solutions to problems of cityhood. . . .

The Dallas center of urban unity is the job or the lobby of the convention hotel. Who are our friends? Our fellow workers. What do we talk about? We talk office gossip and office politics. Yet, we in Dallas have an ambiguous relationship with our job—we like to leave it, literally, and go home.

Even if leaving it and going home involves miles and hours of driving or riding. We don't really *like* to live close to where we work.

The strolling, walking, casual city vision does not operate in Dallas. There is no street tradition to Dallas or to most modern American cities. Dallas has no street life as such. . . .

A Dallas viewer is constrained to point out that it is against the law in Dallas to put out sales displays on the sidewalk, to pass out handbills, to sell fresh food from carts—to sell anything on the streets—to play games in the streets, to sleep in public or loiter on street corners. Dallas is a cautious city; the first time a kite fell, Dallas would have banned aviation.

The automobile has outmoded the street tradition in most of America —certainly in Dallas. There is no open marketplace; there is no park or public plaza if the automobile has demanded that space. The shopping center (the enclosed mall which was pioneered in Dallas) is the American equivalent of the Ponte Vecchio, the Amsterdam market, or the Athenian agora. And as for pedestrian rights—look how we all hate joggers!

The modern American city is a machine which, like all except Rube Goldberg machines, is *more* than the sum of its parts. *People* are its parts—but so are freeways, office towers, parking lots, sewers, zoning ordinances, and sidewalks. . . .

Dallas is a challenging kind of machine, not because it is superior, but because it is at present working better than most other American city machines. . . . The problems of Dallas are problems of attitude, not design or planning. Sometimes Dallas seems afraid of its own human beings. . . .

But the foremost requirements of a modern American city have nothing to do with beauty or urban satisfaction. It is to offer opportunity. Professionals and artists, working alone or in ambient surroundings, may not understand this. Executives and would-be executives do. Unemployed auto workers from Detroit do. *Nothing makes up for lack of opportunity.* . . .

Dallas, do not forget, was *created*, purely and simply. It has no harbor, no river, no natural resource or agricultural pool to draw cityhood from. It sprang from people's minds, yet it never thinks of itself as a people center. A commercial center, yes. No other commodity gets the disregard people get in Dallas. . . .

The artist, the dreamer, the planner —begone. We want doers. And doers don't have time—or the inclination— to look around, to sit down, to stare off into space. The bottom line of Dallas' concern is production. Dallas leadership, also, has not shown a high degree of imagination or a capacity for worldly intelligence. . . .

There is no grace to Dallas city life. You earn your salvation, and civic religion is plain and unadorned—comfortable is a sinful word unless you have earned it, either by your effort or your profession of belief.

If this no-fun attitude isn't bending, at least we in Dallas are making dents. Asking questions about the city is a dent. . . . Dallas street life may not be developed, but it can't keep from being encouraged.

# Street Life

If architecture is the language of the city, freeways the arteries, the city center the heart, the vision and construction the spirit, then the streets reveal the soul of the city.

The street is the commons for the modern city—a ceremonial meeting ground where actions both sacred and profane carry on the ritual life of its inhabitants. The street is also the passageway from one place to another, so that it is both "place" and "path." We tend to forget that the street is a "place" with the possibility that something important can happen there if one takes time and pays attention, because in most modern towns and cities the street has been given over to the automobile. The automobile has encroached as well upon the experience of the street as "path," because "path" implies walking and evokes fantasies of discovery. St. Catherine of Sienna intrigued us by saying, "Heaven is 'all the way to Heaven.'" We say simply, "getting there is all the fun!" Cities are beginning to rediscover their streets and in so doing are allowing the animal life (the animation) of the city to return.

There are many "places" in a city but none with the quality of the street. The street, as commons, belongs to everyone; it is public domain; everyone is welcome there. But, there are laws of the street, a decorum which is observed as part of the memory and tradition of the city. One must always make way for the other, for example, except on the street corner where a group can gather to talk and others must walk around. While common courtesy is expected and almost always observed, the street also invites the unexpected. It is understood in the laws of the street that hawkers can sell their wares and "preachers" can shout their beliefs. At certain times of the day, the laws of the street allow performers to entertain—impromptu musicians, mimes, street tap-dancers or break dancers. What city planners are now re-discovering is that the more spontaneity on the street, the healthier and safer the street becomes. What previously has been considered "loss of control" of the street now is being seen as "lively street life." We are learning that what we had feared in the unexpected as chaotic brings new life-giving forms into the city. If we allow it, this precious quality will come to us without financial requirements, without the burden of planning, without institutional structures to issue invitation; it will come from the unexpected on our lowly city streets.

Like the streets themselves, the following essays invite the unexpected—points of view which tickle the imagination and make one eager to take a walk and have a look.

*Gail Thomas*

# The Life of the Street

## *William H. Whyte*

I am going to talk about the physical street—the experience of the street. My general argument is that many of the things which vex us about a street are inextricably bound up with its great attractions. There is no such thing physically as the ideal street. I would like to talk about what a street might be like, to take a few steps in that direction. First, the physical street. It is interesting how much work has been done attempting to determine the ideal width of the sidewalk. I've always been interested in this because in my own experience, most statistical studies of streets by planners come up with dimensions that are quite wrong, and I have wondered why. Let me make a stab at it. I feel very much at home here in Dallas because your sidewalks are too narrow—about thirteen and a half feet—manifestly impossible, and yet it all seems to work out.

Most of the studies about the pedestrian flow want to find out how long it takes the pedestrian to get from point A to point B—what is the ideal width, the number of people per walkway width. Putting various things together, they come up with an ideal width of thirty-one or thirty-two feet. Many quite large spaces have been designed because of these statistical formulae. If we try to isolate where these studies go wrong, I think we can learn something about the street. Most of these studies are concerned with pedestrian flow at rush hour. To maximize that kind of flow, you need gigantic amounts of space. The problem is, as we have found in our own studies, a lot of people never get to point B— they do not go from A to B. They go part way, stop, may come back. There are also people who just stand there. A great deal of what we think of as congestion is self-congestion. If we miss this very vital point, we miss the essence of a great street. . . .

People like to be in the mainstream. If you have to err between a street that is too wide and one that is too narrow, always choose the one that is too narrow. People adapt to a width. If I had to pick a figure out for the ideal width of a street, I would say that a minimum width would be fifteen feet—a maximum of twenty-five feet. This flies in the face of all logic, but it is extraordinary how people adapt and love the feeling of congestion. . . .

Far more interesting components of the street are the human beings that make up the congestion on it. I want to talk a little bit about the skilled pedestrian. If there is anything wrong with the typical downtown, it is that the spaces are too big. . . . The skilled pedestrian wants lots of people; there is no fun in the game unless there are lots of people. We have done a lot of instant replays of pedestrian maneuvers . . . the skilled pedestrian in a great city is a fast pedestrian—around 300 feet per minute. People in big cities walk faster than people in small cities. Why is this so? Usually, the explanation for the New Yorker is sensory overload. The place is so horrible that you walk fast to get relief from it. I think you can just as easily argue for the opposite. I get the very strong feeling that pedestrians rather enjoy this —it becomes a kind of game; it is exhilarating. . . . Most of our sense of overcrowding comes from a relatively few choke places. In New York City, it is the subway stations with their extremely pitched steps. You get a claustrophobic feeling there—you are no longer in control of your environment.

Let me take a moment to consider the concourse. I know that you plan to extend quite considerably your concourse system here in Dallas. The question I am posing is why? There is a good argument to be made for an underground concourse or for an overhead walkway when you have a great

number of people who really do want to get from point A to point B. Where I would raise a question is if you take the next step and say that you are going to create an underground environment as well—then you have some real questions to ask yourself. Much more time should be spent by those interested in concourses in going to concourses. What you find is:

1. Most underground concourses have a poor climate; it is too hot to wear an overcoat and too cold to be without it.

2. More important, an underground environment is very disorienting; the wonderful thing about ground level is that you know where you are, there are familiar landmarks.

3. The shops that spring up in concourses are mostly junk shops. . . .

To return now to the street, the street is a very sensory experience. I became interested in this because my office is on Sixty-First Street, right off Lexington. Those of you who know that area know that it is very tacky. The sidewalk is a little over fourteen feet in width, and there is a subway entrance in the middle of it, as well as a newsstand. It is so bad that you like it. One of the things that we found is people gather at the most crowded part of this area. At peak time, 3500 people use that part of the street per hour. There is an essential rhythm there, though. And there are wonderful street shops as well as second-story shops. It is just the opposite of the pedestrian flow pattern of the suburban shopping mall. A shopping mall that has two levels has very broad walkways—thirty to forty feet. Lexington and Madison Avenues pack two and three levels of shopping on one walkway. And for some reason, it seems to work. I think that there are some real cues for the design of streets. A good street is a very physical experience. There are all sorts of interactions between people. . . .

A street has life when it is interested in you. It wants your money for one thing—it will thrust a handbill at you; it will beg you for money; it will talk to you; it will waft smells at you; it will ring bells at you; it will whistle at you.

As we get to know a street, we possess it. As we get to recognize its rhythm, get familiar with it, its recurrent patterns, as we learn the idiosyncracies, we get a wonderful feeling of control. The street becomes a little kingdom, highly satisfying—and it is ours for the walking.

# The American Street

## *Robert A.M. Stern*

• It is imperative that we recapture the streets—make them a place where we all like to be. Otherwise, we are prisoners in our cars, in our houses, and in our private shopping centers. We are not really enjoying the rights we have as Americans if we fail to enjoy the public street.

• In the nineteenth century, it was not an issue. People thought of the public street as a place where one had to behave—to use decorum. The first time it became an issue in the nineteenth century was when a demarked area was created away from the city, even though within its boundaries, and was slightly divorced from daily life. That was Central Park, and if you recall Olmstead's park in New York, you know he was obsessed with the behavior of the people in the park. He wrote a code book with "Thou shalt nots" about forty pages long. He understood that the public street was a threat, and that if you pulled it away into a private realm, people would feel freer to behave any

way they wanted, and therefore, rules were necessary.

• The city street is the only place that has been devised where people feel more or less responsible for the behavior in the public realm. The shops on the side of the city streets monitor that street. The presence of people in the shops or in the buildings above coming to windows and catching you dropping your garbage on the street, monitor your behavior.

• This idea in sociological terms was advanced by Jane Jacobs twenty years ago. She started a revolution in city planning to go back to old modes of thinking, but it has been very, very slow to be absorbed into the general way of doing things.

• In the nineteenth century, people built their own individual houses. Today we buy our houses, with predigested messages being presented to us. When people in the last century built their houses, they usually paid attention to two themes of major obligation: one, to shelter their family in the most modern way with the latest plumbing and the most labor saving devices; two, to make the building a proper statement of the family as an important contributor to the community of the city street and of the neighborhood. Houses, all through the nineteenth century, were temples to the family and temples to the town at the same time. The front porch was a preparatory experience, a mediation between the private world of the house and the public world. And you put your best foot forward when you designed the front of that house. You make it say special things about the continuity of the street and about how your family was to be perceived.

• The essence of democracy is that each person has some responsibility to the whole, some civility.

• All the early towns of America maintained a degree of decorum with respect to the street. The street is the single most important public realm. These early towns also understood perfectly well that the role of a public building was to elevate a mundane activity to a public ritual.

• The street is the only public concourse in America, the only forum. It is *not* the mall or the plaza, which are private places. Any individual owner can throw you out of Northpark or the Galleria if they do not like what you are doing, if they do not like your clothes, or if they do not want you handing out pamphlets.

• We hate the public realm of the city streets because they are dirty, there are strange people on them, undesirables sleep in them. It is a fact that we would rather belong to a private club, a place where there are people like ourselves.

• We have lost the sense of the street as the place for the public to be in, and the obligation of the individual builder along that street to do something for the street, to enhance his own ego and to make a gift to the public realm—to be a merchant prince. Why don't we hear of merchant princes anymore? We just hear of people who do leveraged buy-outs. What happened to merchant princes?

# Improvisation
# and the Creative Process

## Albert Murray

In a sense, my topic which is improvisation and the creative process adds up to what the conference should add up to. The conference has not come up with blueprints or prescriptions. It has come up with ideas. I am going to talk about the nature of the creative process; about improvisation, which has to do with how you do what you have to do—how to hang loose and get the maximum. And in order to do that you have to know everything that has to do with what in jazz is called "the break"; and that is what improvisation has to do with.

First, a note or so toward a basic definition, or in any case a notion which serves as a basic guideline for my own procedure as an apprentice to the aesthetic image in general and to literature in particular. Art is the ultimate extension, elaboration, and refinement of the rituals that reenact the primary survival technology; and hence, basic attitudes toward experience of a given people in a given time, place, circumstance, and predicament.

It is, I submit, the process of extension, elaboration, and refinement that creates the work of art. It is precisely play that is indispensible to the creative process. I am so glad that we say "you are going to *play* music." You don't *engineer* it or *work* at it. The word "play" has lost its true meaning. As I am using it here, I want it to be the full meaning of the word "play" as it resides at the very center of all culture, and certainly therefore at the center of art. Play in the sense of competition or contest; play in the sense of chance-taking or gambling; play in the sense of make-believe; play also in the sense of vertigo, or getting high, or inducing exhilaration; play also in the direction of simple amusement or entertainment—as in children's games; and play in the direction of gratuitous difficulty—as in increasing the number of jacks one catches or the height or distance one jumps, or decreasing the time one runs a given course; gratuitous difficulty also in the sense of word play; or play in the sense of sound—as in a Bach fugue. I submit that such play or playing around is precisely what is involved in the process Andre Malraux is referring to when he suggests that art is the means by which forms or raw experience are transformed or rendered into style.

This brings us to stylization. To stylize is to conventionalize. It is to create a pattern which becomes a way of seeing things and doing things. Convention can function both as the container and the thing contained. It provides the structure as well as the content of human consciousness. It is the quality of human consciousness that is the most profound concern of art. What art provides is the most fundamental human equipment for existence. It provides images, representative anecdotes, emblems that condition us to confront what we must confront, and it disposes us to do what we must do; not only to fulfill ourselves but also to survive as human beings in a given place, time, circumstance, and predicament. . . .

So play becomes convention and convention is a pattern of procedure. The convention of playful option-taking is what I call "the blues idiom" and jazz music. I define the jazz musician as one who approaches or creates or plays all music as if improvising the "break" on the traditional twelve bar blues tune. Which brings me not only to improvisation and the creative process but also to blues idiom procedure and the "jam session" as the representative anecdote for life in the United States. By improvisation, of course, I most definitely do not mean "winging it" or making things up out of thin air. The jazz musician improvises within a very specific context and in terms of very specific idiomatic devices of composition. I want to mention several of these devices.

First, there is the "vamp," which is an improvised introduction. This is not unique to blues idiom statement, but it is used in a special idiomatic way by the jazz musician. The jazz composition is also made up of a series of "choruses" which function like stanzas in a poem. . . . Another device for blues idiom statement is the "break," which is a disruption of the normal cadence of a piece of music. The "break" is a device which is used quite often and always has to do with the framework in which improvisation takes place. . . . The break is an extremely important device both from the structural point of view and from its implications. It is precisely this disjuncture which is the moment of truth. It is on the break that you "do your thing." The moment of greatest jeopardy is your moment of greatest opportunity. This is the heroic moment. . . . It is when you establish your identity; it is when you write your signature on the epidermis of actuality. That is how you come to terms with the void. . . .

This kind of improvisation is applicable to educational methods, to scientific method, to inventions. Your knowledge of chordal structure and progression is your knowledge of the experience data of mankind; it is all the wisdom and mistakes of the ages. That is what you "riff" on or improvise on. . . .

The most inventive, the most innovative jazz musician is also one with a very rich apperceptive mass or base, a very rich storehouse of tunes, phrases, ditties which he uses as a painter uses his awareness of other paintings, as a writer employs his literary background to give his statements richer resonances. As a matter of fact, the musician is always engaged in a dialogue or a conversation or even argument—not only, as in a jam session, with his peers—but also with all other music and musicians in the world at large. Indeed, his is an ongoing dialogue with the form itself. He achieves his individuality by saying "yes and also" to that with which he agrees, and by saying "no," or in any case, "on the other hand" to that with which he disagrees. . . . Yes, all of this is as applicable to science and engineering and political procedure as it is to music and literature and all of the other arts.

There is also the very fundamental matter of the "railroad onomatopoeia" that was established by the folk blues guitar and harmonica players—such as Leadbelly, or Robert Johnson. . . .

There is also that matter of the African derived "talking drum." The blues is percussive statement. It is the talking drum that has become the old,

down home American locomotive with its chugging pistons, its ambiguous and ambivalent bell, and its signifying, insinuating, tall tale-telling whistle. The definitive characteristic of Afro-American life style is its tendency to define all movement, indeed all human activity, in the direction of dance beat elegance.

Such is the special nature of the musical convention that I call the blues idiom. This is fine art. The fact that all this is done not in the simple matter of producing music which is simply programmatic, but is consummate skill at producing instantaneous response to life and a matter of improvising, or making up your life or of being perpetually creative as you live your life is what makes this important in thinking about the city.

Improvisation as it functions in the blues idiom is something that not only conditions people to cope with disjuncture and change but also provides them with a basic survival technique that is commensurate with and suitable to the rootlessness and the discontinuity so characteristic of human existence in the contemporary world. . . . However such improvisation proceeds, when it succeeds it puts you on good terms with life. It generates an atmosphere of well-being and celebration. It is music to have a good time with.

# The Blank Wall

## *William H. Whyte*

I have been doing a good deal of traveling the last two years, particularly in the smaller and medium size cities of the country. And it began to dawn on me that there is one recurring scene; and that what seems to be on its way to becoming the dominant feature of the American city landscape is the blank wall. So, I have been studying these and I am going to present to you what, as far as I am concerned, is a definitive study of the blank wall. I will stress the different types, the different materials they are made of, their effect, and so forth. But I want to make one thing very plain at the beginning; the kind of blank wall that I am talking about is not the inadvertent blank wall—the kind such as up on Main Street, that is uncovered by another building going down; the kind that are wonderful for having scenes and what-have-you painted on them. The blank wall I am talking about was meant to be blank from the very beginning, and it has a message for you. It makes a statement about the city and the kind of people you are apt to find on the street.

The blank wall comes in all shapes and forms. Two of the biggest are in New York City: the Fashion Institute of Technology and the AT&T building. Now, if we consider the antecedents of the blank wall, the suburban shopping center is an important model. But there, the blank wall is functional. They need that space for merchandising. They do not need display windows as you need in the city because the patron of the shopping mall has already made up his mind to go inside as soon as he drives in the parking lot. What is interesting, however, is the transplantation of the blank wall form to the city where there *are* passers-by and where there needs to be windows and merchandise within them. . . .

Garages. One of the great differences between the in-town shopping center and the outside shopping mall is the difference in parking. Instead of being spread out all over great sheets of asphalt it is concentrated in garages. Incidentally, I find that a lot of people think they are boring. I think they are visually more interesting than the complexes they serve. They have all sorts of intriguing angles. If you are going to have a garage, let it look like a garage; don't cover it with a blank wall. In a few cities they have adopted the revolutionary idea of actually having stores at street level in these garages, as for example, in San Francisco—or a movie house, as in Portland, Maine. . . .

The convention center is another major contributor to the blank wall. You have a fine one here in Dallas. The orientation is inside, renouncing street life. The day I was there, I went inside and there were 3,000 doctors—3,000, count them, and not a soul to be seen outside. . . . And the same is going on with hotels which are more and more going into convention wings; so you have the blank wall of the Seattle Sheraton, the Hilton in Toronto, the same in Kansas City.

I had to go to a two-day meeting in Seattle on the design of their new convention center. They wanted something that would be an asset to the city, that would look nice, one you could see into and see out of it. And the convention experts—there were seventeen of them, by the way, and to a man they said, "No, it won't work. What you have to have is a great big black box with a lot of parking places for the buses that will take people to the hotels." The people in Seattle said, "But we are going to put our convention center over the freeway right in the middle of town so you won't need the buses to park." However, we were assured that the only thing that would work is not only a big black

box, it must be completely sealed—almost an airlock—so that the natives can't get in, only people with convention badges. If you listen to some of these experts you get the feeling that they would just as soon throw away the key and lock everybody in for the duration.

Now, in Baltimore, they have done the impossible. Their convention center has a lot of glass. You can look out and see Baltimore, and Baltimore can see in. It is a part of downtown and it is right next to Harbourplace. And, quite remarkably, you can enter in there without a convention badge. Just wander right in off the streets and it is perfectly all right. Needless to say, the airlock comes in later when you try to get into the exhibits. And the thing is a great success; and people walk to it. It is extraordinary; they walk to it!

In Toronto, they came up with a model for a new convention center: big box, and completely sealed off at street level. There was a huge hubbub, civic hubbub, and you won't be surprised to hear that Jack Diamond was a part of that. They said that this isn't right; this isn't good enough for Toronto. We are a better city than that. The center was redesigned; complete 100 percent retailing at street level.

Institutions. Institutions have a natural affinity for the blank wall. There is a message here; they are plainly *meant* to intimidate you, or at least to show you the inconsequence

195

of the individual and the power of the institution. The new FBI headquarters makes you guilty just standing there looking at it. And in Boston, the Federal Reserve. The worst new government buildings going up are Federal Reserve buildings in most of our big cities. And the telephone company. In a number of cities they put up new buildings without windows. And, incidentally, when you ask the architects and builders why the walls are blank, you are always told that there is a lot of technical computer equipment in there. But often it seems that the closing off of the windows is something of an end in itself.

The megastructure. Now the definitive, the ultimate expression of the blank wall is the megastructure. These are fortresses to seal you off against the city. The rationale for them goes something like this: So they look like fortresses; they were meant to look like fortresses. You've got to be realists. The only way we can get the middle class back from suburbia into the city is to offer them protection from the city. Those of you that know Houston's center know that you can drive in from suburbia in the morning, into the garage that is part of it. Then there is an upper level walkway; in fact, quite a system of walkways to insulate you from the street. You walk in there, you can spend a day; you can eat, shop, do anything you want. And you leave and go back home without ever having to step into Houston at all. And

the Bonaventure in Atlanta. Many stories of blank wall; quite an achievement in megastructures.

Just imagine that one city decided it would go whole hog and we would have all of these things in one city. I would ask you to think of what would happen to Dallas were it to follow certain trends it is now pursuing and took them to their ultimate conclusion, as they have in Albuquerque. . . .

Now one of my favorite streets is Lexington Avenue in New York. It is the opposite of everything I have been saying. It is smelly. It is crowded. People jostle you. But, my goodness—it has life to it. It has life! And I have been interested in Madison Avenue —upper Madison Avenue which is a great shopping street. Very chic, very expensive; and yet if you actually look at it closely it is a very tacky looking thing in many ways. It is composed basically of a row of five-story brownstones, ten to a block, with a twenty-foot frontage. Because space is so dear, they use the second floor either for displays, or what not; and they are always trying to get your attention and interest. My point is not that we recreate a bunch of old brownstones, but in our new construction I think that we can get some of these timeless sorts of appeals. . . . The street is really where so many things go on; and a great street is a sensory experience. And in those cities which really like their streets, they work with them. There you will find they have open fronts, plenty of window shopping, flowers, food, and plenty of people.

We have been talking about the relationship of economics and taste. Someone has pointed out that taste is social. And here I think is why we can understand the very bad economics of anti-city cities. They are bad economics because they are in bad taste. They are in bad taste because they repudiate the humanness and the mixture and the vitality that are at the heart of the city. Rediscover your streets.

# The Sunny Side of the Street

## *William H. Whyte*

I am going to talk about sun and light—sun and light in the city. My premise is that it is a good thing—sun. It gives us light. It gives us warmth. We use it to get energy. We tell time by it. And best of all, it is free. What we do in cities with this wonderful substance is a very iron test of the real dynamism, the capacity of imagination of the city. . . .

I am going to start with a story about Paley Park in New York City. This is one of the most significant open spaces in the country. It is a very small space—exactly 42 by 100 feet. It has one of the highest ratios of use of any place I have ever studied. On an ordinary day there, a nice day at lunch time, you'll find about 180 people in there. It is a perfectly wonderful place. It is a veritable sort of sun theater. So it was for quite some time. Many people, thinking how valuable that sun was, said that the Paley Foundation should buy the five-story building across the street—to make sure a large structure would not be built there, blocking the sun. But it was not necessary then because everybody knew the city was dead set against building high buildings in mid-

blocks. Only on the avenues; you could go up high there, but not in the mid-blocks.

Then one day we heard about a new building that was going to go up. And by this time we were deep into incentive zoning. . . . This building was higher than ordinary because one of the incentive bonuses was that height could be exchanged for through-block arcades. Now, most of the time, Paley Park is no longer in the sun. Almost overnight, it lost a good bit of its sun, and it has lost more since then. This place is such a wonderful place, it is still well used. . . .

Now, not all is bleak. One of the themes I am going to pick up is that even a little bit of sun can be very very precious. One of the sources for Paley Park is a large building two blocks away, which bounces a fair amount of light against the west wall of Paley Park. . . .

I want to tell of another place—Greenacre Park, which was inspired by Paley Park. It is larger than Paley—60 by 100 feet—and it has a little raised terrace to catch the sun. . . . Several years after the park was completed, we heard about a new building going up two blocks away on Third Avenue, called 805 Third Avenue, and it kept getting bigger and bigger as they figured out all kinds of incentive bonuses. I began to worry that this building was going to shadow Greenacre Park. So we started to do some sun studies. It became very apparent that starting about two o'clock in the afternoon, the building would obscure the sun from the park. In total, it would take only about twenty-four minutes of sun. But it was the most crucial time. We were ridiculed on this, but we thought we had an important case. . . . Well, we got them to cut three floors off the building . . . and now, we have to protect the park from further obstructions. . . .

Now, let's go to Dallas. First, I have to address a point that a number of people tell me. They say Dallas is different—this sun stuff and all this light is not for Dallas. The weather is terrible in July and August. Well, one way you can deal with the sun is to keep the people off the streets. But you can see from these pictures that the underground concourses do not work very well. . . .

You have a place here where some people say there is too much sun— City Hall Plaza. It is a very large plaza, almost twice as large as Saint Mark's Plaza. It is a huge place. On a hot day, it is really hot there. One of the things I was struck by was the seating. It was the worst seating on any public plaza that I have seen

anywhere. It is concrete and not very comfortable. And the placement is very bad. There is no relationship between the shade of the trees and the benches. Exactly three benches are in the shade. . . . The movable chairs and tables are helping enormously, though there is still a way to go. . . .

There is talk that the Post Office might well have a structure built above it. Now is the time to really start inquiring. What would this do to the sun? If it is a tower, where might it go? What is its orientation? Things done now could prevent so much grief later. . . .

The Sculpture Garden at the Museum is turning into a very fine place with a series of quite large open places. It is surely a place that should have sun. But there is a problem. On the left side of Saint Paul Street, a rather large development is due to go up. The base of this new building may be large enough to cast a shadow on the Sculpture Garden. Some important questions need to be asked here. I am not positive, but from two to four in the afternoon, the sun may be obscured by the base of the new buildings—and that is not even figuring in the towers. There is an opportunity here for manipulating bulk so that you can have building and yet, at the same time, not squander this very precious resource. If there is a failure and the buildings block the sun, you have a failure of imagination.

# Hair and the History of the City

## Ivan Illich

The moment I began to think and read on the relationship between hair and the city, so much wealth and strange information began to heap up that all I can do is take a few minutes to introduce some ideas on hair and the city.

When I was a young man, the world was still very much full of bed bugs and lice and fleas. Only well after DDT, bugs became a word for mechanical foul-ups. Lice and fleas and bugs were the regular visitors on the human body. In reading the encounters between doctors and patients in the past, it is clear that people were quite used to living with a festering sore. The doctor couldn't do anything about it, and it is not that people didn't mind—they simply didn't go to the doctor to stop that festering. That is just what the human condition was. But it is always difficult to speak with people about the fact that a festering sore, for example, was something you were stuck with and you had it. That was a pretty common statement until about 1908. Until that time, a patient had about one chance in two that the doctor could do something, anything

at all, about the condition which they brought to the doctor. And, certainly in most of the world, it was quite obvious and normal to scratch and itch.
. . .

Until recently, human beings never lived with their own surface out of contact with animal life. They shared their skin with other animals.

As a historian, I find it very often difficult to explain to a younger generation what was taken for obvious—what could not be changed, what the human condition was like only a couple of generations ago. DDT is interesting because it extended down into the most underdeveloped countries. The poorest people are rich enough in the world now to get effective flea powder.

Living with an uninhabited skin makes us much less aware of our body surface, aware of what hair is—this fuzzy fuzz which we still carry with us, which has always been an extremely important symbol. . . . There is a very strange gulf between ourselves and the way past people lived.

The gulf between past and present, which makes it so hard for us to understand how people have lived, this gulf which makes us separated from ourselves, is a major reason we no longer have in the city a concept of "the commons." We no longer have commons. Today we have private and public spaces. As far as I know, "private" and "public" are concepts which are simply not applicable to a traditional city. The difference between the opposition of private and public is as a sharp line. That line is like we today imagine our body covering, our skin, a line dividing inside and outside. Hair, inhabited hair, belonging at the same time to inside and outside, makes the division more "fuzzy," makes our life and animal life more alike; and when there is a commons, our life and the lives of others are experienced in common; life in the city, a gathering around a commons. . . .

A precise line does not separate me from the rest of the world. Transitions are much more imprecise. In the past, people carried an aura which surrounded them, an aura that had to be washed away, deodorized, to accommodate people in the kind of cities we live in today. . . . Only sometime after washing became possible, lice and flea killing became effective, and therefore we became even more possessive individuals. Fur became then a symbol for luxury, but not any more for the duplicity of inside and outside which the fur implies. In the fourteenth century, it became so important for a person who had an important aura to

carry a fur that trained—for kings and nobles. This royal coat became so large—140 to 200 square feet, weighing about fifty pounds— that one needed assistants to move around. The royal person wanted to shine in the aura which covered him all around. It is a projection of an animal inside—both an expression of the animal as well as an expression of shame of my fur as it is and therefore have to cover it with clothes. . . .

I thought as a contribution to this discussion about growth and undergrowth I want to point out that the undergrowth of the cities is a place where people are aware that the surface of the city, just like the surface of their bodies, is constantly shared for many purposes. A commons is not a public space. A commons is a space which is established by custom. It cannot be regulated by law. The law would never be able to give sufficient details to regulate a commons. A typical tree on the commons of a village has by custom very different uses for different people. The widows may take the dry branches for burning. The children may collect the twigs, and the pastor gets the flowers when it flowers, and the nuts from it are assigned to the village poor, and the shadow may be for the shepherds who come through, except on Sundays, when the Council is held in the shadow of the tree.

The concept of the commons is not that of a resource; a commons comes from a totally different way of being

in the world where it is not production which counts, but bodily, physical
use according to rules that are
established by custom, which never
recognizes equality of all subjects
because different people follow different customs. Their differences can
be recognized in the way they share
the commons. . . .

Once we really have the experience
of an uninhabited skin, it is enormously difficult for people to understand
that commons in the city are typical,
are characteristic of the perception of
space in past time, and not the distinction between private and public space.

# Souls Take Pleasure in Moisture

## *James Hillman*

The mind has a marvelous reach. We can sit here in downtown Dallas, May 1984, and imagine the buried aquifers under the high western plains, the imperial gardens in China, and a gleaming Town Lake in the year 1999. The mind can even reach out and touch old Heraclitus in Greece, 500 B.C.—before Plato and Aristotle—an extraordinary psychologist who said, "Souls take pleasure in Moisture."

Now, of course, Heraclitus wasn't just meaning your ordinary pause that refreshes. . . . He was referring to a system of elements or humors—the moist and the dry, the hot and the cool. And these elemental qualities of water and air, fire and earth composed our bodies and souls and everything else in the world, visible and invisible. For the invisible nature of people too could be preponderantly earth, immovable cold clods; or hot-tempered and overheated; or like a deep pool, or a sap, a drip, a wet rag. But always essential to the healthy psyche of a person or a place was the right proportion of the moist humor. . . .

That fragment—souls delight in becoming moist—meant of course that water symbolizes the arousal of desire: swept away, dissolving, your knees go liquid, your juices squirt, unstoppered, going with the flow, and breaking through the dam.

Commerce and advertising know about the delight of moistening. . . . We do buy moisture: plants all over the house, waterfalls in the restaurants, each receptionist under her tree, gallons in the flush toilets and shower heads, bigger bathrooms, spas, and pools, liquid diets, free drinks, sappy teenagers gurgling sodas, cats purring over moist foods, flow charts not dry statistics, melt, soft drinks, even abstract art is runny and drippy—and of course the ultimate article of faith: the trickledown economy to increase cash flow to build the affluent society.

A common manner of moistening the soul is by dreaming. Dreaming is a nightly dip, a skinny dip, into the pool of images and feelings. . . . Dreams solve problems because all dreams are wet: they dissolve the mental constraints of the dayworld in the flow of imagination. And they affect our humor because they are full of humor themselves.

Not only do they make you laugh if you let them but dreams often have refreshing images. You have probably sometimes dreamt such images as these: entering a pool and feeling the freedom of effortless swimming, going deep and finding something never seen before, drawn to the water by beautiful bathers, or making love under water, being close by a lake and feeling its stillness, or a river and its fullness, walking the margin of the sea. . . .

Water in dreams has different effects and means different things. It may be a sobering cold shower after a hot night; it may offer cool reflection or wash away the stuff we cling to, bringing new thoughts in gushers, doom with floods—that is, flood us with doom forebodings; drown us in hysterical turbulences or provide a body of clear doctrine that holds us up when we immerse ourselves in it fully, naked as a believing child in its greater body.

Above all, water is seductive. Aphrodite, the goddess of beauty and pleasure, is born from the sea, and Dionysos arrives from the waters. Travel posters of Cancun, even Fort Lauderdale, continue to lure us, just as the mythical nixies and mermaids tempted our ancestors into enchantment. . . . Waters were alive, living beings—and one had to know who it was living in the water: a dragon who could suck you in the maelstrom, a nymph who could drown you in her embrace. These fears of capture by

water still echo in our fantasies of pirates, of the great white shark, the giant clam, the enwrapping squid. I wonder what dream figure, what mermaids or dragons, inhabits our Town Lake project? What is its allure? Are we being sucked in? Over our heads? Too deep to get out? Will the taxpayers take a bath? . . .

The dreams in the people of a city are its waters; they make any city an affluent watering place—even Dallas. I suggest to you that Dallas is dry not because it has no big river or bay but because whatever it dreams, it right away places into dry concrete, continually actualizing. Town Lake could make us drier simply by being built, by losing the dream in the project. . . .

If we look closely into the roots of the Greek word for city, *polis*, we find that these roots draw from a pool of meanings related to water. The Sanscrit-Indo-Iranian-Aryan syllable of polis goes back to words meaning pour, flow, fill, fill up, swim. . . . The very word *polis* locates city in the wet regions of the soul. For the true meaning of city is full, pulsating with folk, streaming, subject to waves of emotion, tides of opinion, ripples of gossip, and always feeling too full, too crowded, flooded. The flow must go on. . . .

But does that mean that Town Lake will make Dallas more of a city? Here a word of psychological caution: To a psychologist, a project also means a projection—something thrown out of the psyche and forward into the future, made concrete and visible. Is the dream of Town Lake a projection of our own internal place of reflection, our darker moods and rippling emotions, to become the surface glitter of a new project, another hopeful happy hoopla, only eight feet deep?

I suspect there may be a peculiar law in the progress of our American civilization. The more its dreams are outwardly realized, the poorer it tends to become in soul culture. The more we have located education in schools, the less literate we have become. The more we have externalized into museums our muses and our culture, the less internal musing and cultivation. The more we write morality into laws and regulations, the less internally governed we are. The more we broadcast religion and construct churches, the less internal piety. The fatter our civilization, the thinner, it seems, becomes the soul culture of the individual. . . .

So I worry about collecting the moisture of Dallas into one literal place, laid out there in another huge development. Dallas needs another kind of development—the moisture that gives pleasure to the soul is that flow of life, of people, of juices, of ourselves crowded with dreams, our streets pleromatic, full of folk. . . . The lake we need to build is a lake in the soul of the city, following this path of water, ever downward, ever spreading out to moisten the lowest reaches of the polis, the body politic. . . .

I believe the Town Lake project is a projection of hope for a flowing, mingling, and humorful city that is also a deeper and reflective city. The project projects a wish for a democratic potential that has yet to be built. . . . Whether Town Lake will bring that democratic city, whether it will be built at all, I do know that the longer one can hold in any projection —that is, contain that lake within the levees of the mind and find out more about its nixies and demons, the subtle meanings in it, the dreams of water hidden in the arguments and figures— the more chances there are for images to appear and make clear what this city truly needs.

# Growing Up

## *Thomas Moore*

To some eyes the growth of cities is wondrous. When I came to Dallas nine years ago, I wondered where the downtown or the CDB was. Downtown was fairly flat. But now it has mushroomed, we say organically. Buildings have sprouted, and finally we can come downtown and look up at the growing stems of the houses of commerce as though we were centipedes essaying a meadow of dandelions. . . .

But some are not pleased with the growth of cities. To them, growth in the city is *a* growth, a pathological tumor, on the skin and skeleton of the city. The multiplicity of skyscrapers is akin to or perhaps simply a parallel manifestation of the cancer that makes cells grow wildly in the body. Development is metastasis. The latest tall building is not a golden dandelion gleaming in the vibrant meadow of the CBD. It's Godzilla, an archaic form that threatens the life of the city.

If the modern growth of a city like Dallas is a virulent form of cancer, then perhaps it is right to look for allopathic remedies in smallness and undergrowth. But I want to suggest a different kind of tonic. A homeopathic remedy—treating like with like—for growth gotten out of hand would look for some necessity and value in growth itself. A symptom is an exaggerated form of something that is needed. A depressed person might need some darkening of mood and character, some aging that depression brings. A person whose symptom is alcohol may need something that spirits provide. So, a city tumorous and pocked from excessive growth might actually need growth, but growth in a more solid, more profound, more soulful and effective sense. . . .

Not all getting big is growth. If you build a doghouse, that is not growth. If you add a wing onto your house, that is not truly growth; that is enlargement or development. But, you plant a tree in front of your house, and it will grow.

Growth is not something done with the fingers or the hands. You plant the seed, and growth takes place. But you decide to build housing developments here and there, and the city enlarges. It does not actually grow. Our downtown has mushroomed, but only because we are unconscious of the people who have decided to enlarge the city in various ways. It seems to have grown, but in truth it has been enlarged. Maybe you can watch grass grow, if you're patient, but you can't make it grow. You can't get down on your hands and knees and push it up. Cities may grow, but they don't grow through the efforts of people who set out to make them get big. . . .

Another curious quality about the symptomatic, spurious growth that afflicts our cities is that this is generally growth upward. The growth of cities in our time seems caught in the more general problem that we identify spirituality with upward, airy, bodiless, monolithic goals. Our buildings are so many versions of the cathedral spire that points away from the body of the earth toward the thin-aired skies and which graduates from mass and body to the point where matter is left behind and air takes over. . . .

City growth seems caught in the myth of the Tower of Babel. In this extraordinary image, the people try to reach the realm of the gods by building an enormous tower. But God punishes their hubris by throwing them into the debilitating confusion of speaking in various languages. Usually in religious narrative, divine punishment implies pathology. In our arrogant attempt to capture the spirituality we need by building upward, and calling this growth, we call down the pathology of confusion. We are scraping the sky with our so-called growth, and at the same time suffering the incapacity to understand each

other and express ourselves to each other. . . .

Theology speaks of a special virtue that is apropos of the problem of bigness. The virtue is magnanimity, usually defined as courage or big-heartedness. The word comes from the Latin 'Magna anima,' or 'big soul,' itself a translation of a Greek term used by Aristotle—*megalo-psyche*, great psyche.

We have magnates in our cities, but the virtue of magnanimity seems to have become old-fashioned and therefore neglected. A big soul can hold a great variety of life within it. It is neither small-minded nor narrow in its imagination. . . .

The name Athena, goddess of the city, means 'wide, shallow pan.' Athena, or the city with a great soul, embraces and contains the infinite variety of life, not necessarily with immense depth, but with breadth. This is the city's contribution to growth: to hold the many seeds of life. . . .

Development is not necessarily growth. Growth culminates in the flowering of a city. Every city as Florida, Florence. Every citizen a Leopold Bloom in Dublin. But a flower's bloom is not manufactured. The flower begins, as C. G. Jung says in his commentary on the Chinese *Secret of the Golden Flower*, in a seed vessel that is underwater, unconscious. Growth takes place unseen, on its own schedule, toward its own unique shape and flowering.

A city's growth begins in the seed vessel held in the hearts of the community. If you really want growth,

you tend to these small seeds. Growth
emerges unconsciously. Holly Whyte
comes to town, spends weeks studying
the place, and then gives his report:
put a chair here, don't block the sun
over there, we need a hot dog here.
These are the seeds of growth. After
supplying a chair and a hot dog, we
are happy to see big crowds. Everything in the city is big if it is the
flowering of a seed. No need to build
vast developments displaying our
blindness to the big heart of the
city. . . .

# The Body

The human body, who we most intimately are, may well be the most neglected and abused life form of culture. For the body that is taken in for repair, has parts replaced, deficiencies cut away, parts re-shaped, tuned up in the spa, kept running, is an uninhabited body, a mechanism. Mechanisms do not belong to culture with its inherently symbolic, historical, mysterious, imagistic values, but to technology, which is inherently rational, progressive, futuristic, and perfection-oriented. The technological body endures its own peculiar diseases—stress, cancer, heart-attack, anorexia, bulimia; technological medicine assiduously works to maintain the mechanism and find the causes of its disrepair. With its specialized instrumentation, language, training, medicine has become a sub-culture and has promoted multiple sub-cultures of alternative medicine—wholistic healing, body-work, mental control techniques, explorations into ancient ways, from Greek to American Indian.

Placing culture at the center of concern produces a different sense of the body, of disease, and of health. First, a cultural point of view questions the rampaging health care system which has turned an experience, a state of being, into a commodity; it brings to awareness that such a system is fast approaching crisis. Second, a cultural stance wonders how we got to where we are and thus explores the history of the human body, an excursion making apparent that the present idea of the body is a relatively recent construct. The historicity of the human body also recovers some sense of body experience and of the art of suffering. Third, such a stance revisions disease, looks for its purposefulness without romanticizing suffering.

The following essays are contributions toward the culture of healing and the healing of culture. Modern medicine knows only of cure, of the surface restoration of functional health, which does not constitute a deficiency in medicine, only a limit. Healing, though, is and always has been a matter for culture, sensing disease as something off balance in the whole community. And what follows from the apprehension of a disordered imagination are rites, rituals to restore the soul. In the past healing rituals have always been local, based on the traditions of a particular community. Such practices most probably cannot be applied to a diverse society. What can be restored to medicine, and thus to culture, is a ritual sensibility.

*Robert J. Sardello*

# Health as Disease

## Ivan Illich

One of the threads without which people in Dallas cannot imagine themselves is that strange concept of health which defines the body we have. Now I know that people did not speak this way, they did not *have* bodies that needed health until quite recently. Health services is a very modern expression. There are people among us who remember a time when you would not yet fully speak in the way we speak about health. Dallas health care has become extremely expensive. Medical services consume more than twelve percent of the economic product, and if you add to this other things for which people pay explicitly for the sake of maintaining, regaining, connecting, or protecting their so-called health, you reach a much higher figure. Health invades the economic product of Dallas. When I speak to Mexican peasants about how many hospital beds there are in Dallas and how many doctors, they tell me people in Dallas must be extremely sick. It is not so easy to explain how it is possible to buy so much health care. As a result of this being slowly perceived in the United States, there is

something on the horizon which I will call the health crisis. Just as the energy crisis was easily foreseeable at a certain moment, you can now say we are moving straight into a health crisis.

. . .

We are now moving in a direction which will make more than a quarter of all expenditures in the United States health related—protection of health is more costly than protection against the Russians. . . . Unlike others who argue for redefinition of health needs and a reorganization of the procedures by which health is provided, I am concerned with the importance of reducing our concern with health. I want to argue for ethical and political options that decrease our concern with health, that decrease our perception of health dreams and our attachment to them. I believe health to be a recent social construct. I can prove that it is so. I believe it to be a recent social construct that is now frequently in stark contrast with subjective well being. I feel that the current trend toward preventive health care, the growth sector of the medical business, may increase people's needs for this commodity. . . .

People did not have to die of cancer until about a hundred years ago. Only during the last thirty years have we come to purchase at extraordinary cost the right to die of cancer. . . . We know that one-third of us will die of diagnosed cancer. I know that with a similar group in many underdeveloped parts of the world not more than five or six percent will have to undergo diagnosis and treatment of cancer. We also know that population-wise there will be no differences in life expectancy as a result of the diagnosis of cancer for almost half of those diagnosed. We know that the terminal stage as a result of interventions on your cancer will be much more painful for you than for the people in underdeveloped countries, but we also know that you will be allowed to consume the heinous and most advanced fruits of science because you have the privilege of living in Dallas. Forgive me, we have to face some hard facts. If people come to see that health, not restoration of a person to his own balance, as Hippocrates would call it, but health as a public concern, an issue, was unthinkable two centuries ago, then we can seriously question the sale of this commodity. I challenge you to produce a historical document in which anybody but crazy utopians would speak about health before the middle of the eighteenth century. The history of health has not yet been written—it is certainly not the same as the history of medicine.

If we let the health construct go on,

possibly half, possibly three-quarters of us are those who will not die of accidents or suicides or in very strange circumstances on a trip to India but will die from medicide. I call it medicide because I have no better word for it. The decision of the doctor means no more reanimation; the doctor decides when you will not be reanimated, reensouled, and from this decision you will die. I, at least, have decided that I want to be healthy at the end of my life. I do not want to have to die of a disease. I know very well that for death to be legitimate it became necessary only in 1830 or 1840 to have a disease. Before that you could be buried very easily because you died of your death. From 1830–40 on it became illegitimate to be buried unless you had a death certificate in which a doctor had certified which enemy had attacked you, what you had succumbed to, what disease you had been killed by. . . .

We must be concerned not only with what the social construct of health has given, but also with what it has destroyed. Health certainly has destroyed an old art which can be observed in all societies. In our Western culture it was called the art of suffering. When I mention the art of suffering, especially when in a medical milieu, I provoke three kinds of reactions. The socially engaged people tell me, "Ah, somebody from the elite who wants to tell the poor to suffer; that's easy." And others say, "Oh, I knew it, a preacher; I've heard that before." Then the psychiatrist tells me, "Ah, didn't we know it from the beginning—a sado-masochist." But I speak of the art of suffering as something every culture has either named or practiced in some way. In fact, I would like to call what others call culture the particular style of living, of enjoying and of suffering life. The art of suffering is not the art of wishing to be in pain. In English pain and suffering are two very different words. I suffer my pain; I can't pain my suffering. . . .

The body which we try to recover historically always implied the ability of suffering one's body and its image. Under the age of health we try to imagine our bodies as healthy, and in doing so we neither live our body nor have a culture.

# The Cancerous Body of the World

*Robert Sardello*

We must confront the fact that cancer is not only a medical problem and the possibility that cancer will not find its cure in medicine as currently practiced. Cancerophobia, the fear that death resides in the everyday things of the world, calls for a world-centered cultural psycho-therapy seeking to understand the predicament of cancerous things. There is almost complete agreement in the view of cancer as an environmental disease, a silent affirmation of a chronic illness of the world. . . .

Two peculiarities characterize substances determined as cancerous, primarily things made from synthetic organic chemicals: they do not belong to nature and they make possible the proliferation of mass-made objects on a scale unheard of before. The first of these qualities, a radical suspension from nature, is met by a bodily desire to return to earth, to feel rooted, grounded, sheltered, nurtured—to dwell again in a simplicity that never was. This sentimentality, the body's nostalgia, tears the present from the past, making it impossible to value things of the present world on their own terms, letting them determine what relation to the past they bear rather than dictating what that ought to look like. . . .

The second characteristic of cancerous things, a proliferation of synthetic, mass-made objects, produces a catastrophe of organic form. The instantaneous production of cancerous things hasten or replaces the slow course of organic generation. These things are not rooted in the soil of natural ways —hand-crafted, skilled transformation of earth into art, but are stamped out by computer-directed machinery, understood from inception as commodities made for profit. They appear and disappear almost instantly, more like dream things than natural objects. When approached only as commodities, they appeal to the herd instinct, making cancer a disease sweeping one along with the herd. . . .

In the tradition of homeopathic medicine, disease consists of the materialization in the body of imagination belonging to worldly things. Oswald Croll, Paracelsus's student, states it in this way: "Man is a hidden world, because visible things in him are invisible, and when they are made visible, then they are diseases, as truly as he is the little world and not the great one." The object of therapeutic treatment is to return imagination to the things that have become only physical. If we look at such treatment psychologically, not literally, it suggests a change in cultural attitude toward the world. The homeopathic therapy of cancer employs an extract of mistletoe, administered to the patient because mistletoe resembles the disease, is equivalent to the imagination. Why mistletoe? It is a peculiar plant form because it appears unaffected by either solar or terrestrial forces. Plants satisfy both earth and sky, creating from the tension and balance of that relationship multifarious organic forms. Mistletoe belies those forces: it grows perpendicularly to the branch that bears it, belonging to no vertical direction —neither nature or spirit. It remains green the whole year long, independent of exposure to light. The berries of the mistletoe ripen in winter, without warmth. The leaves are indifferent to their orientation to light. If we feel the imagination of the cancerous world in this unnatural plant, it is a world detached from both earth and sky. Beneficent nature is gone and so is the celestial god. Everything seems barren and abstract. Cancer wants our body. Cancer cells are qualitatively no different from normal cells, so it is as if this disease has the purpose of taking over the flesh; that is to say, the abstract world needs flesh, it needs the imagination of body.

The things of the abstract world, mass-made, unnatural things, need the individuality of imagination's body. The fear of cancer is like the fear of being caught in a mob, where particularity no longer has any part to play. Cancer, then, appears in the body as the uprising of undifferentiated cells destroying the individual structure of the body. Upon close examination, however, a malignant mass shows form. A "ripe" cancer of the ovaries, for example, is not a formless growth, but often shows fully formed teeth. Other cancerous cavities exhibit the growth of hair, or of brain tissue—a body is trying to materialize in cancer, for that is what the world is in need of. . . .

For the human body, uninitiated into psychological perception, living according to the wish of natural, organic life, daily existence is a constant threat and trauma, producing the modern malady of stress. . . . The possibility of body—along with its organic, physiological, and anatomical life—realizing its psychological life, through which the world takes on imagination, occurs with the onset of precancerous symptoms. Medicine gives little attention to such symptoms since they seem like minor psychological difficulties, unrelated to disease. An understanding of these symptoms may be important because any cancer that shows itself as a bodily condition is already an old cancer; in fact, the appearance of a tumor indicates the terminal phase of the disease. Approaching cancer after it already materializes in the body may be looking in the wrong place in the wrong way.

Victor Bott finds two invariable pre-indicators of cancer. The first is the onset of fatigue that will not go away, a particular kind of fatigue, unlike exhaustion from work and also unlike depression. The fatigue can be described as more like a lack of animation, an inability to feel engaged with the world. The second symptom is insomnia. Bott says, "One could even say that any insomnia beginning without evident cause must make one suspect latent cancer." These symptoms appear as signs of the body under attack by a deadly enemy, some unknown virus, only to the materialist eye. The fatigue of the natural body, its apparent loss of animation, calls for a different kind of engagement with the world, one sensing everything in the world as alive, as image, as autonomously animated. Only in our fatigue can the world's animation begin to show. The symptom of insomnia points in a similar direction. The inability to sleep, to enter into the dream world, suggests that the dream world has changed its location from the invisibilities of the night to the appearance of things-as-image. . . .

I do not intend in any way to suggest that realizing the psychological character of the body is equivalent to a cure for cancer. The body of medicine makes us forgetful of the world as suffering things. The organic natural body makes us wish we did not live in the world of abstractions. The psychological body makes a home for the suffering things of the world, allows them to show themselves. . . .

When psychological body is given to the world, will we see a world of freaks—things as crippled, deformed, misshapen, idiotic? There may be a particular kind of intelligence to this monstrous world, for it can show us something of ourselves that has been repressed. In the midst of the urban world, the city of constructions that are supposed to function perfectly, efficiently, we are still village idiots.

# Women's Illnesses
# in the Eighteenth Century

*Barbara Duden*

I am going to speak of my analysis of eighteenth-century doctors' protocols of patients reports of their illnesses, particularly of women patients'. I will be raising three points: first, I want to present thirteen theses, hypotheses on how the body is perceived by the women and also by their doctor; second, I am going to read to you three stories, three examples that record their encounter; and third, I shall say something about the source itself, something about how it is organized.

Now the thirteen theses:

1. For these women patients the inside is indistinct. It contains no specific organs that are distinctly experienced.
2. The inside is a cavity in which knots, congestion, and relief are located.
3. Pain rages freely throughout the insides. It breaks and then locks itself in, first here and then there. . . .
4. The boundaries of the body are vague. The inside opens to the outside in many spots. Those gates are different from those which we would now

perceive. There are more gates, and also the whole skin can be permeable and open up to the inside.
5. The "stuff" which flows from the body gates is ambiguous. Bloody tears can flow from the eyes; the mouth can discharge menses as well as the nose; the stool can be milky; the menses can burst forth from varicose veins.
6. Women explain to the physician that their stool turned white as their breast shriveled and dried up. When their menses ceases, their noses begin to bleed; the body is forever surprising them by the appearance through which it discharges its "stuff."
7. Women approach the doctor full of anguish that their bodies might not open themselves, release discharge, and expel whatever is inside. Women are gripped by the fear that their insides could be retained, hardened, congealed; that the gates of their bodies might be stuck or closed.
8. Women do not bring their diseases to the doctor but the flesh and the

history of their bodies. They relate the history of their flesh, every experience remains engraved in the flesh. For example: a young girl at the age of sixteen hits herself on a cupboard; she gets swollen and nothing happens. After several pregnancies she comes again to the doctor, her menses stops, and she makes the connection between what is happening now and the wound she received much earlier.

9. Fright and anger get stuck in the flesh. The hardening they produce on the inside is feared by the woman who comes to the doctor. Some women come to the doctor for the sole purpose of asking for a remedy for the anger that has become stuck in their bodies.

10. The doctor's main task is the opening of the body. He enables the women to throw up, to shit, to bleed.

11. Women approach the physician imploring help to expel something from their insides. The physician reflects on their stupidity; he sees his task as soliciting their bodies to discharge themselves; he woos their insides.

12. Bearing children is not primarily related to an anatomic context. The regular discharge of blood is not limited to women. Men as well as children can require regular bleeding. Likewise, men and women both discharge milk. Men do not do it as regularly as women.

13. Women approach the doctor when their bodies swell, after their menses has stopped. However, there is no way for the women or the doctors to verify pregnancy. They seek help and advice for opening their body or deciding that opening it is not necessary at that point.

Now, a story: A choleric, phlegmatic woman, about forty years of age; she had been married after her thirtieth year. In the autumn of 1738, her son dies. "About this death she became exceedingly sad, and she started thus to become irregular in regard to her monthly discharge." She claims in the following periods to have suffered coughing, flying heat. This coughing receded for some days, but then she felt pain under her breast. Later she again felt sweating. After drinking some burgundy wine, she complained of fire in the face, inward heat, cold hands and feet. Days later, she suffers from what she calls "mother-anxiety." In February she has burning pain in the lower parts of the body. She has nights full of anxiety. Also, she complains of stiffness in one arm and still later that her breast was constringed and of signs of her menses receding and stopping again. In March, burning pain in her breast and stomach and much thirst; later, constipation.

Another story: A woman from her youth has a discharge which manifested itself in the beginning as a small rash under the nose. From her thirtieth year on, it appeared also under her breast, especially under her left breast. This discharge changed sometimes, with a slight oozing from the navel.

When she felt it from these two places, she was well and healthy. But when it didn't show itself, she would become ill of "hard" disease. In her fortieth year she suffered from stones and had by her fiftieth year collected a small supply of stones.

These stories and the theses derived from them come from the case reports of one Dr. Storch, an eighteenth-century physician. He began practice in 1705 in Germany. He started a diary when he began to practice. In the reports he records when he sees the women and what the women say. He seems to have been a very ordinary physician, quite respected and very concerned with being scientific.

# Cancer and Body Development

## Arthur von Hochstetter

The development of the organism, the appearance of a new organism through the phenomenon of birth, displays many of the features considered to be characteristic of malignant growth. Seen in the light of morphology, there are so many similarities between onto-genetic and neoplastic development that they may be seen as variants of one fundamental process, namely growth and development.

The analogy taken at face value is, of course, absurd and may point out no more than the limitations of mor-phologic criteria in the assessment of malignancy. After all, the appearance of a child and that of a tumor are ob-vious. The analogy is absurd because it compares the normal development of an organism, the natural life history, the constructiveness of its growth, de-velopment and differentiation, to the destructiveness of a malignancy. It draws parallels between that which en-sures the continuity of life to that which heralds its end. If the absurdity becomes obvious toward the end, be it the termination of gestation or of ter-minal cancer, where in the respective life histories of organism and tumor may the crucial differences become ap-preciable? . . .

The notion of growth must not re-main restricted to volumetric increase through proliferation only of constit-uent limits but be expanded to signify growth through increase in number and in structural organization. Increas-ing structural organization in a living system implies functional differentia-tion.

The development of the human body is a study of structural and func-tional differentiation. Neoplasms, cancers, however, also display differen-tiation, often to a surprising degree. . . . On a histological level, where cells and noncellular structural elements are woven into a fabric, neoplasms may attain high levels of maturity, com-parable at times to that of mature adult tissues. . . . Malignant tumors . . . in the case of germ cell tumors, i.e., tumors thought to arise from the precursor cells of gametes in both ovary and testis, imitate in aberrant ways stages in the development of the embryo. They sometimes continue to develop fully differentiated and mature tissues, such as nervous tissue, bone and cartilage, gut and teeth. . . . The appearance of germ cell tumors is an incomplete and aberrant morphological echo of ontology.

Proliferation and differentiation are inversely related. If cells are to differentiate, they must refrain from dividing; the ability to replicate is lost with increasing structural and functional complexity and organization. . . . In the 1960s Hayflick and Moorhead and others observed that normal human fibroblast strains have a finite lifetime; when cultured in laboratory glassware (in vitro) they are able to double their population a finite number of times, about fifty times. . . . In other words, cells have a limited lifespan, and a memory of how long they have lived, which resides in the nucleus. . . .

Germ cells, the cells of reproduction, on the other hand, are considered immortal, since they ensure the continuity of life through the generations. The soma, the physical body, is in that sense a side branch off the main sequence of life. According to the "disposable soma theory" of aging, an organism must optimally allocate its resources, to maximize its fitness, among a variety of metabolic compartments. For a higher organism which reproduces repeatedly, the optimal allocation of energy involves a smaller investment in somatic maintenance and repair than would be required for the soma to last indefinitely. Thus, there will be an accumulation through life of unrepaired somatic damage, hence senile degradation and death. In contrast, the germ cells are immortal. In the words of some reductionists, an organism like the human being would be the germ cells' way of making more immortal germ cells.

The germ cells are not the only immortal cells, however; cells cultured in vitro from a variety of malignant neoplasms display similar "immortality." The most famous human cell line, called Hela, was derived in 1952 from cultured tissue from the uterine cervix and is still available today. In addition, cultured human cell strains can be transformed into an immortal cell line by being treated with the cancer-causing monkey virus SV 40. The transformed cells are clearly abnormal in such characteristics as number and shapes of chromosomes, chemical properties, and staining characteristics. Most of the transformed cells give rise to tumors when injected into laboratory animals, whereas normal cells, of course, do not.

Recent experiments have shown that transformed, immortal cell lines fused and hybridized with mortal, normal ones give rise to mortal hybrids, suggesting that mortality is dominant from a genetic standpoint.

From the point of view of aging, the phenomenon of cancer suggests a Faustian pact: achieving localized, regional immortality at the price of one's life.

# Ritual Separation and the Humanization of the Body

*Bernd Jager*

To begin with I want to focus attention on the famous story of Prometheus as we read it in Hesiod. I propose that we read this story in a manner so that it will highlight the birth and the emancipation of mankind following the original separation from the gods. The story is cast in the form of a contest of wits between Zeus and Prometheus at the time when gods and men chose to go their separate ways. Prometheus is charged with slaughtering a bull and making an equitable division of the portions that were each to be given to the mortals and to the gods as presumably they sat down to have their last banquet together. We might understand Prometheus as charged with the task of dividing in an equitable manner what only shortly before had been held in common:

> He took the meaty parts and the
>   innards
> thick with fat, and set them
> before me, hiding them away
> in an ox stomach
> but the white bones of the ox he
>   arranged

with careful deception
inside a concealing fold of white fat
and set it before Zeus.

When Zeus chooses the deceptively displayed bones Prometheus has placed before him we stand at the threshold of human emancipation. A line is drawn between two parties; each is assigned his separate portion from what was once their common place and their commonly held property. The knife of Prometheus carves a border which both separates and relates mankind in a new way to the gods. It is important to understand this border not as a total separation. . . . The line appears ambiguous; it appears where it is not drawn, and it is drawn there where it does not immediately make its appearance. What appears on one side of the line (the meat) actually is hidden on the other and vice versa. Thus a first deception has taken place, some advantage is taken and recriminations are set into motion. Because of what he considers an uneven distribution of the goods Zeus decides to withhold fire from mankind. Prometheus illegally crosses that same dynamic line when he steals the fire from what is reputed to be Zeus's hearth. In return Zeus sends Pandora, the first woman, across the line of division as a kind of Trojan horse intended to weaken an opponent. . . . The separation of man and the gods can thus be seen to be repeated in the division between the sexes. . . .

If we permit ourselves for a moment to condense Hesiod's story to a mere schema and if we keep in mind the notion of Prometheus as the god who makes a difference and who institutes a border, we come to the following outline. At the beginning when mankind was formed by means of a fateful separation from the gods, a number of crucial borders were created that together form the limit and the place of human kind. There is first of all the division between nature and culture in which the former (nature) no longer is accessible except through the mediation of the latter (culture). The emblem of that difference is *fire*, and the particular border manifests itself in the *hearth*, which gathers the family around itself, as well as in the blacksmith's forge from which craft and industry proceed. In both cases, in the focus of family life as well as in the hearth of the blacksmith, we are confronted with a contained and domesticated fire. Aeschylus and Hesiod both speak here pointedly of an *entechnon pur*, in distinction to a mere natural fire that is undeserving of that epithet. The fire carried by Prometheus is cul-

tural, contained, domesticated fire capable of serving social and technical ends, and as such it differs from fire to which man may have had access in his original state.

We find a similar pattern within the sexual division where an earlier, maternal, uncomplicated relationship between men becomes replaced by a mysterious, delightful, insecure, ever changing relationship between the *sexes*, which is understood here as a relationship between those who have been cut (*secare*) and made to differ by the knife of Prometheus. Finally, there is the division between gods and men, mortals and immortals, and where the bordermarker presents itself in the form of an *altar*. This altar is the place where is reenacted forever the separation of mortals and immortals in a form which honors the border and makes possible a communication, an exchange of gifts. . . .

Within Hesiod's treatment the *hearth*, the *phallus*, and the *altar* all can be seen as bordermarkers from which stretches a life of the past and the beyond that remains forever inaccessible to direct confrontation. If properly approached, these borders become a place of upsurge of human life; from the hearth flow the cohesiveness of family life and the necessities of societal life; from the phallus flow abundance, fertility, procreation, and from the altar comes to us a new attitude to limits which brings us into a relationship to what lies beyond the realm of the mortals.

# Fat and the Female Body

## Gail Thomas

I am trying to see the female body. Simply that, attempting to see the female body. Not, of course, as a packaged product ready for delivery to the highest bidder, a concept peculiar to the age we now live in, but as a manifestation of the mysteries of life itself. I think the biggest problem is that the body is disappearing—the female body. I mean the body that is carrying on the mysterious life of the universe every moment. That body is disappearing. . . .

How can it be that almost all women today hate their bodies? Adrienne Rich says in her book *Of Women Born*, "I know of no woman —virgin, mother, lesbian, married, celibate—whether she earns her keep as a housewife, a cocktail waitress, or as a scanner of brain waves—for whom her body is not a fundamental problem."

How is it that the repulsion is so widespread that young girls claim openly to want to cut off their breasts and utter sounds of relief when, after excessive running or starvation, their menses ceases? Why is it that fashion conscious women have the nerve to take male hormones in order to reduce the size of their hips and breasts and increase shoulder width? Why is it that what used to be called simply "woman"— all those body parts which define her, breast, tummy, hips, buttocks, thighs—are now revoltingly referred to as "fat"? . . .

The female body, because of its primordial innate power, triggers our compulsions. In the twentieth century, the consumer power of the female body reigns, so that almost every enterprise uses as an advertising ploy the sumptuous woman as a promise to fulfill some deep unconscious hunger in the consuming public. Who is it who is smiling from the billboards, from the TV screen, or book jackets and boxed packages of food? The body of the great mother is still our bounty. In order to get through the complexes of our consumer culture, we must be able to see how her image and her surrogate, the female body, has become packaged, consumed and degraded—an economic entity.

It is my belief that "fat" is at the root of this complex. . . . We are so accustomed to thinking of fat as an evil, as something to be scorned, that it is difficult to acknowledge that it has undergone an enormous change within the last few centuries. Like woman herself, fat has had a transformation. And, amazingly, the two hold much in common.

A quick look at the definition of the word shows us that fat is described as the glyceride of the fatty acid. It occurs in the organic tissue, especially in the subcutaneous connective tissue of animals and seeds, nuts and fruits.

Under its scientific name, lipids, it constitutes the principal structural material of living cells. Lipids, indeed, are the most important storage form of chemical energy. Fats (tricyglycerols) are the most abundant forms of lipids. On the average, forty or more of the daily energy requirements of people in highly developed countries is met by dietary tricyglycerols.

Obviously, fat is quite important to our well being. How can it be that we have come to despise it so? Blamed for one of the main causes of heart disease, fat in the company of its companion cholesterol is a modern killer. A fourteen-member panel, recently convened by the National Institute of Health, has issued a statement calling obesity a deadly disease. . . .

The notion that fat causes serious illness and premature death is, in fact, new to the history of body imagery. Before the twentieth century, people were stout, ample, and chubby, but the condition was a state of being and certainly not a threat to life.

The word "fat" and the female

body have much more in common than expected. One of the oldest forms of the word means "to hold and contain." In early use, fat is a vessel, that which contains the essentials for life—a silver vessel holding holy water, a large cask of wine, a pot storing dried grains. Until the middle of the last century, the word "fat" conveyed that which is full-bodied, substantial. When fruits are spoken of as fat, they are thought of as full of juice; wood, as full of resin. Fat was also used as a measure of capacity—a fat of leather traded for a bale of hay—and as a measure of good condition. (In the usage as measure, fat was sometimes used interchangeably with fate—a person's "lot" or "portion.") The fat part of anything implied the richest and most abundant, the most nourishing, the choicest produce—to eat and live on the fat of the land.

Suddenly, in the middle of the nineteenth century, the notion of fat changes radically. Fat is defined anatomically. In the year 1846, fat globules are detected under the microscope; in 1847, a deposition of fat corpuscles is noted; in 1866, fat glands are identified; in 1883, fat engendering repose and dangerous fat reducing systems are noted. Also in this year a mechanical device is invented to catch the fat in drains (plumbing) so that it will not stop up the pipes.

The fat of the nineteenth century has lost its bountiful nature and comes as an intruder, an invader of the body system. Gone is the notion of holding and containing; gone is ripeness and juiciness, richness. No wonder we no longer desire it. Fat has become the enemy. . . .

As fat becomes identified through anatomy, so does the female body; the womb (house of the child) becomes a uterus, a reproductive organ, in the eighteenth and nineteenth centuries. During the same period, midwives and female physicians lost their status and rights to practice. The "old ways" of caring for and curing the female body were forgotten. Consequently, the rites, taboos, and mysteries which have accompanied menstruation, conception, birth, lactation, and menopause went underground.

The womb as mysterious source of life itself and fat as the vessel which contains those elements essential to life have suffered the same fate. It is no wonder the anorexic and the bulimic young women are saying "no" to twentieth-century silicon, look-alike, female bodies.

# The Body in Stress

## *Robert Kugelmann*

In an illuminating book, the sociologist Aaron Antonovsky links stress to an experienced lack of coherence in the world. The significance of this insight is that it connects stress, which we experience daily in ten thousand ways, with the very core of modernity: its assault on traditions, its revolutionary spirit, its quest for the new and the undiscovered and the future. The contemporary meaning of "stress" originates only in the eighteenth century, that age of revolutions. Stress is the experience of destabilizing change, a change to meaninglessness. . . .

It is little noticed that stress functions for us as religion and myth did in earlier times. It provides a frame of reference and bestows meaning on suffering and pain. Unlike earlier frames, however, stress is explicitly nonreligious and accommodates any religious meaning that an individual would want to add. Stress provides only the functional meaning—the way modernist architecture provides only the functional necessities for a building.

Stress is a strange kind of totemism, and in this way too, distinguishes modernity from other ages. This totemism is an identification of the soul with the materials and products of modernity. It is a felt kinship with plastics, reinforced concrete, steel, and aluminum; a felt kinship with skyscrapers, freeways, automobiles, computers, supermarkets and parking lots. These materials and products—so unnatural, so distinctively the fruit of human labor—are ourselves writ large, even as the raven and the killer whale and the cedar are the very soul of the Indians of the northwest coast. . . .

In a landmark book, *Psychological Stress and the Coping Process*, Richard Lazarus writes that the first major study of psychological stress was Roy Grinker and John Spiegel's 1945 book *Men Under Stress*. Grinker and Spiegel worked as psychiatrists with aviators during World War II. These pilots, navigators, bombadiers, and gunners were the first to suffer stress. . . . These soldiers of the air forces have transformed the nature of warfare and changed our place in relationship to war. Total warfare is now possible because of the success of these men. Now no one on earth is safe in time of war. War now comes from the sky. . . .

A bomber crew delivered the first

atomic bomb and ushered in the atomic age, which thus coincides with the age of stress. The existence of nuclear weapons ensures the militarization of modern life. We all know the terror that formerly only the soldier on the front line knew. And terror is essential to the emotional charge of stress. For stress, as an experience of modernity, has its feeling tone: it oscillates between boredom and terror, the two faces of a pervasive anxiety.

The boredom reflects the monotony of a technical world, with its many equalizers, such as TV, radio, hamburgers, shopping malls. This boredom is punctuated with moments of terror . . . to the possibility that a descending human creation will blow modernity to atoms. . . . David Bakan has written that the stress response resembles Freud's idea of the death instinct. . . .

An early form of stress occurred during the Civil War. It was called "nostalgia," and it affected the minds of soldiers, making them incapable of performing their duties. In this first modern war, the early inhabitants of a mechanized military suffered from "home-sickness"; what an ideal term for stress, which is the suffering of homelessness. It clarifies our situation to accept "nostalgia" as a synonym for "stress.". . .

Modernity is not all technology, bureaucracy, and pluralization. It is also a nostalgia, a longing for the natural, when a man could act decisively, heroically. Millions of dollars are spent each year in the cultivation of the natural: for fitness, for biofeed-

back, for resort vacations. . . . This is not to say that modernity's nostalgia is ultimately beneficial. . . . Under stress, we exploit our bodily nature with as much thoroughness as we do the earth's resources.

The other return to nature is the turn inward, to the psyche. Again, this turn is as old as modernity, originating with Mesmer's magnetic sleep, the first secularized form of meditation. Regardless of how one turns inward, be it active imagination, yoga, psychoanalysis, one does so with the idea of turning to one's soul. This turn is made in order to balance the pressures of reality. . . . Psychology is another of modernity's answers to the sense of homelessness. It is the discovery that home is within. . . .

To conclude: I have tried to show a network of fantasies that we call "stress." Stress is the experience of and the suffering of modernity, when we imagine our lives as moderns.

# The Body's Range of Indeterminacy

## *Donald Cowan*

Science has a history from which the body is by no means absent—it is of course extension and can be measured, as volume in a tub of water for Archimedes; or mind, a knower with a point of view for Einstein. The story of the growth and refinement of concepts in science is fascinating, important to the understanding of a culture. And yet, as physicist, I set aside that treasure trove, that accretion of social wisdom, to face afresh the innocent phenomenon.

It is not the business of physics to prove anything true or false. It *is* the business of physics to find what is true in experience and to drag it into the light of rationality—not infrequently having to extend rationality to encompass that which is recognized to be true.

There is a region bordering rationality, a realm that Gaston Bachelard labels the *surrational*, similar to the surreal in art. "And it is here," says Bachelard, "if anywhere, that the physicist dreams." For me it is the land of insight where outcroppings of truth occur, seemingly detached from the body of accepted rationality.

Truth, however, is never discarded for want of explanation. Rather the borders of rationality are extended to encompass the island, to make it a peninsula, and Europe is the greater for it. The process of connecting the new territory must have the property of being sufficient for anyone who follows in its path to reach the identical conclusion. The idiosyncrasy of the discovery must be rendered universal.

Most children of the West, Professor Alfred Ziegler has pointed out, are sunworshippers. It is in the *light* of reason that we know rationality. The distance between two points is measured along the track that light takes between them. Straightness is defined by light. Geometry constructs what can be *seen* in a rational world. Our models are visual images.

It is no wonder that primal authority is granted to that information communicated to us by light. Light is the all-pervasiveness of the universe. We are embedded in an electro-magnetic potentiality, bound to it by an energy $E = mc^2$, where $c$ is the speed of light. And light has the surprising property that if measured by anyone, any-where, in any condition of motion, it has the same velocity, although the colors so received are indeed altered by the relative velocities between source and observer. If rulers must shrink or time extend to make such a condition rational, so be it. That was the remarkable assumption that Einstein made to regain rationality in the observed universe—Special Relativity (1905), one of whose consequences is the aforesaid $E = mc^2$.

Light, then, is preeminent in rationality and was certified theoretically by Maxwell (1890), Planck (1900), Einstein (1905), Heisenberg (1925), during those fruitful years when the proof of the pudding lay in its alterations. Light, the medium of measurement, became discrete in energy and momentum, and measurement itself was found to have limits in accuracy—that is, our knowledge of reality cannot be wholly exact. Indulge me a moment to expound on this uncertainty. Phenomena, events, are changes in states of particles. A state of a particle is described by its position and its momentum—where it is and where it is going. On a two-dimensional graph of momentum against position, any state would be a point. But as it turns out, we cannot know this point precisely— only somewhere within a small area of size no less than $h$, Planck's constant. The more accurately we know momentum, the less accurately we know position. Energy and time are similarly interrelated. This indeterminacy is not the fault of our instruments or our own incompetence. Nature herself demands it, quite apart from our desire to know.

Now $h$ is extremely small and of no significance in ordinary experience. But for elementary particles such as electrons or photons it looms quite large. Within the nucleus of an atom, communication at the speed of light between entities takes little time; therefore large energies can be exchanged and in such a manner that the gluons bind together the quarks. Within the range of indeterminacy, neither energy nor momentum need be conserved. The laws of logic are observed only outside the borders of indeterminacy.

This uncertainty principle allows us to invent a little creation fable for our time. It would go like this: God was bored sitting in eternity where nothing happened without space or time, so He decided He would make just a teeny weeny bit of time to see what it was like. He did so, keeping it as near zero as he deemed safe, and whammo! —an immense amount of energy exploded from a point. "Wow!" said God. "I didn't expect that."

To speak more soberly, we might say that He saw the light and called it "good" in that little instant of time, and it was His word that made creation stable, allowing it to expand in space and time from that single point, with matter condensing from energy, forming stars and galaxies, earth and sky—and it was indeed a pretty good day's work.

Somewhat less playfully but more speculatively, I would say that what concerns me about indeterminacy for our present purposes is how the body knows itself. If we peer down from our high tower at this asinine body we inhabit, we know it in the light of reason with no noticeable uncertainty. It is what light reveals it to be. But there are ways of knowing other than sight, other modes to dwell in. "We live in a forest of models," says Michel Serres; "rationality is only one of them. Sometimes we stand so close to our model that we cannot see the forest." Serres was indulging in synecdoche in using models for modes: there are many ways of knowing, he was saying, and we can quickly think of several. Each of the senses has its medium of communication, and though the detailed interactions can be reduced to electromagnetic ones, the actual transmission of information travels at a characteristic speed much less than light. Sound, for example, is of the order of a million times slower.

Like light, sound is a wave motion —longitudinal, not transverse; and local, not universal but having many common characteristics. Atoms, seemingly, are bound in a solid with an energy $E = mc^2$ where $c$ is the speed of sound in the solid, just as matter is bound to the electromagnetic realm. Certain phenomena, such as sputtering, wherein surface atoms ejected into the back space seem to violate conservation of momentum, can be ex-

plained by treating the velocity of sound similarly to light, thereby restoring the simple connection to rationality that physical explanation demands.

What I go on to now is speculation. Each mode of communication, I say, has its own indeterminacy interval. I suspect these intervals are of a size inversely proportional to the velocity of communication for each mode. For sound in a solid, the interval would be a hundred thousand times that for light, which, as it turns out, would yield about the separation distance of atoms in a crystal, the shortest wavelength propagated for sound. Information by sound, as in sonograms, is less precise than by light, as in x-rays. Atoms, so to say, know each other with an imprecision characterized by the velocity of sound.

To a physicist, this way of thinking is interesting, even exciting. But for this conference all I want to do is to suggest the possibility of there being indeterminacy intervals other than the value of Planck's constant $h$ associated with light. The human body knows itself by many modes, by touch, by chemical reactions, glandular responses, with varying nerve transmissions. The uncertainty intervals may be quite large. And within the uncertainty realm ordinary logic does not apply. There can be virtual presences within the interval, hordes of them on the head of a pin, flitting about accomplishing the task of viability under the cloak of indeterminacy. Rationality would have to be matched only at the borders.

Now I think this speculation is all true and might have practical consequences, but for now we can let it go as a morality tale, a metaphor that is meant, a plea for sympathy toward the body in its own terms. "My own heart let me more have pity on," as Gerard Manley Hopkins wrote. "Let me live to my sad self kind." The body's lumbering presence in the world knows and is itself known, not so much in the brilliant electromagnetic glare of light as in a more gelid, opaque medium that nonetheless communicates the reality of what is *there*.

# The Wasting Body of Anorexia

## *Joanne H. Stroud*

Today, anorexia is no longer the exclusive province of a minority of young women. In less debilitating forms, we have all caught the disease. This symptom in a few presaged a general drive in the direction of distrust of food. The bounty of the earth was once considered a gift of the gods. In recognition we gave thanks and sacrificed some portion in appreciation. Once food had lost its soul, it became first devalued and then demonized, attacking us from all directions. It is impossible for us to go through a single day without thinking about the danger of ingesting something. . . .

Anorectics want to rid themselves of the stuff or matter or mother that is choking them inside. Since the fast as a religious observance has waned in importance, anorectics have adopted a private ritual of fasting. They are sacrificing on the altar all that is symbolic of being feminine. They are sacrificing body and blood—their own. They don't need the doctor for bloodletting. They stop their own flow. They are sacrificing their fertility, their generation, their creativity to sainthood through skinniness.

Anorectics are terrified of letting go. And they are afraid of opening the gates of the body and letting anything alien enter. Control is vital. They detest going to any therapist or physician. Attempts to treat either the psyche or the soma feel like forceful invasion, rape. Anorectics become fearful of any food that enters their mouths, carefully studying what little they can get by on. Often this meager portion has to have a special visual appeal. Equally, in the field of relationships most are incapable of the letting go that a truly satisfactory sexual relationship requires. . . .

The word anorexia has a root connection with the word "to span"—"an" (without) plus "orexia" (a longing) to reach out. The anorectic has no bridges. A bridge takes us from here to there. She can't visualize the possibility in her life of going any place. Only the empty void seems real. Her determination to remain physically empty reflects her view of the macrocosm as a void. That emptiness craves being filled but fears equally any contact. Such a longing might encourage a forceful invasion. The anorectic feels herself in lonely isolation, in a place bereft of body. Who needs a body anyway, if there is no place to go? . . .

The phenomena of bulimia and anorexia, which are presently assuming epidemic proportions, reflect a cultural lack of respect, lack of love for the female body. We allow a surgeon to cut on our faces, take out our breast tissues as prophylactic preventive for cancer, and remove our wombs. We could make a case for the lack of respect for the male body as well, or just the body. In the West our lack of attention to the needs of the body extends to our daily habits. We don't have the Oriental's respect for the space around our bodies. We bump into one another on the street or elevator. In other ways we are living as if our bodies were lifeless and unfeeling, instead of recognizing that all our sensing, experiencing is mirrored through the body. . . .

Looking at the human form in popular art, we can determine what an age admires. What we now admire is the adolescent figure, Twiggy or Brooke Shields. Oddly enough, the other extreme, the buxom Playboy bunny who blows up her bosoms with silicone, is gawked at. Both extremes have an unreal plastic quality.

The growing girl who wants desperately to be admired and doesn't see herself as a Marilyn Monroe chooses the other extreme. She finds any weight gain alarming. Her shaky sense of identity at puberty becomes a battle to remain forever an adolescent, a

*puella aeterna*. Absorbing the communal lack of respect for her body, she goes one better and detests it. No amount of mortification or denial will suffice. She tortures her hated body and treats it like an enemy. Its only meaning is in terms of numbers on the scales which she consults obsessively for any deviation upward. She exercises until exhausted. Her body, if it displays any roundness, implies softness, tenderness, receptivity, femininity, to her all the things she fears to be. . . .

The plight of the anorexic girl alerts us to what we have forgotten. This small lost creature carries our collective shadow. She provides us with the haunting image of what our culture fails to see about itself. She images our abusive lack of understanding of the treasures inherent in life or in love. . . . We ignore these simple truths at great risk. The anorectic becomes our propitiation for our forgetfulness and our abuses. She is akin to the young virgin in the "Sacre du Printemps" who dances herself to death so that the community can be assured of the return of the green of spring. There is renewal through the sacrifice of the virgin. But in our ever-busy, ever-manic world we have no reverence for the lessons of depression or for the acceptance of death and renewal. We run away as fast as we can from them. The anorexic girl forces us to turn around and see the dark, suffering face of depression and the mysterious energy of death from which life issues.

She alerts us to something we have
forgotten. In the world of extroverted
and incessant activity, where the
"doer" is idolized, we need a time for
self-preserving, self-sustaining introver-
sion as well. In a world of restless
movement, we need a space for
limited achievement and an appreciation for small acts of courtesy and
care.

# The Abandoned Body

## *Robert D. Romanyshyn*

I begin with this curious observation: the body toward which we have become so attentive, the body with which we are even obsessed—health, sports, medicine, science—is a body with which we are unfamiliar. It is the specialist's body, the body as object of knowledge, the body which one has. It is also the anonymous body, the body which is the same for all, the democratic body, the body for everyone, anyone, and, therefore, no one. It is finally the body which has lost its place in the fabric of the cultural-social world, a body which has been displaced from the world and compressed into itself. I call this body the abandoned body. . . .

My thesis is that the invention of linear perspective construction in the fifteenth century arranges the space of the world in a new way and in such a fashion that the body can and must be abandoned. The space of linear perspective begins with Leon Battista Alberti in 1435, where we are given for the first time in human history the method for the creation of a three-dimensional spatial depth on a two-dimensional plane. Alberti says:

First of all, on the surface on which I am going to paint, I draw a rectangle of whatever size I want, which I regard as an open window through which the subject to be painted is seen; and I decide how large I wish the human figures in the painting to be. I divide the height of this man into three parts, which will be proportional to the measure commonly called a braccio. With this measure I divide the bottom line of my rectangle into as many parts as it will hold—then I establish a point in the rectangle wherever I wish; and as it occupies the place where the centric ray strikes, I shall call this the centric point. . . . Having placed the centric point, I draw lines from it to each of the divisions on the base line.

We should note that the centric or vanishing point, as that point toward which all parallel lines converge, has become our assumed, natural way of envisioning the space of the world and our place within it. What does this vision, this assumed innate geometry in our eyes, presume? First, it presumes that we, the perceivers, are looking at the world as if through a window. Second, insofar as Alberti's placement of the vanishing point is intended to insure that all objects in the painting and the viewer of the painting will lie on the same plane, this vision assumes that the depth of the world is a matter of spatial distance from the viewer, horizontal rather than vertical depth. Third, insofar as Alberti's procedure intends the heads or tops of all figures which lie on this same plane to be placed on the horizon line, this vision presumes that with increased distance the figure (the body) will and must shrink from the bottom up. Alberti specifies other assumptions, but let me point out the cultural-psychological implications of those set forth. Seeing the world through a window, our engagement is already specified in a certain way: there is a detachment, the detachment of one who has become an observer, an onlooker, a spectator if you will. . . . Second, when the world's depth has become a matter of distance, reality has already been explained—that is, the world and its space has been made a level ground, even, flat, clear and distinct. In such a level space, in a space whose depth is horizontal, depth as a matter of levels, vertical depth, will be eclipsed and all those beings and things of the world which belong to such levels will be displaced—beings like angels and those creatures which haunt the landscapes of Bosch. They will disappear from the world explained and will, of necessity, retreat inside. They will become our dreams and our nightmares. Third, this world of horizontal depth— it stretches to infinity, which is farther than human legs can ever walk but not farther than the eye can see. In an

infinite world the body is a hindrance, to be abandoned.

# Beyond the Monster

## *Alfred Ziegler*

It is not self-evident that man possesses an ability to judge that allows him at first glance to distinguish human symmetry from the sick and monstrous. He has a sense for proportions. Moreover this power to judge not only works in a neutral manner, but most of the time is supported by a whole series of emotions, which range (according to ethnic differences) from a self-forgotten admiration to aversion and disgust. The norms of anatomy and physiology are not only statistical figures, but also objects of an immediate feeling of value.

When for us the proportional is exalted as the outstanding element, then it easily becomes the superhuman. The experience of proportionality leads to the experience of the likeness to God; at least to the likeness to that god who is thought to be the supreme god of Western monotheistic religion. God the Father is never monstrous or misshapen but always well-built . . . apollonic.

This pleasure we take in human proportion now seems to be altogether a part of our solar faith. We see God himself as a descendent of the sun.

And for all chosen people we use solar or solaroid descriptions. Movie figures beam as stars, and when we do especially well we feel splendid or our mind is brilliant. We are the *insiders*.

On the other side we perceive every misshape and monstrosity with aversion and often with disgust and a shiver. They become for us the subhuman. Here is where the evil in the horror movie or Shakespearean theater begins. Here, as well, it turns religious or quasi-religious (devilish). Here is the realm of the *outsiders*.

It was not too long ago when in our European world everything monstrous and all things misshapen were thought to be basically non-Christian. Monstrous human beings were not really Christian human beings. Rather they were alien heathens. This was especially true for the so-called "small people," who lived in secluded parts of nature, in the woods and the far mountain valleys. These heathen people lived in the wilderness and very often consisted of strangely shaped people. Since they were in reality somewhat abnormal, they were imagined to have tails, look like roots

and have wrinkles, be midgets and
hairy, have the faces of birds, wooden
feet or the feet of goats, or green
teeth. They were often in bad moods,
vengeful, and without manners. They
loved to make a "heathen-noise." . . .

# The Marquis de Sade and Erotic Suffering

## Thomas Moore

The contemporaries of Sade dealt with him by keeping him shut up in a prison or asylum for the greater portion of his life. In modern times Sade's imagination has been similarly imprisoned in the bastille of a well-built and maintained system of morality and health. Sade is now not a mere perversion but a sickness as well—sadism, that inexplicable manifestation of human inversion. One effect of this modern form of incarceration has been to obfuscate any genuine search for insight into the potential psychological meaning and value of the vision Sade espoused. . . .

Sadism as defined in the textbooks is only a small portion of the imaginal world to be found in Sade's novels. . . . A brief examination of a few of the foundational elements that make up that cosmos reveal a cosmogonic eros in place of plain sexual perversion and a rather extensive and varied set of motifs that surround and serve that central erotic creation.

Paradoxically, for example, we find in Sade a genuine reverence for virginity. The most obvious appearance of this theme is the consistent and unex-pected predilection on the part of the libertines for virgin girls. . . . Yet the unbridled, cruel libertines do not take virginity away; in fact, they consciously protect it, an advantage of anal intercourse.

The time of virgin containment is elaborated in other images of enclosure. Sadian revels are celebrated in remote places, usually chateaux or monasteries surrounded by forests and far from the town. The walls are sealed by a moat and thick stone; locked doors and isolated chambers are common. . . . In this sense, to be sadistic is to imprison oneself or at least to understand that the psyche requires such imprisonment in order to enjoy visions otherwise precluded. . . . A depressive mood can turn sadistic when one closes oneself off from others, keeping even close friends out and imprisoning oneself in one's blackness. . . .

Erogenous zones are usually understood to be those parts of the body that generate eros, but in Sade the quest for erotic response generates a world, a microcosmos, of what Roland Barthes aptly designates as the "amorphous body." Every article in Sade's creation is there because Eros wills it; every technique of approaching the human body is conditioned by its erotic power. If we understand eros and sex in Sade to be metaphor, we might see that, from a psychological viewpoint, Sade is exploring in his fiction psyche's necessities, meaningful movements of the soul often misunderstood and undervalued due to moralistic and egoistic prejudices. . . .

Sade's work is a psychopoetics, an imaginal statement dissolving perimeters of the psyche beyond the horizon of moral vision. Psyche requires torture and violation, ineffable crimes, but these do not have to be brought into action. . . . Those who refuse to acknowledge the horrors that imagination holds are condemned to act them out blindly. . . .

If orgy is defined as abandonment to excess, then one finds little genuine orgy in Sade's writing. There is indeed excess in a sense, at least a seemingly abnormal attention to erotic activity; but one must keep in mind that this is imaginative literature, not chronicle. Furthermore, the excess is carried out within the limits of ritual, with excessive detail. . . .

With respect to painstaking details, this kind of taking pains is pleasurable, as if the saturnine emphasis on ordering, number, precision, limit, and rule has finally found its pure erotic form. . . . Other details of the sadian ritual suggest as well that Saturn is the god of Sade's imagination; the anal focus, the proximity to death, the instru-

ments and paraphernalia of torture, the dominating males, the insistence upon authority, and so on. . . . By exposing this saturnine eros imaginally, Sade is offering a way of tempering its destructive literal enactment. . . .

Critics have complained that the novels of Sade are not interesting; they seem to lack all dramatic form. Indeed, sometimes the novels read more like books of rubrics, giving all the rules and exceptions, the ordered movements and gestures of some complicated liturgy. But the effect is to design a drama, a ritual drama that attempts not to duplicate life but to give image to its underlying patterns— Sade's ritual style abstracts from the personal and the temporal, giving us a view of the archetypal *dramatis personae*: Eros, Saturn, the Bishop, the virgin, the dramatic set, the incidental players. There are no flesh-and-blood people in his imaginal world—only essences. . . .

In life one can hardly move without being sadistic. The teacher needles his students, prodding them to learn. The wife hurts her husband by asserting herself against his romantic wishful illusions. . . . Rejecting the imaginal world Sade crafted with such precision and overwhelming power, we are left with a literal society which feels victimized by a completely mysterious and uncontrollable tendency toward crime and violence. Ignoring the dark god of sadistic imagination, we live out a saturnine severe existence of law and order attacked by a corresponding saturnine mania for violence.

# Body, House and City

## *Bernd Jager*

The house, the body, the city all form a privileged unity of mutual implication. It is here that human life becomes situated, where it centers and unfolds. . . . One of the most interesting challenges of our time is to intertwine these three primordial terms, to rekindle their long forgotten relationships, to re-experience their underlying unity anew in modern thought and in modern architectural practice. . . .

It would promise to be instructive to think through the interrelationships maintained between the body, the house, and the city or village at various times and in different cultural settings. We could pose the question whether attitudes toward the body are frequently or invariably reflected in attitudes toward buildings and vice versa. Would, for example, a purely functional mechanistic approach to the body find an echo in an equally functional approach to the building of houses and cities? Would a conception of the body as a material envelope of an immaterial soul reappear in an architectural conception for a house and city as mere material containers of a human cargo? Could a professed disinterest in the beauties of the flesh find

its parallel in a loss of esteem for wood and stone? Could there be a relationship between a contemporary overemphasis of the medical view of the body and the fact that so many apartment buildings look for all the world like hospitals and so many universities like surgical wards? . . .

If we ask the question what it may mean to inhabit or embody the world, we come upon what we may experience with the French philosopher Merleau-Ponty as the central mystery of the body, namely, that it belongs to the visible, that it can be seen, while at the same time it also remains a source of vision. The body is a visible source of vision. This duality is also visited upon that part of the world that we inhabit or use. A house or a city, when properly inhabited, will not merely remain something seen, it will itself become a source of vision and light according to which we see. . . .

To approach inhabitation in this manner means no longer to be able to make such a radical distinction between flesh and matter, between bodies and mere things. Bodily existence floods over into things, appropriates them, infuses them with the breath of life. A fully inhabited world is at the same time also a fully embodied world. . . .

Like a certain bodily attitude, a building opens a particular world of tasks, of outlooks, of sensibilities. The windows guide and frame our outwardly directed glance; they may offer us the possibility of seizing a majestic surrounding landscape or they may gently place before us a secret spot of nature, an inner court, a protected porch, a tender little garden. . . .

Our discussion of the interrelationships of the human body, of the house and the city now moves in a direction where it becomes possible to speak of buildings as quasi-bodies and to experience the material presence of a house or a city as we would the carnal presence of a person. It becomes then possible to begin to formulate demands which we can make on buildings which are not unlike the demands that we make on other people. We will then not only speak architecturally of canons of beauty or of functionality, but we will find it legitimate to ask ourselves the question how a building makes us feel as we walk past it, as we enter and use it, as we come to live in its neighborhood. And it will no longer be quite so ridiculous to think of buildings as narcissistic, or self-absorbed images, forever performing before the camera without giving much genuine attention to the living needs of the inhabitants and the passers-by. . . .

All this should inform us that a house, a neighborhood, a city is never merely a visual object. But nor is it a mere tissue of functions. A building that is too preoccupied by its functions, that is forever too busy to look up from its tasks, is merely a bore and a nuisance besides. Those who pass by buildings have the right to be acknowledged, to be received and greeted.

Both extremes of narcissistic building, forever worried about losing its good looks, awaiting any day the ruin of a weather mark upon its perfect and endless façade, and that of the so-called functional buildings, perpetually flexing its tubes and wires in exaggerated fake servility, both types of buildings remain oblivious to their context, incapable of gracefully receiving rain and wind, too removed from the true world of civilization to become for the pedestrians or the inhabitants the starting point of an interesting reverie or a novel plan of action, of a poem or an equation or a thought.

Both types of building, while catering to abstract needs, disembody those who attempt to inhabit them because these buildings have themselves forgotten that they are bodies, that they must become flesh of our flesh if there is to be a living city, an inhabitable home and a truly human body.

# Lost on Circe's Island, or,
# The Enchanted Hero
# Each Evening Recalls the Body

*Eileen Gregory*

*And I am known for decorous deceits*
*from which neither bruise nor wailing comes,*
*just refusal to observe the perishing.*
*I know there is loss in the heavens even if,*
*fixed on enchantment, I stare only at colors*
*abridged from history and from the history of awe.*

Ann Lauterbach, "Between"

I must speak now from this domain of
the boundary, shaping the landscape of
this strange place as feelingly as I can.
I appear to have no other way of
moving. Though I wish to be apart
from this world, to be capable of seeing it whole, from a safe distance, it is
not possible. This protean place cannot
be known from a distance or persua-
sively reported by a casual traveller.
This is not a place of distances, of
demarcation, of abstraction, but of
nearness and immediacy. My body
and the bodies of things are vivid and
full, and moments occur with distinct-
ness, but there is no separate body or
measurable instant. For here time and
identity are not the unequivocal realities they presume to be in ordinary

life. They are indeterminate. It is en-
chanted, after all: the course of the
sun delimiting the sequence of moments is obscure; and the shapes of
things are radically mutable. The
boundaries are always shifting.

To undo the habit of decorous deceit, this is what I wish, to admit the
perishing. At dusk the sun falls beyond
the boundary of the world, falls into
Ocean, the Greeks would say, accustomed to wide waters. Things move
into darkness, revealing themselves.
And then "we see . . . that deep in the
shine/of the perceived landscape is a
chain of events/like a handcuff of
stars, or pebbles." Deep beneath the
shining "enchantment" of surfaces is
an inexorable action, "a chain of
events/like a handcuff," a history.
That story is my own, but also the
story of each who witnesses this daily
fall, this slippage of light signaling the
fragile tangent of the heart. Only deceit, refusal, can abridge this event

"from history and from the history of awe." It is an occurrence of intimate and yet cosmic scale, this "loss in the heavens," an old memory persistently awakened: "Now goeth sonne under wood:/Me reweth, Marye, thy fair rode." The sun always dies, the light fades from the earth, and the woman grieves, as if for a son or a lover. Yes, we know this. It is familiar, it has happened.

Myth is at this juncture between "history" and the "history of awe," between personal experience of body and spirit in time and those mortal mysteries always and continuously occurring. Only surrender to life at the threshold, life at the margins of the world, brings us into the stream of those histories simultaneously flowing. Is this, then, what they meant by the Ocean Stream, which for the Greeks encircled the known world, beyond which was a vast, unknown, and yet vividly imagined landscape, belonging to no one because belonging to everyone? Is this where the histories flow together, within this circle at the outer edge of time and place, marking the source and end of the diurnal course of the sun: out of the Ocean it rises, and into Ocean it descends? Within the boundaries of Ocean life goes on, following the course of the sun, but beyond its edge, only death, disintegration, mysterious change. But so much of what matters, so much of what is essential within the ephemeral passage of life, happens just there, at this juncture, where what is failing shines out. Where we come to witness: not only

to observe but to grieve the perishing.

Memory recalls another circle earlier than Oceanos, the ancient Mother of all, the Uroborus, the dragon biting its tail. Men say that history, action, consciousness, identity begin with the breaking of this circle, the slaying of this woman. But this cannot be true, that the bitter dragon could pass away, and men's lives then be firm and purposeful. She can no more be slain and dismembered than the Ocean can. It is the hero who rises and falls, dimly and suddenly recalling his mortality. She lets us go, speechless and innocent, and she brings us back when, failing, we have no way but through her healing bitterness, and we are drawn in memory and in persistent longing for her touch and speech. "[S]ea, brine, breaker, seducer,/giver of life, giver of tears," she governs these times at the edge of the known world, when things descend to and rise out of darkness, teaching a mothering mind and mothering language.

# Contributors Notes

**Mortimer Adler**, author, educator, philosopher, is chairman of the Board of Editors of Encyclopedia Britannica. He is director of the Institute for Philosophic Research in Chicago and is a senior associate of the Aspen Institute for Humanistic Studies. He is author of *Ten Philosophical Mistakes; Six Great Ideas; How to Think About God; Aristotle for Everybody; How to Speak/How to Listen;* and the famous *Paideia* series.

**Jacques Barzun**, one of America's most distinguished intellectual leaders, served for many years as Provost of Columbia University. Two of his works, *Teacher in America,* and *The House of Intellect,* have had a major influence on American education. He has written twenty-two books, has edited nine, and has translated Flaubert, Diderot, Mirabeau, and Berlioz, among others. Mr. Barzun has collaborated on the *Paideia* project which re-visions American education.

**Wendell Berry**, poet, critic, and philosopher, is an active farmer in Kentucky. His most famous book, *The Unsettling of America,* stresses the in-divisibility of culture and agriculture. The insistent theme of his writing is the interdependence of land, weather, animals, family, and thoughtfulness. His writings include: two novels, *A Place on Earth* and *Nathan Coulter;* two books of poems, *The Wheel* and *Collected Poems;* two books of essays, *Standing by Words* and *The Gift of Good Land.*

**William Burford**, a poet, a writer, and a teacher, has taught at the University of Texas, Austin, the University of Montana, and the University of Washington. His publications include *A World,* a book of poems, and *On Reading,* a translation of Marcel Proust's *Sans la lecture.* He is completing a book, *Proust on Ruskin,* for Yale University Press.

**Donald Cowan**, former President of the University of Dallas, is an acclaimed educational theorist. He has been concerned with the re-definition of the university in our time and the re-animation of the role of education on all levels of our society. His discipline is physics; he continues to write and perform research in this field. His current writings focus on educational theory, physics and the city.

**Louise Cowan**, teacher, author, and literary critic, is author of *The Fugitive Group: A Literary History*; *The Southern Critics*; and *The Communal World of Southern Literature*. She is editor of *The Terrain of Comedy* and has contributed chapters to numerous other books and journals. She is currently writing on Dostoevsky, Faulkner, and the city as symbol.

**Barbara Duden** is Professor of the History of Technology at the University of Berlin and also teaches at Pitzer College of Claremont University. She is engaged in research on the historicity of the female body.

**A. C. Greene**, author and historian, has brought to life the story of the Southwest in his works, which include *Personal Country*; *Dallas, the Deciding Years*; *Highland Park Woman*; and *Dallas U. S. A.* Mr. Greene has been active for many years in all areas of the media. He is a Paisano Fellow of the University of Texas.

**Eileen Gregory** has taught literature for many years at The University of Dallas. Her recent research has been on women's poetry, focusing primarily on H.D., Emily Dickinson, and Sylvia Plath. She has published several essays on William Faulkner. A monograph of her work,

*Summoning the Familiar*, has been published by The Dallas Institute Publications

**Roy P. Harrover** is head of Roy P. Harrover and Associates, the architectural firm in Memphis responsible for the design and construction of Mud Island, a park on an island in the Mississippi River at downtown Memphis. Mr. Harrover conceived of the island park as a tribute to the history, folklore, music, and culture of the lower river and its valley.

**James Hillman**, one of the most seminal depth psychologists, is editor of *Spring* and Spring Publications. He is a practicing analyst and a prolific writer. Among his books are *The Myth of Analysis*; *Suicide and the Soul*; *Re-Visioning Psychology*; *Insearch*; *The Dream and the Underworld*; *Inter - Views*; *Freud's Own Cookbook* (with Charles Boer); and *Anima*.

**Ivan Illich** is one of the world's most astute observers and critics of culture. Born in Vienna, Austria, he has lived and worked all over the world—in New York City, as founder of the Center for Intercultural Documentation; in Cuernavaca, Mexico; and in Göttingen and Berlin. He is author of *Deschooling Society*; *Tools for Conviviality*; *Energy and Equity*; *Medical Nemesis*; *Towards a History of Needs*; *Celebration of Awareness*; *Gender*; and *$H_2O$ and the Waters of Forgetfulness*, published by The Dallas Institute Publications.

**Jane Jacobs**, writer and urbanist, has been writing about the vitality of cities for over twenty-five years. Her books have influenced, through planners and architects, the making of urban life. They include: *The Death and Life of Great American Cities; The Economies of Cities; Cities and The Wealth of Nations.*

**Bernd Jager** is professor of psychology at Sonoma State University. His numerous writings focus on the psychology of dwelling, the imagination, the cultural implications of the psychoanalytic tradition, the psychology of the body, and psychological interpretations of myth.

**Dan Kiley**, a landscape architect, is currently assisting Criswell Development Company of Dallas in the Fountainplace project. Mr. Kiley also deigned the courtyard for the Dallas Museum of Art. By his own admission, Mr. Kiley's approach to design comes to him from the works of world philosophers Emerson, Thoreau, Goethe, Herodotus, and Jung.

**Robert Kugelman** is Chairman of the Psychology Department at the University of Dallas. He is the author of *Windows of the Soul*, a phenomenological study of glaucoma. He is currently at work on a book on the phenomenology of stress.

**Charles Moore**, renowned architect, teacher, and writer, currently occupies the O'Neil Ford Chair of Architecture at the University of Texas at Austin after sharing his time between firms in Los Angeles and Connecticut. His books include *The Place of Houses; Body, Memory and Architecture; Los Angeles, The City Observed;* and *Water in Architecture.*

**Tom Moore** is a counselor in private practice and a teacher of archetypal psychology at Lesley College in Boston. Dr. Moore's writings include two books, *The Planets Within*, a work of Renaissance psychology and imagery, and *Rituals of the Imagination*, published by The Dallas Institute Publications.

**Edwin T. Morris**, an authority on Chinese studies and horticulture, teaches at the New York Botanical Garden, the New School of Social Research, and New York University's School of Continuing Education. Fluent in Peking Mandarin, he has led numerous tour groups to China. His book, *The Gardens of China: History, Art and Meanings*, was published in 1983.

**Albert Murray** is author of numerous books which tell a profound story of American culture. They include *The Omni-Americans, South: To a Very Old Place; The Hero and the Blues; The Train Whistle Guitar;* and *The Story Teller as Blues Singer.* His most recent book is the biography of Count Basie.

**Christian Norberg-Schulz**, head of the School of Architecture at the University of Oslo, enjoys an international reputation as scholar, lecturer, and writer. Among his best known works are *Intentions in Architecture; Existence, Space and Architecture; Meaning in Western Architecture;* and *Genius Loci.*

**Lyle Novinski** is Chairman of the Art Department of the University of Dallas. An acclaimed artist, Professor Novinski additionally serves the discipline of art as teacher and lecturer in art history and art education. His works of liturgical art, located in numerous chapels and churches throughout Texas and other states have received wide recognition and honor.

**Bill Porterfield**, a journalist for over twenty-five years, has made an important contribution to almost every branch of the media: radio, television, newspaper, and magazine. He is the author of four books, the most recent of which is *Texas Rhapsody.* He is presently a columnist with *The Dallas Times Herald.*

**Kathleen Raine** is one of England's most renowned poets and a literary and cultural critic. She is the author of eight books of verse, a three-volume autobiography, and a seminal study of the philosophic and religious sources of Blake. She is editor of the international journal *Temenos.*

**Robert Romanyshyn** is professor of psychology at the University of Dallas and a clinical psychologist in private practice. He is the author of *Psychological Life: From Science to Metaphor* and has published numerous articles on psychotherapy, the psychology of science, memory, architecture and technology.

**James Rouse** has an international reputation as a master planner and master developer. Founder of the Rouse Company, he pioneered the concept of "festival marketplaces" which are visible today as Boston's Faneuil Hall Marketplace and Baltimore's Harborplace. Mr. Rouse is currently Chairman of the Board of the Enterprise Foundation, which concentrates on solutions to low-income housing.

**Robert Sardello** is a psychotherapist and Co-Director of the Dallas Institute. He is the author of two monographs, *Money and the Soul of the World* (with Randolph Severson), and *The Healing of Things* (with Larry Dossey). He has published numerous articles on the psychology of medicine, architecture, urban life, nuclear threat, death, aesthetic experience, and violence.

**Denise Scott Brown** is an architect and planner with the Philadelphia firm, Venturi, Rauch and Scott Brown. In her writings and in her professional work she brings a special